Learning

to Fly

Learning to Fly

A Memoir

KARMEN BERENTSEN

LINDT
PRESS

Denver, Colorado

ISBN: 978-1-7352350-0-4 (print)
Library of Congress Control Number: 2020910918

Published by
A Line Press

Editing by Melanie Mulhall, Dragonheart
www.DragonheartWritingandEditing.com
Cover design by David Drummond, Salamander Hill
www.SalamanderHill.com
Interior design by Bob Schram, Bookends Design
www.BookendsDesign.com

First Edition
Printed in the United States of America

For Reese

I felt your soul before you came into this world,
and your presence in my life is my greatest joy.

CONTENTS

PART ONE
Innocence and Hardening

Part Two

Awakening

PART ONE
Innocence and Hardening

CHAPTER 1

Learning to Fly

Tinker Bell could fly, so why couldn't I?

I SAW MYSELF TAKING FLIGHT and soaring over the houses, the streets, the kids on bikes, and the barking dogs. There was no question in my mind that I could do it, even though I hadn't done it yet. With my knees bent, calves pressed together, head tilted back, and eyes closed, I prepared to lift off, my blond hair glistening in the sun like that of any other fairy princess.

My status as fairy princess was mostly invisible to adults. I didn't care if my shirt was on backward or inside-out. I didn't care if it was food-stained, and at the moment, my pink tee shirt with ponies on it was splotched with spaghetti sauce because I had used it to wipe my face off during dinner the previous evening. And even though it was still morning, the bottoms of my feet were already black, not only because shoes were a nuisance but because I knew that shoes would be little more than an encumbrance during flight.

Full of self-confidence and trust that this was the day I'd become the fairy princess version of Superman, I gathered my will, pressed my toes into the landscape log that served as my launch pad, readied myself for the leap.

Even though it was only spring, the temperature neared one hundred degrees in Phoenix. Mom and Dad were at work, my sister Kyla was sitting in her first grade class, and I was home with Grandma. Being a three-and-a-half-year-old alone with Grandma all day required imagination and creativity. My little mind could only be entertained so long with card games and cooking. Unlike other girls my age, I had no desire to help Grandma in the kitchen while she cooked and baked. I was too much a tomboy for that. The only time I came into the kitchen was when there was brownie batter to clean out of the bowl. I magically appeared the moment the batter was poured into the pan and the sweet, sugary smell of it permeated the house.

It had been a typical morning. I slept while everyone else in the house showered and rushed off to work and school, limbs sprawled out in every direction among tangled blankets and stuffed animals. Around 9:00 a.m., I stumbled half-awake from my bed to the couch and began watching Grandma's favorite morning show, *The Price Is Right*. Grandma would yell out prices from the kitchen and squeal when she was right, and she usually guessed better than the contestants on the show. After fully waking up, I half-bounced, half-trotted toward the kitchen table where Grandma served me homemade oatmeal with brown sugar, fresh berries, and cream. After breakfast we usually played a game of Skip Bo before she returned to the kitchen to attend to whatever baked goods or casserole was coming out of the oven.

When Grandma returned to the kitchen, I returned to my bedroom and pulled off my pajamas, which remained wherever they landed regardless of how many times my mother pointed out the laundry basket in which I was supposed to deposit them. As far as I was concerned, what she called a laundry basket found better use as a fort, sled, or other tool for my adventures. I grabbed a pair of shorts and a tank top with no concern for style, color, or pattern. The change of clothes was only to appease the adults who valued "getting dressed" before going outside. And making my way outside was important because I wanted the expansiveness of the open sky to engage in my favorite activity: learning to fly.

The front yard was my training ground. In the corner of the yard were three logs creating stairs to the sky. The longest log was almost longer than I was tall. They were meant as decoration, not as stairs, but I climbed them until I was standing on the tallest log. Seeing the ground far below me, I closed my eyes and began moving my arms up and down, mimicking what I had seen birds do as they took flight. When my legs felt power-charged and my entire body seemed light enough to lift off as easily as a balloon released to soar, I bent my knees and leaped into the air.

I had done this countless times before. Each time, I expected to soar across the grass, climb high above the houses as the wind pulled me skyward, and watch the world from a vantage point among the clouds. Yet, regardless of imagination, desire, dreams, or effort, my little body ended up in the grass a few feet from the log. I'd sit for a second before standing up and trying again. Each time, I shut my eyes harder in an effort to see myself flying through the air like the fairies on television and in books. Tinker Bell could fly, so why couldn't I?

After dozens of attempts, I would give up for the day, determined that the next day might be the day I figured out the secret to flying. I never doubted that I would fly. It was simply a matter of practice.

With no doubt about the inevitability of eventual success, I abandoned flying practice for the day and allowed myself to be drawn to the next adventure. Shifting roles from fairy princess to tap dancer was predictable because my signature dance move was a lot like flying. I returned to my bedroom and put on my tap shoes, ignoring the fact that my feet were more than just a little dirty.

The tile in the entryway provided the perfect stage. I lined up my stuffed animals on the living room couch, guaranteeing a full house for my performance. My tap shoes echoed throughout the entire house as I shuffled across the tile. I always ended the performance with a series of wings, a most impressive step that produced a beautiful three-beat sound made louder than any other step because both feet were moving out and in to make the sound as the arms circled to achieve the height necessary for three beats in one jump.

I loved catching Grandma smiling at me, her eyes sparkling as she peeked around the corner of the dining room. It didn't matter if I nailed the steps or simply made noise. Her smile remained the same. I liked that she sneaked those backstage views, and I loved performing wings perfectly because it was a big accomplishment for a little girl, a learned skill that took practice and coordination—not to mention the fact that just for a moment, I was airborne during the move.

But the best part was simply the joy of expression without inhibition. Some days I mimicked Bert, the tap-dancing chimney sweep in *Mary Poppins*, and I lost myself in the fantasy by using Mom's makeup for soot on my face. "Chim Chim Cher-ee" blared as my body moved with spontaneity and utter freedom. I loved the magnitude of noise thirty-five pounds could make with tap shoes on a tile floor.

My emotions were completely available to me. I cried when I got hurt or scared and laughed when something was silly. My feelings and body flowed together without my brain or emotions getting in the way. I was free and innocent.

My mom and dad both grew up in rural Minnesota, and I was born in Bemidji, Minnesota, a town twenty-five miles away from Bagley, which was the closest town with a Target, chain restaurants, and a hospital. Bagley had one stoplight, one church, one school, one bowling alley, one five-and-dime store, and multiple bars.

We lived in Arizona during the school year, but my sister and I returned with my dad to Minnesota each summer to work the RV resort my parents had bought years earlier. My mom had the steady, corporate job and stayed in Phoenix for the summer while my sister and I played concierge, waitress, cook, wrangler, caretaker, and janitor at our humble 180-acre resort with twenty-eight RV hookups and a small convenience store with one gas pump and an undistinguished restaurant.

As soon as we arrived each summer, we jumped in the pickup and found the closest livestock auction. The summer when I was four, we bought two Shetland ponies, a goat, a calf, two kittens, and a huge rabbit. We loaded the calf and goat onto the bed of the pickup and simply held the kittens and rabbit on our laps. The ponies were being brought in a horse trailer. But before we got home, it started raining, and I began to cry because the goat and calf were getting wet. I imagined them scared because it was stormy and they were trying to keep their balance in the bed of a pickup truck with metal grooves in the floor that were not hoof friendly. Moments later, my dad, my sister, a calf, a small goat, two kittens, an enormous rabbit, and I were scrunched together in the truck cab.

Life with my dad was an adventure, and it was never serious. He was more like a big kid than an adult or parent, tickling me until I thought I would throw up, allowing me to order dessert before my meal, and often going along with my every whimsical wish.

Summers included my sister and me playing a tag version of hide-and-go-seek while riding bareback on our ponies. The fields around the resort were filled with rolled hay bales that resembled huge loaves of bread. They were six feet in diameter—plenty big enough to hide behind on a pony. One of us would close our eyes and count to a hundred while the other one rode hard to a hay bale or clump of trees in the pasture. It was exhilarating to hide, ready to bolt. The seeker's strategy was to race around the bales to flush out the sister who was hiding. The hider's strategy was to hear her sister's pony approaching and dart off before being caught. More often than not, our ponies collided. Sometimes we managed to keep our seats while the ponies reared and bolted; other times we fell to the ground laughing.

After an adrenaline-charged game, I would lie back on my pony and rest my head on his rump with my legs dangling over each side. There I would fall asleep as the sun beat down on my face and my pony grazed, slowly eating his way through the grass, his big tummy moving in and out in a rhythmic, soothing way. I was in tune with my pony's spirit and felt everything from his perspective. When we took trail rides, I knew when a bear or fox was near because his demeanor changed from lackadaisical to alert. I knew, instinctively, that his joy and enthusiasm matched mine when we played hide-and-seek. I knew when he felt safe and relaxed enough to graze. I was present and unselfconscious with him.

In the simplest terms, I was a little girl who was fully in the moment and fully alive.

Skepticism and Doubt

Peter Pan had left town.

THAT SENSE OF ALIVENESS on the back of a pony was something I shared with my dad, as well as my sister. Back in Phoenix, weekend horseback rides became a tradition for the three of us.

Mom was outside sunbathing one Saturday when the three of us returned home. Her body glistened with suntan oil as she floated in the pool on a yellow inflatable raft, her eyes covered with cotton balls under her sunglasses. Oblivious to our arrival, she seemed completely at peace. Dad instructed Kyla and me to be quiet as we watched her through the sliding glass door. Then he turned and disappeared. Within seconds, a human cannonball jumped from the roof, making a gigantic splash in the pool right next to the bathing beauty. As Mom came off the raft, I began to laugh—until I saw the look of disgust on her face. She grabbed her top, which had been untied to avoid tan lines, but she couldn't manage to salvage her sunglasses. As they sank to the bottom of the pool, the fight began. It wasn't the first yelling match between my mother and father.

Mom and Dad were very different. My dad was always talking about the future and how we were going to be millionaires. My mom was focused on making sure there were groceries in the fridge and a coat on my back when it got below seventy degrees in Arizona. Dad talked animatedly about the deals he had going that were sure to make millions. It was every bit as grand as the stories of kings, castles, princesses, and knights he told me before bed. My mom felt the burden of simultaneously trying to raise two little girls and dealing with a man who, like Peter Pan, refused to grow up.

I was innocent to any struggles between my parents until I was five and my dad was served with divorce papers. Kyla and I were in the car with Dad, ready to leave the house for school, when a stranger pulled up, got out of his car, and came over to us. "Are you Clark Stave?" he asked before handing my dad papers and asking him to sign a sheet attached to a clipboard.

In rage, my dad flew out of the driver's seat and charged the stranger. The poor man ran for his car as my dad screamed at him in language I *was* too young to understand apart from knowing that he was using "bad words." The man jumped in his car and started his engine, but he was not going to get away that easily. Dad rushed back to our car and flew out of the driveway, chasing him down the road. My sister cried hysterically as we chased the stranger through the streets. At every stoplight, Dad jumped out, ran to the man's car, pounded on his window, and screamed more bad words.

The drama finally ended (for my sister and me, anyway) when Dad dropped us off at school. When we returned home after school, Dad was gone. I never got to say good-bye. Mom seemed relieved; I was devastated.

My playmate was gone. I was left with a mother and an older sister who behaved like a second mother. The pillow fights disappeared along with the Saturday morning horseback rides. For me, the house had turned solemn and lonely.

Any sympathy I expressed for my father was invalidated with comments such as, "You're too young to understand." I *was* too young to understand, but I still missed my dad. There was something about his departure that changed the entire landscape of my life. I had felt sadness and fear during my short time on Earth, but I had always felt safe. My father's departure was an earthquake that rattled everything. Spilling my milk, which happened often, disrupted life. The crash and breaking of glass was loud, but it was contained. An earthquake, on the other hand, upset everything. Dad's exodus was the first event in my life that rattled the safety my soul was born with. The trust that there was order and safety to the universe cracked and the wide-eyed, curious, carefree girl looked at the world with skepticism and doubt for the first time.

Nevertheless, Mom became happier as the days turned into weeks and the weeks turned into months. And with that increased happiness, I began to experience a new side to her, one that was never present when my dad was around. She became more available, affectionate, and fun. Some invisible wall that had been like a force field around her became permeable. She seemed lighter and less guarded. Seriousness sometimes gave way to tickles and cuddles. I had a bedroom of my own, but most nights, I slept in her bedroom with her arms wrapped around me as we spooned one another.

Mom demonstrated her love for Kyla and me through her ongoing concern and presence. She wasn't a helicopter mom, but she always seemed to know everything that was going on, even though she was an accountant by day and was going to school at night. If some school drama involving gossip and pettiness upset me, Mom served as my rock, providing an infusion of wisdom and the common sense that can only come with maturity.

During Thanksgiving weekend, she also demonstrated her love through gastronomy, transforming from a foreigner in the kitchen to a gourmet chef. Thanksgiving became a time of family connection around food. From the Wednesday before Thanksgiving to the Sunday after it, our kitchen emanated delectable smells. Everything from pies to sauces was homemade. My normally fast-moving, perfectly polished, half-listening, driven mother pulled her hair back into a loose bun, skipped both makeup and footwear, and donned an apron. She slowed from whirling dervish to someone moving with quiet ease.

Thanksgivings were priceless to me. The food was memorable, but it was the energy engulfing the house that made it special. For those few days, it was like living in a perfect little cottage within a cozy snow globe. Rushing and perpetual lateness were replaced by the luxury of time. The mother who usually juggled work outside the home with making lunches, doing laundry, tending to the dog, and making sure we practiced the piano and did our homework could drop the corporate role and just focus on being a typical northern Minnesota mom in Thanksgiving holiday mode. There was still productivity, but everything felt organic and relaxed instead of forced and stressed. Mom was never so present as at Thanksgiving time, but even when it wasn't Thanksgiving, she was more present than ever before.

But while Mom was present, Dad was out of the picture. Peter Pan had left town, and four year after his departure, he seemed like a distant memory—right up to the day when he made a reappearance just long enough to strip me of my regained sureness.

I was in fourth grade. It was January, and I had just gotten my latest report card. I couldn't wait to show my mom. I had received an A+ in both math and science, my favorite subjects. I got an A- in art, which I hated. What was the point of taking clay and crafting it into an object that was supposed to resemble a turtle, firing it in an oven, and painting it only to give it to my mom, who had to pretend to love it and want to display it? It didn't make sense to me. I loved being competitive and thrived physically, so the A+ in physical education was no surprise. Eye-hand coordination came easily to me, and I had the drive and determination to run until my legs dropped out from under me. In reading and social studies, I received an A-. Studying history and facts bored me. What was the purpose of memorizing facts? That Africa was almost an island, save for the Sinai Peninsula, and that China had twenty-three provinces meant nothing to me. How would those facts serve me in life? But even with subjects I didn't care for, an A- was the lowest grade I received. I wasn't brilliant, but I worked hard, and I knew how to study, memorize, and perform.

That day, Mom was not alone when she picked me up after ballet practice. A man was with her. "Karmen, your dad is in town. He's excited to see you," she said through a forced smile. Her words were telling me to welcome him, yet her entire body was tense and rigid.

I thought of my report card. This would be *great*. I hadn't seen my dad since I was five years old, and I was about to show him a straight-A report card. That was sure to melt the cold energy in the room. I ran over to my backpack, which was shoved under one of the little ballet studio benches, grabbed my report card, and returned, beaming.

"All A's!" I proclaimed, smiling at my mom while handing the report card to my dad.

Slowly, his eyes scanned my report card. "What percentile are you in the class?" he asked without looking up.

I was confused by his lack of excitement. I fully expected him to tell me how smart I was and how proud he was of me. "I don't know," I replied decisively, glancing at Mom.

"It is imperative that you be in the top five percent of your class," Dad said without hesitation. "You will amount to nothing in life if you are not in the top five percent." He announced that he was going to speak with my teacher and find out what percentile I was in before he had any further conversation with me about my grades.

My ballet body—dressed in pink leotard, pink slippers, and a pink tutu—felt heavy instead of light. I was more army tank slogging through mud than cotton candy floating on a stick. I hadn't seen my dad in a long time, and I'd dreamed of him sweeping me up in a fatherly homecoming embrace. I'd dreamed of having my family back, of my parents magically recoupling. But in one sweeping inquisition about my class ranking, the father

I'd seen as my playmate became an accuser, judge, and jury for some wrong I could not even comprehend.

There was a physical weight to the silence. Mom did not know how to respond. The last thing she wanted was a fight in the ballet studio. She put her arm around me and smiled, communicating with her eyes that *she* was proud of me. I loved my mom, but in that moment, all I wanted was for my dad to be proud of me and want me as his daughter.

The next evening, Dad took Kyla and me out to dinner at an expensive steak house. He informed me that he had spoken to my teacher and learned that I was in the top seven percent, not the top five percent. In one cold, unfeeling gesture, he pulled out my report card and ripped it into pieces. Then, as he sliced into his medium-rare porterhouse steak, he told me to get into the top five percent. "Your classmates are your competition, not your friends. When you get older and have study groups, you are never to *share* anything with them, but you are to *use* them. When you walk into a class, your job is to determine who the competition is and *beat* them."

I held my breath in an effort not to cry. My eyes became moist, but before any emotion was released, determination and anger found its way in. My mind raced to quiet my hurting heart. I came to a simple conclusion: To be loved and wanted by my dad, I could not be average, or even above average. I had to be perfect. My sister was perfect. She was number one in her class. I needed to be like her to gain my father's love.

Every cell in my body *wanted* a father. I knew that crying about it or begging him to stay was useless. I had sobbed the day he originally left, and it had done no good. What I needed was to prove to my dad that I was worthy of being his daughter. I was going to get into the top five percent no matter what it took. I could do that. I could and would do it!

From that moment, I began rejecting anything but scholastic perfection from myself. Average would not do. Above average would not do. I had to be the best. My friends could no longer simply be friends. They were now instruments to attaining my dad's love. Everything had to be conquered. Nothing could simply be enjoyed. I had to master everything.

Shortly after that dinner, Dad disappeared again to chase another promise of business prosperity.

I didn't understand my girlfriends' fathers. They were captivated by their daughters—even the average ones. Ashley was a girlfriend who struggled in school. She was sweet but extremely plain. We went to her house to play one day after school. As evening approached, her dad came home from work, and Ashley jumped up and ran to him. I sat on the floor and watched as her dad picked her up, beaming with delight. He sat down on the couch with her in his arms, and he listened intently to every detail of her day, mesmerized by her. I didn't get it. Why was her father so excited about her? She was a B student. She hadn't even made the school play. It baffled me. I had no awareness or cognizance that fathers love their daughters simply because they *are* their daughters, not because they are stars at school or on the playing field.

For the rest of elementary school, my dad was in and out of my life. He appeared when he struck it rich and was on top of the world, swooping in, bigger than life, and dropping thousands of dollars. His arrival was like a circus coming to town. Overnight, a big tent would materialize. Within it, wonders would be performed, mesmerizing me as I shifted focus from one of the three rings to another. Exotic animals would do tricks and contortionists would perform superhuman feats. Then the tent would come down and the troupe would leave town overnight, as magically as it had arrived, and I would walk around the empty field wondering if it had all been a dream.

One weekend, my sister and I met him in New York City, where we stayed at The Plaza Hotel. The entire weekend was extravagant, but the finale was a trip to Bloomingdale's. Dad reached into his wallet and pulled out hundred-dollar bills—twenty of them. He handed a thousand dollars to me and another thousand dollars to my sister. Then he sat down in an upholstered chair with a paperback book and told us to go have fun. Without concern, he reclined, opened his new book, and made it clear that we were on our own to explore the entire eight floors of Bloomingdale's in Manhattan.

After New York, Dad disappeared yet again. He was still the gambler—not in casinos, but in business. He wanted to make millions in one deal. He would take all the equity in a company and gamble it on an opportunity he was sure would make him rich overnight. It was a game to him. The problem was that when he lost and had no worldly wealth to show for his efforts, he disconnected his phone and moved without leaving a forwarding address or phone number. Over and over, my sister and I lost our dad. We were abandoned time after time. He never apologized or even acknowledged his absence when he returned, raving about his latest deal.

My dad's every action told me that he was not going to protect or love me unconditionally. Instead, he was constantly toughening me up like Mr. Miyagi did to Daniel LaRusso in *The Karate Kid*. Mr. Miyagi was relentless and harsh with his young student, yet the training resulted in the twiggy boy winning a karate tournament and being able to handle himself in a fight. Maybe my dad's training would make me tough, resilient, and mighty.

CHAPTER 3

God and the Fragile Human Body

I was the grownup now.

LIFE WITH MOM WAS STEADY, consistent, and newly full of God. Mom had found the Nazarene Church, and the church had heroes with wild adventures. Noah heard God's voice, built a boat, and saved his family and all the animals. Moses touched his staff and the Red Sea split in two before crashing in on Pharaoh's army. My soul eagerly devoured the feeling that there was more to this life than just what I saw.

I was ready for the mythical. When my father lived with us, life had been adventurous and playful, but with his departure, all sense of fascination and mystery had been replaced with order and control. There was no time for wonder when we had schedules to keep and there were accomplishments to be had. The magic was gone. His leaving had dovetailed with my first experience with socialization: school. In school, my teachers quickly corrected me when I chose a crayon color other than yellow for the sun. According to them, the sun was yellow, not pink, despite the fact that every Arizona sunset I saw was rosy pink. There was no room for creativity that was not confined to set social standards. The magic and thrilling enchantment of the world I had known evaporated.

But hope and the supernatural were implicit in my mother's newfound faith in God, and I embraced faith with open arms. I welcomed the spiritual dimension I felt when singing worship songs to a mighty God. I loved the *Star Wars* movies because of the Force, a source of power extending beyond human capabilities. The Force gave Luke Skywalker intuition and supernatural abilities. I related the Force to the Holy Spirit in the Christian teachings, and I loved the idea of something that transcended everyday living. I was drawn to the idea of being part of an eternal story about the battle between good and evil. God was big and glorious, the creator of spectacular sunsets and terrifying thunder as well as the ultimate warrior for good. I was introduced to a heavenly father who loved me unconditionally, and I was taught to know him personally. The word *Abba*, which means *daddy* in Aramaic, was used in church to describe God. I was taught that I had a father in heaven who adored me, a daddy who was constant—unlike my earthly father, who was in and out of my life.

Faith produced confidence and hope that the miraculous could happen, and the stories of faith in the Bible always included adventure and courage. A puny shepherd boy named David killed a giant with a slingshot. If you were brave enough to obey God, you got to be on the winning side when he made towers tumble and floods overtake the face of the planet. My pastor constantly challenged the congregation to seek what new "lands" God was calling them to, just as he had called Moses to a new land. I loved praying, being still, and listening to God's voice inside me. That voice promised to show me

my mission and my purpose in the everlasting battle between good and evil.

On the flip side, I was a sinner and needed saving. My
soul was equated to "filthy rags" without the blood of
Jesus Christ. Miracles were allowed, though most seemed
to have occurred two thousand years before my birth.
Magic was not allowed. It went against God. The rules
were black-and-white, and from the moment I accepted
the church's position on how the universe worked, I found
myself growing up in a black-and-white world.

Sex outside of marriage was a sin. I was told that the
emotional scarring caused by premarital sex, should I engage in it, would haunt me forever, inhibiting me from
enjoying sex with my husband. I was terrified of that. As
I left childhood and became a teen, I was petrified that
one night of passion would ruin my sex life forever and
leave me fatally stripped of eroticism and sexual excitement. There was no acknowledgment that an unmarried
person was even a sexual being. Not only was masturba-
tion seen as sinful and of the devil, for the unmarried, *anything* smacking of eroticism was wrong. This approach
essentially castrated anyone outside the sacrament of
marriage and then miraculously returned their sexuality
to them as a blessing from the Holy Spirit once they took
the marriage vows. Alcohol was prohibited. It was dangerous and it led to promiscuity.

Wearing provocative clothing was a sin. It was my
fault if a guy lusted after me or had impure thoughts. I
was told that the devil prowls like a lion looking for souls
to destroy, and I was to be on guard. In youth group, a
common weekly gathering for church teenagers, they

played a Led Zeppelin record backward, blaring the demonic messages hidden in the music and scaring the daylights out of all of us by telling us that if we listened to secular music, we could be possessed by the devil.

On one hand, I had rules and restrictions, and on the other hand, I had unconditional love. How I reconciled the seemingly opposing views was simple. I had a heavenly father who had created me. I was the creation and he was the creator. Because he loved me, he gave me boundaries and rules so I would not hurt myself. Having a guide felt good. I didn't have to figure it all out by myself. The Bible was a rule book containing everything needed to guide me to the "promised land," which was as much a condition I longed for as it was a place. The church and its Christian message promised adventure and mysticism leading to the safety, happiness, and peace of heaven. That promise was both intoxicating and comforting.

Those who do not grow up in a black-and-white Christian home often picture it as repressive. The truth is that I didn't know anything else. My world was a Christian world of the fundamentalist variety. My friends were from the church. I went to a Christian school, a youth group, and church camp. Everyone around me believed that God had sent his only son to die for the sins of the world, and if we confessed our sins, we would be saved and go to heaven.

Trusting in a God who had a plan for me was empowering. Believing that I was part of a greater plan, something bigger than myself, inspired me and gave me courage.

The church taught being "sensitive to the Holy Spirit," the part of God that lived in those who were "saved." For me, being sensitive to the Holy Spirit meant that I listened to the quiet voice that often told me things I didn't want to hear. It was the voice that told me to give up my window seat and move to the middle seat in the airplane so a family could sit together. It was the voice that told me to hug someone because they needed a hug. While my heart called me to give the woman a hug, my mind said that she was going to think I was crazy. But each time I listened to that small voice, I ended up as blessed as the person I did something for.

My body and soul were connected when I was three and a half, sure that I could will myself to fly. I had lost that sense of connection for a time, but I regained it with the church. The church provided a vehicle for getting connected and listening to the voice of God inside me. When I was a teenager, all seemed peaceful. I had matured, and while I no longer thought I could fly like Tinkerbell, I did believe that there were powerful forces with which I could align myself. I was fighting a mighty, unseen battle for God.

When Kyla went to college at Point Loma Nazarene University, a private college on the cliffs of San Diego, my mother and I moved to Irvine, just south of Los Angeles. JD Edwards had repeatedly offered Mom a consulting job after she was on the project team implementing JD Edwards' software at Del Webb. Kyla hadn't wanted to move, so we stayed in Phoenix until she graduated from high school. JD Edwards was growing rapidly, and Mom finally accepted a job offer at their Orange County, California, office. I couldn't have been happier to be leaving Phoenix after my freshman year in high school. I was going to be the cool Cali girl.

We quickly found another faith community in the Nazarene church in Anaheim. I was welcomed into the youth group with enthusiasm. That was nice, but it did not really feel necessary because my internal coolness barometer had been instantly elevated with the move to California. At fifteen, being from Orange County seemed way better than being from Phoenix.

Even though the church taught that beauty was contained inside you, I loved fashion. I couldn't go anywhere without being fully done up, and that meant I had to get up at 5:00 a.m. to be ready to leave the house with my mom at 7:00 a.m. My mom's alarm clock didn't go off until 6:00 a.m. I had a head start by getting up at 5:00. It was a simple routine in a life that was full of simple routines. Life was good in California . . . until it wasn't.

That day I heard my mom's alarm clock go off as usual, but I didn't hear her shower running a few minutes later, which was a part of the routine. Curious, I walked into her bedroom. She wasn't in bed. I found her in her bathroom, where she was hunched over the toilet throwing up. I viewed my mother as beautiful, confident, and strong. She was tall and sleek, with riveting eyes and a confident gait. She was as powerful as Superwoman to me, yet there she was, hugging the toilet, spewing vomit. Apparently, even Superwoman could get sick.

I reached to hold back her hair as she did for me when I was sick, but to my shock, I got elbowed. This wasn't like her. Stunned and confused about what I had done to warrant the elbow, I silently stood over her, afraid to say or do anything else. Finally, I regained my composure and reverted to my role as a typical, supercilious teenager.

With a shrug and a roll of the eyes, I responded, "Fine," before walking back to my bathroom.

She just has the flu, I told myself as I sat on the bathroom counter, inches from the mirror, applying my eyeliner. But why would she elbow me? It wasn't like her. In all my life, my mom had never rejected me as she had just done. Being on the receiving end of aggression and unkindness from her was a totally new, totally bewildering experience.

I couldn't breathe. Something wasn't right. My mind flew through all the logical explanations. None fit. I hated the panic rising in my throat. My mind searched for an answer that would quiet my heart. None helped. Exhausted, I gave my head a physical shake, as if my thoughts and worries could literally be thrown aside so I could return to applying my makeup. She just had the flu; that was all. There was nothing more to it than that.

When I heard a peculiar thumping sound coming from my mom's room, I slowly uncrossed my legs and touched my feet to the cold linoleum. Holding my breath, I slowly tiptoed toward her bedroom. As I turned the corner and entered the room, I saw her upper body sticking out of the bathroom, violently thrashing around on the floor. Her beautiful green eyes were far back in her head. Her mouth was open, spewing foam as she choked on her own saliva.

I stood there, frozen, staring at her as she jerked and seized on the floor for what seemed like minutes. I knew it was my mom. I was standing in her bedroom. But my head had to convince me that this was, in fact, my mom. Only minutes earlier, I had been in this very bathroom watching her throw up.

Call 911!

It felt like a voice outside me. I had removed myself from the scene and was now the director telling an actor what to do. I watched myself staring at my mom convulsing on the floor. A voice kept telling me to call 911. I finally replied to the voice. *I am to call 911 only in case of emergency.* And then I realized that this *was* an emergency.

I ran to the cordless phone sitting on my mom's nightstand and dialed 9-1-1.

An operator answered. "State your emergency."

"My mom is flopping around, foaming at the mouth, gagging."

"I need you to roll her on her side," the operator replied.

I hesitated. She was halfway in the bathroom. "There isn't room to turn her over. She's wrapped around the toilet."

The operator instructed me to take her arms and pull her out of the bathroom.

My heart dropped. I had to touch her? I had to pull this thrashing, scary body that held no resemblance to my mom? I breathed, put down the phone, and grabbed her arms, making no eye contact with her foaming mouth or rolled back eyes as I pulled her body until she was on her side and free to thrash in the open.

I picked up the phone and said, "Okay, she's on her side."

"Do you have any pets?" the operator asked.

What? My mom was lying unconscious and the 911 operator was asking if we had any pets!

"Yes, we have a dog," I replied, confused.

The operator instructed me to put our cocker spaniel, Taffy, in the garage so the firefighter-paramedics would not have a dog to deal with when they came into the house. I understood the operator's request, but I was conflicted. How could she expect me to focus on anything other than the only parent who had been—until this moment—always in control? I stared at my mom. Her eyes were still rolled back. She looked dead. Taking one big breath, I realized that there was nothing I could do for her. I got up, walked downstairs, and put Taffy in the garage.

With the phone wedged between my neck and shoulder, I said, "Okay, our dog is in the garage."

The operator continued down her list of standard questions, asking if there was any furniture that would be in the way when the paramedics brought the gurney into my mom's room.

A gurney? My mom was going to be put on a gurney? The paramedics weren't going to simply waft smelling salts under her nose, give her some juice to drink, and leave? As I moved end tables, the reality of what was happening began to set in. My mind was spinning, trying to comprehend all that was happening.

I was brought back to reality by the operator's voice. "I need you to go to the front door. The fire truck just pulled up."

I looked out the window and, sure enough, there was a fire truck outside. In fact, there were two fire trucks, an ambulance, and a red SUV. As I stared at the surrealism of emergency vehicles lined up in front of my house, I felt like I had been awake for days, even though I had only been up for a little over an hour.

I opened the door and was greeted by a team of firefighters. I led them upstairs and into my mom's bedroom.

The seizing had stopped. She lay lifeless with her eyes rolled back. Her face was covered in vomit and saliva foam.

This was the woman who had been laughing uncontrollably the night before as she mercilessly killed me in a game of Uno. She had been dealt the perfect hand. In one play, she put down a string of draw two, draw four, and reverse cards superlatively lined up in a way that allowed me to only play two cards during the whole round. She hadn't been able to contain her laughter. In that one hand, she had managed to catch me with over a hundred points. My mind was lost in the picture of the healthy, radiant, beautiful face that had been so full of life less than twelve hours earlier. Now I stared at her lifeless looking body on the floor as firefighter-paramedics worked on her.

Lost in thought, I was oblivious to the fact that the chief's hand was on my shoulder. He wanted to know if my mom was a diabetic or had any allergies, but I was too much in a state of shock to pay much attention. Finally, he grabbed my shoulders, turned me toward him, and gave me one firm shake.

"If you want your mother to live, I need your help."

I looked around me as if expecting to find an adult to help him. I had just turned sixteen, and while I saw myself as being old enough to make decisions for myself, I couldn't imagine dealing with a life-and-death situation as the adult in charge. But Kyla was away at school. I was it. The scared teenager standing in the hallway with tears streaming down her face vanished. I took a deep breath, wiped the tears from my eyes, and began answering all of the chief's questions. No, she was not diabetic. No, she had no allergies. She was five foot nine tall and 127 pounds. She was thirty-nine years old. She didn't smoke or drink. She was a senior project manager for a software company. As I answered questions, a gurney rolled out of my mom's room. I saw her out of the corner of my eye. I wanted to run and curl up in her arms and have her hold me, but the time for crying and being scared was over. I was the grownup now.

I finished answering the fire chief's questions as Mom was being wheeled out on a gurney. I needed to lock, grab my mom's purse, mobile phone, and planner because we were heading to the hospital. I grabbed it all in a matter of seconds, walked down the stairs, opened the door to the garage—releasing Taffy from her captivity—continued out the front door, locked it, and sat down in the front seat of the ambulance.

What had begun as a routine day had become anything but.

At the Hospital

A large vacuum had suddenly appeared
and sucked all the oxygen out of the atmosphere.

THE DRIVE TO THE HOSPITAL WAS DREAMLIKE. Outside the small world called *ambulance*, everyone seemed normal. Cars contained people singing to the radio, women putting on makeup, and kids being yelled at by their parents. But my world had stopped. In a moment, the test in biology, my archenemy on the cheerleading squad, and the beautiful football running back were all irrelevant. In fact, they were nonexistent. I stared out the ambulance window, watching the world continue as if nothing had happened.

In stark comparison, a lot was happening in the ambulance behind my seat. My mom was regaining consciousness. I could hear the fear in her muddled grunts and slurs. I wanted to unlatch my seatbelt and jump into the back, but only adults were allowed to ride in the back with the patient. And at sixteen, I was not considered an adult. The closest I could manage was a seat up front, and I had to negotiate for that. The alternative had been to ride with the chief in his SUV, but I was having none of that. I refused to leave my mom, and while I wanted to be in the back with her, the closest I could negotiate was a seat in the front.

"Mom, don't fight them! They're trying to help you. It's okay," I yelled from the front seat while stretching my neck as far around the seat as possible.

But my voice only seemed to exasperate her as she struggled harder and harder to sit up. I wondered why the paramedics had to be so rough. Couldn't they see she was scared?

"Don't hurt her," I yelled as I began to shake with tears.

But the struggle only continued to escalate, and I began sobbing harder and harder. I was helpless and alone. If my dad were still around, it would all be different. I wouldn't be alone, trying to be strong. And because we would be following the ambulance in our own car, I would be insulated from the medical drama happening in the back of the ambulance.

Finally, things settled. I figured she had become cognizant enough to realize that she was in an ambulance and was going to be okay. I thought it was best for me to keep as quiet as possible to avoid agitating her and risk sparking another episode. When we arrived at the hospital, I jumped out of the ambulance, ran to the back, and watched as they lowered the gurney. She was awake! Her eyes were open!

"Karen, do you know who this is?" a paramedic asked, nodding toward me. It was a ridiculous question. Of course she knew who I was.

"Mom, you're okay," I said with the most courageous and encouraging smile I could marshal.

Her head followed my voice, moving from the paramedic to me, but instead of laughing at the paramedic's ludicrous question and saying, "This is my daughter," she looked at me with a blank stare. My own mother was staring at me, expressionless.

Where had she gone? What had happened?

I wanted to breathe but couldn't. A large vacuum had suddenly appeared and sucked all the oxygen out of the atmosphere. I knew I couldn't collapse because if I did, the paramedics would have another patient on their hands. So I willed myself to breathe, focus, and get my mother admitted into the hospital. A switch located deep within me flipped—the same switch that had flipped when the fire chief put his hand on my shoulder earlier. With one decisive shake of the head, I rolled my shoulders back and marched into the hospital to find admissions as they rolled my mother away in another direction.

"Hello, my name is Karmen. My mom was just brought in by the paramedics. What paperwork do I need to begin filling out?"

The nurse behind the counter looked up. The worry in her eyes said it all. She had to be wondering why a teenager was at the counter to admit her mother instead of an adult. Unmoved by the look, I waited for her to do her job and hand me the clipboard so I could do my job and get my mom admitted. Mom's social security number and insurance card were in her planner. I found her driver license in her wallet. I even knew the date of her last menstrual period because we were on the same cycle.

I completed the forms and returned them to the desk. Now it was time to make some calls. First on the list was

Mom's boss. I informed him that she had been taken to the hospital and would not be at work that day. Second, my school. I recounted the same facts I had given my mom's boss and provided the name and number of the hospital so they could validate that I was not skipping school. Next on the list was Point Loma Nazarene University. I needed to locate my sister and tell her to come home immediately. We were up in Orange County, ninety miles north of San Diego. I gave a college secretary the hospital name and address and enough details so she could find my sister.

Next came the harder calls. My grandmother, my mom's mom, was vibrant and energetic at sixty-three years old, still living in northern Minnesota with my grandfather. I knew she needed to know what had happened, and I knew I needed to be calm and self-possessed when I talked with her. I didn't have the option of falling apart. But the questions careening through my mind were too much to deal with on my own. What was wrong with my mom? Was she going to die? Was she already dead? The unknown was a tsunami, and I needed to pretend it was just a beautiful, sunny day in Orange County, California.

Two hours flew by as I called family and friends, but it felt like twenty minutes. I was reviewing my to-do list when my sister and her boyfriend walked into the waiting room.

Kyla's face reflected all the feelings hidden deep within me: panic, uncertainty, and gut-wrenching fear. But I had buried my emotions deep in my belly, so my face was plastic and emotionless.

A man in a white coat appeared, asking for Karen Berentsen's family. With the divorce, Mom had dropped her married name, Stave, and had reclaimed her birth name, Berentsen. He was looking for us, and his timing was perfect. I wasn't going to have to explain anything. Kyla would see it all for herself. I wanted to warn my sister that Mom wasn't going to look or act like Mom, but what energy I had was needed to hold myself together and keep my guard up. Kyla would find out soon enough.

The doctor escorted us into a space sectioned off by a curtain in the ER triage area and pulled back the curtain. Mom was sitting up. Her eyes were bright and clear, and a smile was on her face. She immediately reached for us. Except for the IV in her hand, she appeared normal. My sister immediately went to her. I stood, frozen. I felt imprudent for calling my sister and her boyfriend and making them leave school hurriedly to come home in response to what I thought was a dire emergency. I was perplexed.

"Karmen, come here. I'm okay," she said, her voice warm and confident.

She was back. I fought tears in an attempt to stay strong for my mother, but as relief swept over me, I gave in and collapsed into her arms. For the first time in hours, I was able to breathe deeply. Maybe it had all just been a bad morning.

After a few minutes in my mom's arms and the normalcy of listening to Kyla and James talk about school, I began to question what had happened. What had caused the seizure? Mom told us that she had gotten out of bed too quickly and that the lack of food had caused her blood sugar to be too low, which caused the seizure.

I couldn't make sense of that explanation. The previous night had been like a million nights before it. Mom never ate much. She never ordered anything when the three of us went out. Kyla and I each had a chronic case of eyes bigger than stomach, and Mom always just finished what we did not eat. At home, she often exchanged the calories of dinner for a glorious bowl of Häagen-Dazs ice cream with just a drop of Hershey's syrup to give it a hint of chocolate. The last ingredient was just enough milk to create a chunky, thick milkshake served in a bowl. My mom was a master of staying skinny without being on a constant diet. Knowing how many calories she could eat came as naturally as knowing the letters of the alphabet.

She didn't starve herself. She didn't let her blood sugar get too low. If her doctor had proposed low blood sugar and getting out of bed too quickly as the diagnosis, I was ready to challenge it. But I was both physically and emotionally exhausted from trying to be a sixteen-year-old-adult for hours during what had felt like a real crisis. And who was I to question a doctor's assessment? It didn't make sense, but I decided to accept it and stepped back into the role of teenager. It had never felt better.

I was ready to go home, but Mom wasn't dressed. Why? If this was just a blood sugar problem, why was she still in a hospital gown? -

As if reading my mind—or the scowl on my face— she said, "I want you and Kyla to go home, eat something, and take a nap. They're going to transfer me to another hospital for a few more tests."

Tests?

Before I could argue, she continued. "Karmen, I'm fine. They just want to make sure. Go home and rest."

I left with my sister and James.

The mess in the house captured the drama of the morning. End tables had been pushed against walls to make way for the gurney. Lamps were lying on the floor. Rugs were twisted from the commotion. My sister and James retreated to the kitchen while I retreated to my mom's room. My mom's unmade bed beckoned me. I told myself that it was just a bad scare, that she was fine. All was going to return to normal. She would be back in her own bed that night.

Laura, a friend of my mom from Arizona, called to say that she and everyone else in the office was worried and praying. The word seemed to have spread quickly on its own. I was exhausted and my mind wandered as she continued to talk. But my attention snapped back to Laura when she said, "We are all praying for your mom and her brain surgery."

Brain surgery? Mom had told us that she had just gotten out of bed too fast. The panic I'd felt earlier came crashing back in, but this time, it felt as if all the blood was draining from my body. "Laura, what are you talking about?" I screeched.

"Oh, my gosh . . . you don't know!" she said, sounding completely panicked at having said something she shouldn't have revealed. "I have to go."

And then she hung up.

CHAPTER 5

Brain Tumor

My world had collapsed.

I SAT ON THE BED WITH THE PHONE IN MY HAND. My world had collapsed. The tsunami *had* hit. It wasn't just another day in sunny California. It wasn't just a bad morning, never to be repeated. My mom had collapsed on the floor because she had a brain tumor.

I dialed the hospital and asked for her room. She answered, and without saying hello, I recounted the conversation I'd just had. "Is it true? Did you lie to me? Do you have a brain tumor? Are you having surgery this afternoon?"

Mom told me to come to the hospital and we could talk about it.

"No! I want an answer *now!*" I insisted.

"Yes, I have a brain tumor," she blurted. "Now, really. Come to the hospital. We can talk about it."

I hung up and marched downstairs in anger. Without regard for my sister's feelings, I announced that Mom had a brain tumor, that I was headed to the hospital, and that they were welcome to join me.

What I most feared was the sight of my mom being scared. For sixteen years, my mom had always been calm when I was scared, strong when I was weak, and wise when I was confused. She had been my rock, and I was terrified of seeing her crumble.

Her hospital room was filled with close friends and our pastor. Everyone greeted us with hugs and encouraging words. I found my way to a corner and waited. I needed everyone to leave before I unleashed my anger about being lied to. I waited and watched my mom sit in her bed and laugh with friends as if nothing had happened. I wanted to be cynical. I wanted to see her as a fake. But the more I watched and listened to her, the more perplexed I grew. Mom was laughing with authenticity. She appeared to be sincerely at peace.

"Are you on drugs?" I asked when everyone had finally left.

"No, why?" she asked with a chuckle, surprised by the question.

"I don't get it," I replied. "You have a brain tumor. You're having *brain* surgery and you're acting like everything is okay."

Even dressed in a hospital gown with an IV in her arm, she seemed self-possessed. "Karmen, every weekday I wake up, go to work, manage clients, attend meetings, and drive home. On the weekend, I teach Sunday school and sing in the choir. Finally, I'm going to be *used* in a mighty way."

I could not believe it. I was angry, and she was excited. Somehow, she saw purpose in her illness. She believed this tragedy was going to give her an opportunity to bless, encourage, and impact a multitude of lives. She was not scared, even though her world had just collapsed. Instead, her personal sliver of the world had just become exciting and meaningful to her. I couldn't possibly be angry with God when my mom was praising him. She didn't know what life had in store for her, but she trusted that it would be good. She believed that God was good. She didn't see her sickness as punishment, nor did she see the universe as being against her. She saw it as an adventure, an opportunity to be part of a bigger story.

I simply did not understand. My mom's wisdom was far beyond my black-and-white, literal world. At sixteen, my daily life had been driven by things like my perceived level of popularity and whether or not my hair looked good that day. That superficiality and innocence had just been stripped off in one quick and painful tug, like a bandage being ripped from a not-yet-healed wound, and I was terrified. But my mother was completely unafraid. She believed with certainty that the brain tumor would merely be one of many experiences in her life that chiseled her into the next version of the woman she was to be. And she had no doubt that she would be an even stronger woman after defeating the brain tumor.

My mom's brain surgery took place the next day, but it was months later before a nurse told me about it. My mom had requested to be kept fully alert and awake all the way into the operating room. The usual practice was for the anesthesiologist to sedate the patient before surgery, but my mom had requested that not be done. Once she arrived in the operating room, she asked all the nurses and doctors to gather around her. In her mind, it was simple. The doctors and nurses were operating on her head, and she had every right to have a few words with them before they opened her skull.

"I have no idea what your religious backgrounds or faith consist of," she said once they had gathered around her, "but before you perform surgery on my brain, I get to pray for you." She asked them all to bow their heads or stand quietly. She prayed and asked God to give them wisdom beyond their years, insight beyond their experience, steady hands, and calm hearts. She reminded them that they weren't really in control, and if God was going to take her home, there was nothing they could do about it. My mom believed in a bigger world than the visible one. She believed that if it was her time to die, no doctor could stop or change it. And with that, she was anesthetized and the surgery began.

About five hours later, her surgeon came out to the waiting room to talk with the family. Overall, the surgery had gone incredibly well. But the tumor was cancerous. It was the size of a plum and its tentacles had permeated her brain. If the neurosurgeon had removed all of the tentacles, he would have severely disabled her. The plan was to begin aggressive radiation in a few weeks, but she probably had only three months to live.

I was thrilled that she hadn't been disfigured by the surgery. In my shallow sixteen-year-old mind, being disfigured was worse than being given three months to live. She would beat cancer. She was Superwoman. She had married right out of high school, had babies at twenty and twenty-four, modeled briefly between birthing the two of us, and then boldly divorced at twenty-eight. As a single mom, she had put herself through night school to get her accounting degree. She got her college diploma and began as an accountant, then she was promoted to accounting manager, which opened the door to being on the project team when they were implementing JD Edwards' software. That led to her being offered a consulting job, and she was quickly promoted to project manager, a position paying six figures a year. She had proven she could do anything. Surely, she could beat a brain tumor.

My sister returned to college and my mom came home from the hospital. Taking care of her became my full-time job. I quit dance. I had studied dance since I was three years old, dancing five hours a night since age ten, but dance was now out. I also quit cheerleading and resigned from the student council. There wasn't anyone else to take care of Mom. During my junior year, I missed fifty-two of the 181 days of school. Overnight, my childhood was replaced with adult responsibilities.

The three months she was given to live turned into six months. Her headaches were intense, but they could usually be soothed with ice packs and drugs. Unfortunately, the drugs were not always enough to stop the seizures. I became intimately familiar with seizures. That meant I also became intimately familiar with trips to the hospital because Mom lost consciousness when she had a seizure. When that happened, I called 911, put Taffy in the garage, met the firefighter-paramedics at the front door, and gave answers to their questions before they asked them. Upon arriving at the hospital, Mom was admitted and sent to a room on the oncology floor. Usually, she regained consciousness shortly after arriving at the hospital. The nurses did their routine checks of her vital signs every ten minutes as she came to.

One particular night, however, Mom wasn't recovering like she normally did after a seizure. I left her side, went out to the nurses' station, and told them she wasn't becoming alert. The nurses saw a child talking to them and told me they would check on her in a few minutes. I returned to her room. Thirty minutes went by without a nurse appearing, and my mom still was not alert. I returned to the nurses' station, this time more aggressively stating that something was wrong. I was met by the same condescending response. They suggested that she was fine and I should go home and get some sleep.

I couldn't articulate what was going on with my mom, but something deep within my gut knew things weren't okay and she needed help. I demanded to speak with her doctor. Annoyed, they decided to let her doctor be irritated with me and dialed his number at 3:00 a.m. Fortunately, her doctor knew I was familiar with Mom's seizures and was not a drama queen. He ordered Mom to be transferred to the ICU, where she would have a dedicated nurse, and he promised to be at the hospital within the hour.

I saved my mom's life that night. Her brain had swelled, and if she had been left for the night as the nurses suggested, she would have either been dead or severely brain-damaged by morning. At sixteen, I had become an adult fighting with medical professionals. I read medical journals from UCLA so I could speak as intelligently as possible with my mom's team of doctors and nurses, but what saved my mom that night was the wisdom of my intuition.

I wasn't nearly as in tune with my intuition as I'd been as a small child when the same innocence that made me think I could fly had made me open and available to the wisdom of the universe. Logic, science, and my mind now guided me most of the time. Thankfully, there was still some connection to that inner voice located deep in my belly, because it was intuition that saved me from being motherless that night.

CHAPTER 6

The Death of Superwoman

"You're going to miss me more than you think when I am gone."

ONE YEAR AFTER FINDING HER on the floor in a grand mal
seizure, Mom surprised almost everyone when a CAT
scan showed all signs of the tumor gone. One more time,
she had proven herself to be Superwoman. The radiation
had worked; the tumor was gone. Cancer cells had not
spread to her lymph nodes or anywhere else in her body.
She was cancer free, and she began talking about going
back to work in the fall.

I could not understand why no one seemed to be
questioning what had caused the cancer and made it grow
so quickly in the first place. I saw nothing in her lifestyle
that should have contributed to its development, so there
was nothing obvious to me that could be done to prevent
cancer from redeveloping in the future. My mother did
not confide in me about it. She simply focused on returning to the same high stress job she had before her collapse.

It appeared that my mom viewed her tumor as something God had given her so she would have the story of
her illness and cure as an example of the power of faith.
She would have physical, documented proof of a miracle—a rare, incurable cancer being cured. She would be

a living testament for God. She had been excited to be "used by God" in a mighty way when she was diagnosed and given three months to live. A year later, she was alive, healed, and ready to return to her role as Superwoman.

The missing part was any personal accountability. If God had allowed the cancer, and if God had cured the cancer, she bore no responsibility for it. Therefore, she did not need to make any changes in her life. I had no desire to dispute God's miracle, but something just didn't resonate.

Her announcement that she would return to work in the fall left me unsettled and scared. My gut was trying to tell me something, but it seemed irreverent to question the miracle God had wrought. I wanted to live soulfully and faithfully. A spirituality that embraced trusting my intuition was beyond my ken. At seventeen, to trust my intuition before trusting the church would have contradicted faith as I understood it. So I never challenged my mother's plan to regain her strength over the summer and return to work in the fall.

But just as real hope began to take root, Mom's color began to change. Her skin began to have a dull, sick tone to it. I knew the tumor was back, but I tried to convince myself that it was just in my head. Then she had a horrific headache one night and asked me to bring her an ice pack and prescription pain pills. That hadn't happened in months.

I could no longer deny the fear that was gaining a foothold in my soul. Before I knew what I was doing, I made a detour and went to the downstairs bathroom. I turned on both the fan and water faucet to mask the sound and sank into the corner, sobbing uncontrollably.

In anger, I began to talk to God. "I can't do it again. You tested us. We praised you. Please, don't make me go through this again."

I sobbed until I was drained, feeling tired and alone. I told myself that sitting there and crying was not going to change a thing, and I willed myself to get up, keep moving, and stop feeling. I stood up, splashed water on my face, left the bathroom, and headed for the kitchen. There I prepared a beautiful tray with Mom's meds, an ice pack, and frozen fruit. Resuming the familiar role of nurse and caregiver, I returned to my mom's room.

But as I placed an ice pack across her head, covering her closed eyes, she began to pull me toward her. I knew I could not hold back my emotions if she held me. I gently resisted her tug, but she persisted. I finally compromised and sat down on the bed. But I kept my body rigid and tight, as if I had magical powers that could transform my skin into cold, hard metal—a protective armor. I was determined to suppress any piece of the child who was drowning in terror from the fear that the cancer was back and her mother's death was foreseeable. The simplest way to do that was to become as cold as steel—not just outside, but also inside, where my heart ached with dread.

My iciness didn't dissuade my mother. Instead, she began to pull on my arms in an attempt to get me to lay my head on her chest. How I craved to curl up in her arms and be held and comforted. I yearned to once again be the carefree child, but instead of seeing her love and protective arms reaching for me, I saw death. I felt like Snow White, who innocently reached for the shiny red apple. Apples are healthy and delicious, but evil had poisoned the apple Snow White was offered, just as cancer had poisoned my mother. I wouldn't be tricked into being vulnerable. My mother's arms were temporary and fleeting. Mom was sick. She had cancer and was dying. I *had* to remain taciturn and callous.

I needed to excuse myself from her room, but as I moved to rise, her frail fingers squeezed tighter around my arm. Her eyes were covered with the ice pack, but I could see the physical pain in her tightened jaw. And yet, she was using all her strength to gently coerce her seventeen-year-old daughter into her arms. Her persistence won. As my head hit her chest and I became engulfed in her arms, my armor melted and the terrified girl was again exposed.

Minutes passed as I lay on her chest sobbing. Over the past year I had been learning the art of living emotionally detached. I had survived by stepping out of my role as a teenager and into the role of adult. But now I had been stripped of all my weapons. I was exposed and defenseless, but it was freeing to be able to drop the adult persona, if only for a while. In my mom's arms, I again became a simple teenager and my mother's youngest daughter. I didn't need to pretend I was tough as nails. I didn't need to pretend God had cured her. I didn't need to pretend that I could coolly bring her ice packs and take care of both her and me without breaking a sweat. I could just let her hold me while I sobbed.

I felt the rise and fall of her chest and the steady beat of her heart.

I enjoyed feeling the rise and fall of her chest as she breathed in and out. Our toes wiggled next to each other now that I had fully moved up into bed and was cuddling with her. The sobbing had subsided, and I could feel all that was in me and all that was around me. The freed up energy felt like wind under my wings.

We were quietly resting when her chest moved as she took in that intentional breath before beginning to speak. I was sure she was going to finally express her anger with God and the universe, but she did nothing of the kind. "Karmen, God must have something really big in store for you to put you through all of this." There wasn't an ounce of anger or pity in her words. There was anticipation for how this was going to shape my life and mold me into the woman I was to become. Her voice was full of faith and hopefulness.

All this time, I had thought that I was the one in control, that I had become the adult managing her medical treatment plan along with the house and bills. But as her words penetrated my heart, I realized that I was still the little girl who needed her mother—even when that mother lay with an ice pack on her head and had a malignant tumor rapidly encroaching on her brain.

We both knew the tumor was back, but by morning Mom had reapplied her own persona—that of the strong cancer survivor who would be back in the corporate world with her corner office. I matched her, persona for persona. I had gone from tough adult to vulnerable child the previous night. The shapeshifting was exhausting, but it was now time for me to shift again, just not back into my adult persona. All the vulnerability and suppleness disappeared, and all our energy was focused on portraying the healthy mom and unaffected child.

It was Saturday, and I was supposed to leave for church camp the next day. We had made this arrangement when she had been feeling better and regaining her strength. Now everything was different because I knew the cancer was back. My head told me I needed to stay home, but my heart ached for a week of normal teenage gossip and fun. This was the first time in over a year that I was going to be physically distanced from the cancer and my mother. I was going to camp at Big Bear, and I was going to have a chance to *play*. I went to see one of my mom's friends and talked to her about going to camp. She advised me to go. I was scared. I asked her what would happen if Mom died while I was gone. She gently shook her head back and forth and told me that Mom wouldn't die while I was away.

I left Sunday morning on a bus with dozens of other teenagers and headed up to Big Bear. I tried to act silly and carefree like the other kids on the bus. I tried to care about petty gossip, but this persona was as counterfeit as the strong, unfeeling caregiver façade. My true self was happy to be away from illness and everything that accompanied it, but it was simultaneously terrified that my mom would die. And who wants *that* girl on the bus up to summer camp? I didn't want to be a recluse, so I acted like Mom was beating the cancer and I was a regular high school girl. I got one full day of camp with that portrayal.

I was on the volleyball court that Tuesday morning when I saw a swarm of camp counselors come running out of the office and spread out in an obvious search for one teenager among the fifteen hundred at camp. I knew they were looking for me. I stood still, watching the search as the volleyball game went on around me. Finally, one of the counselors caught my eye. A yell went up from her to the others searching, and all the counselors began running toward me. I was sure Mom had died, and I collapsed in the sand. They informed me that she was in the hospital and I needed to return home. Surrounded by the camp staff and all the kids who were now fully engulfed in the drama, I sat up and asked if I could stay until the evening campfire service had ended. I wasn't ready to go back to the nightmare of doctors and hospital smells.

The evening campfire service proceeded as normal, starting with loud, fun songs to get us engaged. That was followed by a message and the typical Nazarene altar call. The altar was a sacred place, and an altar call was an opportunity to pray and be prayed for by pastors and other church members. Everyone expected me to go down and pray. I slowly got up and walked down the stone amphitheater stairs. A herd of teens, ministers, and camp counselors followed me. I bowed my head. Everyone around me was crying. I couldn't find a tear. I was mad! As the prayer session ended and everyone was blowing their noses and wiping their eyes, my youth pastor—the one about to drive me down to Orange County—asked my permission to ask a question. I nodded yes.

"Do you know what your mom wants?" he asked.

I was enraged! What *she* wanted? What about what *I* wanted? For months, I had been holding it together and trying to be emotionally mature. But my hold had been precarious, and my fingers were losing their grip. I felt that my whole life had become about her, that nothing was about me. And I was not happy about it. I had lost everything. My days were filled with nursing my mother, not high school drama or dating. All of my hobbies and pleasures had been replaced with doctor visits and hospitals. I was too young and too immature to handle the responsibility, but I had been pretending to be Superwoman, just like my mom. My Superwoman cape was sliding off me. How dare he ask me if I knew what she wanted.

The youth pastor waited as I struggled internally. "I encourage you to find out what your mom wants," he finally said, softly.

I arrived at the hospital in the early hours of the morning and sat next to her bed, where I watched her sleep for about an hour before she woke up and smiled at me. Without speaking a hello, I asked, "Mom, do you want to die?"

She lay on her side studying me, saying nothing in reply.

"If I were you, I'd want to die," I finally added. "You know you're going to heaven, and it is a better place, a place without pain. Why wouldn't you just want to die and stop suffering?"

She continued to study me for a time before answering. "I realize I will never be the woman I once was. I will most likely never be an executive again, and I may be confined to a wheelchair, needing one brain surgery a year. But I will accept all of that to watch you and Kyla grow up." She paused before continuing with pain in her voice. "You're going to miss me more than you think when I am gone."

She was right, but I didn't get it. I didn't understand the loss that came with death. I didn't have any idea how much I would miss her. My naïve, seventeen-year-old mind thought life was contained in doing and accomplishing things. I didn't realize that her presence, her wisdom, and her unconditional motherly love were just as real in a wheelchair as they were in the stunning body and outwardly successful life she'd had only a year earlier. I also didn't realize something else: My mom's presence, wisdom, and love were the most precious things about her, and they would be what I would miss when she was gone.

She had her second brain surgery at 7:00 a.m. The first tumor had returned, along with a second one. After the surgery, she went in and out of coma for weeks. When she returned home, we knew it was only a matter of time. She began talking to me about going to college early instead of returning to high school for my senior year. Before she had become ill, my plan had been to go to Georgetown and study to become a lawyer. Now I was set on Cornell to become a neurologist. Her sickness had swayed me to the medical field, and Cornell was my top pick. I had received letters from Ivy League colleges because I attended one of the top prep schools, and despite all that had happened and all the school days I had missed, I still had a 4.0 GPA.

Mom asked me to think about going to Point Loma Nazarene University. I couldn't believe she was asking me to consider a small, private, Christian liberal arts school. I responded with disgust and shock. I had spent my entire academic existence taking the classes and getting the grades required for an Ivy League university. I had the scores, grades, and extracurricular accomplishments to get into one of the best schools in the country. Why would she ask me to think about going to a liberal arts school that anyone could get into?

No longer having the energy she'd once had to debate with me directly, Mom decided to accomplish her goal another way and asked her younger sister to talk to me about going to Point Loma. My aunt was almost closer in age to me than to my mom, and because she was more like an older sister than an aunt to me, I rolled my eyes but promised to pray about it.

That night I knelt next to my bed and started negotiating with God. I knew the Bible well from all my Sunday school classes and Christian education. I began by telling God how, in the book of Matthew, there was a parable about talents. The lesson of the parable was not to bury them but to use them, and by doing so, they would be multiplied and blessed. I made the argument to God that he had given me many talents, and it would be a sin to bury them in the ground, as the bad steward had done in the parable.

My clinching argument was that the Bible contained the Ten Commandments. One of the commandments was to honor your father and mother. My dad had literally disowned my sister when she decided to go to Point Loma. He told her that she no longer existed as his daughter, and for two years, he treated her as if she were dead. During that same period of time, he at least called me sporadically. I was my dad's prize possession now. I was his last hope for a child of his to attend a university he could brag about to his West Point buddies. My dad was going to blow a gasket if I even mentioned thinking about going to Point Loma. There was no way I could honor my dad and his wishes and go to Point Loma. But I told God that if, by some miracle, my dad wanted me to go to Point Loma, I would go. This was my private prayer with God. I didn't share the prayer with anyone, including my aunt or my mom. I simply prayed, confident that I had checkmated God and could pursue an Ivy League education with no guilt.

Point Loma had offered me a full ride academic scholarship, and I didn't even have to finish high school. I could simply take the GED. My grades and SAT score were sufficient to be accepted with a GED. Mom was thrilled because she knew she would soon be in hospice. She wanted me at college with my sister, not living alone my senior year.

We decided to talk to my dad, who was remarried and had moved from Texas to California. He was relatively close, in San Juan Capistrano, so he could meet with us in person. I was petrified. I expected him to respond in anger, sending the kitchen table flying as he burst out of his chair, and I played this scenario over and over in my mind.

When the day came to have the talk, I sat on one side of the kitchen table with my head down, body trembling. My dad sat next to me and my mom sat across from me.

"Clark, we've been talking about college," my mom said.

I watched out of the corner of my eye.

My dad started to smile as his mind conjured up the list of Ivy League schools his daughter was considering. When my mom stopped speaking, he turned his attention to me. My throat was frozen shut. My eyes paced from my dad to my mom and back to my dad. His impatience was growing.

I finally blurted out, "I've been offered a full ride to Point Loma," and quickly looked down, shutting my eyes, preparing for the table to go flying. After sitting hunched over, eyes squeezed shut for what seemed like eternity, I finally looked up at my dad.

"I think going to Point Loma might be good," he said. "You would only be ninety minutes away from your mom, and your sister seems to be very happy there."

What? I couldn't believe my ears. My dad, the one who had disowned my sister when she had decided to go to the very same school, was now in agreement that I, his last hope for unapologetic fatherly pride, should attend Point Loma. I sat in disbelief, realizing that I was heading off to a small, liberal arts, Christian college in a few weeks.

∞∞

I went off to college and Mom was admitted to hospice to die.

On December 10, 1991, my sister and I got a call from the hospice telling us that Mom probably wouldn't live through the night. We had received the same call many times before. Each time, we had left college together and driven north to Orange County. Each time, my mom had miraculously lived through the night. My sister and I each had one more final the next morning, and because we thought this was just another false alarm, we decided to stay, take our exams, and then head home for the holidays. Within seconds of making this decision, the telephone rang again, and I answered it. The woman on the other end of the line introduced herself as a nurse at the hospice. I said hello, expecting to hear that Mom's condition had improved and that we could drive up whenever it was convenient.

Instead, I heard, "Your mom is gone. She died a few minutes ago. I'm sorry."

Without a word, I hurled the cordless phone across my sister's dorm room and collapsed into a sobbing ball.

CHAPTER 7

The Burial

*I breathed in the acrid scent of power—the power that
comes from needing no one.*

MY MISSION WAS SIMPLE when I drove to the mortuary
the day before the funeral. I wanted to say good-bye to
my mom. The lady at the front desk escorted me to an
enormous room and closed the door behind me. At the
opposite end of the room sat a coffin on a stand. I wanted
to turn and run. The room was cavernous and stark, with
no intimacy or life to it. Everything about it seemed hollow and empty. The finality and austerity of it all was almost palpable, and for several moments, I was frozen in
place, terrified and dreadfully alone.

Would she be stiff and puffy? I didn't know what to
expect. I held my breath and nervously walked across the
room, knowing I needed to say good-bye. People had told
me that I needed to see her dead body to have closure,
but I wondered why. I wanted to remember her as a
healthy woman who was full of life. Sadly, I hadn't seen
that woman since finding her on the floor more than
eighteen months earlier. The steroids she was given had
made her body balloon. Her beautiful cheekbones had
disappeared and her face had puffed out like a chipmunk.

It was fluid, not fat. Unfortunately, the result was the same. My mom had morphed significantly.

More than her physical features had changed. Her physical weakness had seeped into her mental and emotional selves, sapping her of parenting strength. Even before I had left for college, the mom who had been intensely engaged in my life prior to being sick had lost the strength to ask me about my date when I returned at midnight. She hadn't challenged me on the friends I chose or the boys I dated. She had become too weak to focus on anything other than her own internal journey toward healing or death. It was the right focus, but it was accompanied by a shift of attention from the world that contained her daughters to the invisible world that held her fate.

Her death had been the external sign of her departure, but the mother who had been intensely engaged in raising me was gone months ahead of that final disappearance. I knew that pity would be projected on me at the funeral because everyone saw me as a motherless daughter. What they didn't understand was that I had been motherless for over a year.

Returning to the task at hand, I willed myself forward. I crossed the room and saw her. She was in a suit, and her hair and makeup had been done. I stared at her body lying in the cream silk that lined the silver casket. It wasn't her. She was gone. I couldn't feel her anywhere nearby. Her soul had left her body. The woman lying in front of me was no longer my mom. The person I had known as my mom was gone. My mind didn't understand it, but my heart felt it.

As I stood there, I was jealous of heaven and God. I *needed* her. God didn't need her. She was nowhere in sight and nowhere I could get to. She was gone to the invisible realm that was inaccessible to the living, and I felt *alone*. I was seventeen, alone, and terrified. I wanted to collapse, but who would comfort me if I did? In the past eighteen months, I had been held once. My sick mom, the one now lying dead in the coffin before me, had been the only person to hold me. Who was going to hold me if I started crying? Who would put me back together if I came apart?

How did this happen? Life wasn't supposed to turn out like this. I wasn't supposed to turn out like this. Where had the summers up in Minnesota wildly playing on ponies gone? What had happened to the wonder of tap dancing on the entryway tile for an audience of stuffed animals? The hours of tap dancing on the entryway tile were in the past. The heart that had dreamed of and believed in flying was grounded. As I stood before my mother, I felt my soul making a decision. Little Karmen, innocent Karmen who had once been vulnerable, sensitive, transparent, and open to being touched by everything, was going to be buried right alongside her mom. Immediately, I felt Little Karmen being siphoned right out of me and joining my mother in her casket. And once all the childhood enchantment was drawn out of me, I felt my body filling with pragmatism and reason. Standing in the place of Little Karmen was a hard, practical, tough, invulnerable, and impenetrable woman. The sheath growing around me felt dense and protective. My heart was going to be insulated from the potential of ever being wounded again.

It was decided. I was fleeing from myself because my survival depended on it. The child full of hopes and dreams had been buried, and a woman had emerged. That strong, unbreakable woman now stood in front of the casket and said good-bye, not only to her mom, but also to herself.

My new self—practical, calculating, and invulnerable—quickly devised a plan. I would return to college, get my degree, and become an autonomous, successful adult who needed no one. A new Karmen had been born, a Karmen who didn't need the magic of flying to ascend above the world. I would build a real empire and soar through the air on a Lear Jet—dominant, exclusive, and of course, fashionable. I would amass enough wealth to be loved and wanted by all. I would show the world a commanding woman, full of energy, with an eternal smile on her face.

I had seen the world's fascination with my mother's strength, coupled with her beauty. I had watched men enticed by her vivacious smile and independent nature. I would use my sensuality to entice men to adore me, desire me, and spoil me the way I'd wanted my dad to. And I would do it without allowing them anywhere near my heart.

The old Karmen had fought the idea that she needed to view her friends as competition and do whatever it took to get ahead in the world, taking no prisoners. The new Karmen was now ready to achieve the perfection in grades Dad demanded, fully inhale his schooling, and embrace the skill of manipulating people. In an instant, people descended into the role of pawns in my personal game of chess. For years I had played chess with my dad and had sacrificed the pawns as needed to win the game and declare checkmate. A gale force wind was blowing through my heart and eradicating any warmth and compassion for people. Everyone—friends, professors, and employers—needed to become as utilitarian as the marble chess pieces my father and I had played with, and I would use them as I saw fit. It was my game now. There was no magic, only strategy and calculation.

As I walked out of the memorial home, I breathed in the acrid scent of power—the power that comes from needing no one. The pain of my mom's death would ease over time. And as it eased, I would become a desirable woman who held all the power because she neither needed nor wanted anything from anybody.

CHAPTER 8

The Disappearing Father Act

I would never again be fooled by love.

I HAD BARELY INITIATED MY TRANSFORMATION when my dad asked me to come live with him instead of returning to school after the holiday break. He suggested I take a semester off and return in the spring. My newly forged internal armor began to slip from my psyche. Maybe everything was going to be okay. Maybe I wasn't completely alone in the world. My answer was quick. The morning after the funeral, I agreed to move to San Juan Capistrano and live with him and Betsy, his wife.

My sister and I had first met Betsy five years earlier when we visited for the summer. I was twelve and my sister was fifteen. My dad had picked us up from William P. Hobby Airport in Houston, Texas. As we drove, he told us that he and his girlfriend, Deane, had broken up. He was now living with his new girlfriend, Betsy. We arrived at the house to find Betsy waiting at the front door. She was much more polished than Deane, who had been silly, easygoing, and laid back. Betsy stood at the door with shined penny loafers, a long pleated skirt, an embroidered sweater, and perfectly styled hair. A smile covered her face, but something about her wasn't welcoming. Unlike Deane, who radiated kindness, Betsy's smile seemed forced, even strained.

Kyla and I had on jean shorts and Keds tennis shoes that were far from white. Our hair was a little messy after sleeping on the early morning flight. Betsy led us upstairs to the guest room of the old Victorian house she owned near Rice University in Houston—a prestigious neighborhood. The house was filled with antiques. My dad put our suitcases in the upstairs bedroom and left to unload the remaining suitcases from the car. Before my sister and I could follow him downstairs, Betsy shut the door, blocking our exit. Kyla and I looked at her, confused, and waited.

Betsy stared us up and down. "I am only going to say this once, so you better listen well. No one is going to separate me from your dad's money, including his two little grubby daughters. I can see that you obviously live like pigs at your mom's house, but you won't live like that in this house. Mess with me and I will make your life miserable."

Terrified, my sister and I stood motionless.

Betsy opened the door and in the sweetest Southern voice called, "Clark, let's sit down at the table and enjoy the girls over a glass of tea and cookies."

Kyla and I looked at each other. We had just entered twilight zone hell.

Betsy went downstairs and took my dad's hand. With a big smile on her face, she said, "Come on, girls. We want to hear all about school."

We sat at the table with her and my dad for the next hour. Betsy smiled at us like we were the cutest things she had ever seen and asked us questions in the sweetest voice. Having no idea what had just transpired between Betsy and us, my dad reprimanded us a couple of times when we hesitated before answering. We were utterly perplexed and trying to understand who this woman at the table with us was. Dad told Betsy that we were a little tired and jet lagged from the flight but promised that we would be more polite and talkative later.

Thanks to Betsy's opinion that we were uncivilized hicks, my sister and I got to attend Tiffany Jewelry Manners School. It was a prestigious weeklong manners school for children. I was thrilled to be out of the house, away from my wicked, soon-to-be stepmother. That week I learned how to sit at any table with dozens of dishes, flatware, and glasses and know exactly which one to use for each course. I also learned the art of writing a proper thank-you note and how to answer the phone correctly. My typical phone greeting, "Hi. Who's this?" wasn't even close to the proper greeting, which was, "Hello, this is the Berentsen residence. Who may I say is calling?" I also hadn't known that it was *never* appropriate to lick one's fingers at the table, even with finger foods. "Food is for the mouth and the napkin is for the hands," my instructor told me repeatedly.

At the graduation meal, where we showed off our newly learned manners for our parents, we were served chocolate-covered strawberries as the finger food. It was the ultimate test. It is cruel to serve chocolate-covered strawberries and expect children to wipe the chocolate off their hands with a napkin rather than lick one more delicious morsel off their fingers! If children could be served chocolate-covered strawberries and not lick their fingers, they had become civilized.

Dad and Betsy married the summer after that first visit with them. Years later, I learned that the night before their wedding, Dad called Mom and asked her if she wanted to remarry him. He still loved her. To my mom, remarrying would have been unthinkable. She had put herself through night school, gotten a great job, and was providing a good life for her girls. Remarrying was anathema to her. Dad married Betsy the next morning. Betsy wore a black sequined dress. She looked like the bride of Frankenstein.

After the wedding, I tried to build a relationship with Betsy. My mom encouraged me, often reminding me that Betsy was not the only difficult person I would have in my life, and the sooner I learned to deal with difficult people, the easier life would be. She painted Betsy as a *lesson* for me instead of something *done* to me. I was never allowed to be a victim who blamed other people for my unhappiness. Mom encouraged me to call things what they were and then figure out how to change, manage, or brave them. I was in control and responsible for my happiness. But my refusal to give Betsy power over my happiness only infuriated her.

Betsy's ability to change demeanor on a dime, depending on whether Dad was around or not, made me wonder if she had some sort of mental illness, like multiple personality disorder. And after Mom's death, I wasn't sure which Betsy would greet me that first morning at the house. But what I was met with that first morning was a quiet Betsy who seemed to respect that I was grieving the loss of my mother. It was a relief.

I also didn't know if my father would be around or busy with work. My sister had already made her escape back to college. As I walked past my dad's home office, he surprised me by springing out of his chair, greeting me enthusiastically, and asking what I wanted to do that day.

I wasn't sure how to respond. I knew I needed to attend to the chore of packing up the house Mom and I had shared, so after a pause, I said, "Um, I was planning on going to the house and packing it up. Don't you have work to do?"

He suggested that we take the bikes and ride to breakfast. A bit confused by his express desire to spend time with me, I agreed. As we rode our bikes, he behaved like Superdad. He listened attentively to every word I spoke, seemed interested in me, and actually behaved as if he wanted to be with me. This was not the father I had become used to.

At breakfast, we talked about everything from business and politics to boys. After breakfast, he asked if I wanted to ride by the golf course and maybe stop for ice cream. I agreed. My adult responsibilities over the past eighteen months had given me an adult voice, and I somehow summoned the courage to speak boldly to my dad once we had gotten our ice cream. "I don't understand you. You have been absent most of my life. At times, you threw around money like it was candy, but you made Mom fight you for every penny of child support. And now that Mom is dead, you spend the entire day with me, acting like I am your only care in the world."

His answer was slow in coming. "I was never needed when your mom was alive. She could do everything—and do it better than me. I was so afraid I was going to mess you guys up, I thought it best to just stay away."

Tears sprouted in my eyes. "It would have been nice to have you around."

That day was just the beginning. The quarter went by in a blur. Betsy remained polite and respectful, for the most part. She seemed to have pulled in her need to be the center of attention, and she did not get in the way when Dad and I spent time together.

And we did spend time together. Dad and I spent hours together each day, cycling, eating, playing chess, and reading *The Wall Street Journal*. After twelve weeks, Mom's house was sold, the boxes were packed, mostly by my uncle and grandmother, and I was ready to go back to school. I told Dad that I was planning on driving down to school the next weekend in preparation for classes on Monday. He surprised me by saying that he thought I should take another quarter off and return to school after summer break.

I wanted to go back to school. I missed my friends. I loved that my dad wanted me around, but I told him that I thought I should go back. A couple of days later, I packed up my car and drove back to college. The weekend flew by as I caught up with friends. But I missed my dad and phoned him on Monday, after my first day of classes. It had been days since we had spoken.

He answered after two rings. "Clark Stave."

"Hi, Dad. It's me," I said.

He responded in a brusque, serious voice. "What do you want?"

Stunned, I tried to conceal my hurt. "I just wanted to say hi. I miss you."

"I'm busy. I'll call you in a few days," he said impatiently. And then he hung up before I had a chance to reply.

His words felt like a left hook to the jaw that I hadn't seen coming. Maybe Betsy wasn't the only one with multiple personality disorder. How was it possible for him to be cold and unfeeling after months of closeness and affection? His tone and words were shocking and unexpected. We had grown close over the past twelve weeks. I had let my guard down and shared my heart without reserve. Surely, he was simply having a bad day. With an imaginary eraser, I made quick, strong strokes and purged the entire phone call, along with my fear of being rejected by my father. I decided to call him again in a few days, and then I put my attention back on my books.

Three days later, I awoke with a plan. Dad was a morning person. If I caught him in the morning, all would be right again. Maybe we could even spend the weekend together. I dialed his phone number with nervous anticipation. After half a ring, it picked up. *The number you have dialed has been disconnected. Please check the number and dial again.* I hung up. Assuming I had dialed the number wrong, I dialed again, only to hear the same recording. Were the phone lines down? My dad's house was less than two hours north of my school. I would simply drive up and get to the bottom of this wackiness.

Ditching class, I jumped in the car and drove north. To my utter disbelief, I found the house he had rented empty. His furniture and personal belongings were all gone. The house where I had slept for the past three months, the house that had provided warmth and stability after losing my mom, the house where I had lived with my dad and laughed and cuddled . . . was hollow, void of any soul or sign of life.

I felt like a character in a disaster movie in which an asteroid has hit Manhattan and the lone survivors are surrounded by carnage, bewildered and disoriented. Yes, Dad had disappeared repeatedly in my childhood, but that was before the adult connection and bond we had forged over the past three months together. Less than six days earlier, I had been living in this now-abandoned house with a father who had been allowed into the deepest parts of me. I had shared my dreams, and I had flung open the gates to my heart. I had welcomed him into the inner chambers of my soul because I had come to understand that he had always loved me but had simply stayed away because my mother was expansive and self-sufficient.

Had I been duped?

Before I closed the book on my dad, I had to confirm that he had actually packed up his house and moved away without a whisper of good-bye. Swathed in humiliation, I knocked on a neighbor's door. George, the neighbor, answered. Feeling trepidation but wearing a mask of calm, I asked him if he knew where my dad and Betsy had gone.

With sad eyes he said, "Yes."

"Where have they gone?" I asked.

George looked away from me, embarrassed. "He asked me not to tell you where he has moved to."

My father's behavior when I called that Monday had merely knocked me out, but George's words were the coup de grâce. I stood, stunned, feeling like a knife had just gone through my stomach. I couldn't breathe. Only days earlier, we had ridden our bikes to our favorite breakfast place as father and daughter. What had I done that had been so awful? What had compelled him to leave and not let his daughter know where he had gone?

I wanted to burst into a zillion pieces that could never be put back together again or, even better, eradicate any evidence that I had ever existed and vanish, like vapor. I had been fooled again! I had believed that I was worthy of love and was finally loved and cherished by my dad. What I thought was real hadn't been more than an illusion that I had bought into, a chimera. I felt like an alien on Earth who had no aptitude for understanding the environment, let alone living in it. I didn't even know how to begin processing the fatal blow my heart had just experienced.

I pulled myself together enough to realize that I did not want to expose George to any more of my family disaster. Crumbling into a ball on his front stoop was not an option. I needed to steel myself against hurt and wrap myself in an imaginary mantle that would shield and safeguard me. Without that, I wouldn't be able to excuse myself and make it back to school. I took in a deep breath of chilly, stone-cold, hardheartedness. Once transformed and feeling strong and impassive, I looked straight into George's eyes. With a perfectly constructed synthetic smile, I thanked George for his time, turned, and walked indifferently to my car. I would never again be fooled by love.

CHAPTER 9

College and Dating

I was going to survive and thrive.

I WAS AN ORPHAN. My mom had died and my dad had vanished, but I was determined to survive and thrive. I returned to my classes with fierceness. My goal was to amass enough prestige, power, and money to ensure that I would need no one. My dad had fooled me for the final time. The last shred of innocence had been expunged from me.

Maybe my dad's business had been in financial trouble and he shouldn't have been spending time with me. Maybe he couldn't face any type of rejection and saw my decision to return to school as rejection. I had given him my heart and all of my love. He had been the center of my attention for weeks, but the plan had always been for me to return to school. I needed an education and a degree. I needed my friends. I never imagined that he would be impulsive and disappear without a good-bye. Yes, he had done it before, but that was when Mom was alive. This disappearing act would be his last magic trick at my expense because my heart now had callouses on its callouses.

My days of being duped were over. I would exploit all that I could out of my full-ride scholarship at a

Nazarene university to become a world-class doctor who was respected and in demand. All the magic of the church and the supernatural had disappeared, but I still needed an education, and I needed a community.

Fortunately, Point Loma was not just a girls' school, and I planned on reveling in the men there. I wouldn't allow myself to become attached to and deceived by any of them as I had done with my father, but I also would not be without male attention. Flirting was fun, and male attention would give me some validation about my attractiveness and desirability, but I would keep my brain engaged and never let my heart run wild. I was sure that I had hardened my heart enough to use the same kind of command and control in my relationships with men that I would later employ in my career. I zeroed in on a popular varsity tennis player who was attractive and popular, but no match to me intellectually. We dated for a while, and I found myself becoming friends with his roommate. Peter was neither hip nor particularly popular, but he had something my boyfriend lacked: He was intrigued with my intellect. He also had a dry, self-deprecating sense of humor, and he carried himself with carefree lightness— two qualities that belied an underlying maturity I found calming. He was grounded and secure.

I continued to date the tennis player, but by sophomore year, Peter and I were studying together Monday through Thursday nights. When I broke it off with Peter's roommate, I spent weekend nights with other guys on dates, and then our Monday night study session often included some harassment over my choice of weekend dates.

Peter's focus on the guys I dated seemed to come from a place of brotherly love, not jealousy. We were implausible as anything but friends. Peter was practical and disciplined; I was a woman whose life was filled with drama and noise. He didn't care much how he looked; I was into fashion. We were like brother and sister, and I felt unconditionally accepted by him.

One night while we were studying for sophomore finals, he nonchalantly reached over to my side of the library table, took my planner, wrote something in it, and returned it. He went back to studying, and I looked to see what he had written. Penciled in on Friday was "dinner date with Peter." I stared at the page in confusion, unsure what to think at first. But because having dinner with him seemed harmless, I smiled at him and nodded in agreement. We were buddies. Maybe I was misinterpreting his intentions. Back in my dorm room, I conferred with my roommate Julie. Was this just dinner with my buddy, or was it a date?

She rolled her eyes at the absurdity of my question and replied, "Of course it's a date. And there is no way *you* are going on a *date* with Peter Smith."

Irritated by the fact that my roommate was predicting my actions, I grew a few inches taller. "And why exactly wouldn't I go out with Peter on Friday night?"

Julie didn't sugarcoat her response. "You think he's beneath you."

She had nailed me. She was exactly right. Peter was not popular and would definitely not elevate my social status. He was smart and quick-witted, but he was neither cool nor trendy. He was someone I studied with, not someone I went out with on Friday night. On weekends I was seen with guys who held student council positions, were captains of sports teams, or were surf gods.

The problem was that I didn't want to be the shallow girl who was proving that she wasn't self-confident enough to go out with someone like Peter. The image I worked hard to project was that of a confident, independent, self-assured woman. But the brutal truth was that I got so much of my worthiness from the guys I was dating instead of searching for any of it in myself. My dad's rejection had convinced me that I didn't have innate value, and I was working hard to manufacture it. The confidence and lightheartedness that I had at three years old while dancing for my stuffed animals was buried so deep within me, it would have taken a team of geologists to unearth them.

Of course, my only conscious thought in that moment was that I was not going to prove my superficiality, so I looked Julie right in the eye and said, "Watch me."

On Friday night, Peter picked me up and took me to a restaurant in the Gas Lamp Quarter of downtown San Diego. My strategy was to keep my hands in my pockets to ensure no accidental hand brush that could lead to handholding. This was going to be the only date with Peter Smith. I would prove that I was confident enough to go on a date with someone off the popularity radar screen, but I would also find an acceptable reason for not being compatible with him so I could avoid a second date.

By the time we ordered, I realized that this date wasn't like other dates. I didn't have to *pretend* to be anything. I usually asked my date questions to ascertain what type of girl he was attracted to. Then I morphed myself into that profile. Peter already knew me. I couldn't pretend to be a surfer or a blues aficionado. I couldn't pretend to be anything. All I could be was me. It was easy and authentic. Three hours flew by, and we closed down the restaurant.

When we left and got into the car, Peter handed me a bandana. "I need you to put this on," he said.

Immediately my body tightened in resistance. I was praying that he wasn't going to drive me to the beach for some stargazing. He pleaded with me to trust him, and I gave in, blindfolding myself with the bandana. As seconds turned into minutes and minutes turned into half an hour, I began to relax. I realized that we could not be headed to any of the popular make-out spots because too much time had passed. Just when I was beginning to stop worrying and enjoy his company again, the car came to a stop and Peter told me to stay put as he came around the car to get me. He opened the door and led me a few steps.

"Ready?" he asked.

"Sure," I replied, though I honestly could not concoct the tiniest hope of whatever he had planned ending well.

I removed my bandana. Standing before me was a Dunkin' Donuts. I turned and looked at him in disbelief. I loved Bavarian Kreme donuts, and he knew it. But I had never seen a Dunkin' Donuts shop anywhere in Southern California.

Peter smiled. He knew he had done well. He had found a Dunkin' Donuts in Escondido, a town twenty-five minutes from San Diego.

As I stared at the fluorescent Dunkin' Donuts sign, I felt cherished and known. I was standing in front of the shop that held my favorite treat because Peter had listened to my genuine and silly desire for a greasy, air-puffed, five-hundred calorie, cream-filled donut. And he had gone out of his way to get it for me.

We decided to take our donuts to the beach. There we sat and talked until the sun came up. I was stumped. I had just had the best date of my life with a guy I had never imagined dating.

Peter dropped me off in front of my dorm at 6:00 a.m. and gave me a hug before saying good-bye for the summer. He had a 10:00 a.m. flight to Colorado, where he was going to work in the kitchen of a dude ranch for the summer.

I was in a state of confusion and delight as I went back to my dorm room.

As I quietly crawled into bed, trying to avoid waking my roommate, she lifted her head and said with a smile, "I assume it was a good date."

CHAPTER 10

Marriage and Compromise

*I had made my own hell by doing what I thought
would get me a family and babies.*

UNLIKE PETER, I HAD NO FIRM PLANS for the summer. I bummed around Southern California for a few weeks before deciding that a trip to visit my aunt in Fort Collins, Colorado, was a great idea. I decided visiting her would be the perfect excuse to "run into" Peter, even though the dude ranch where he worked as a chef was more than three hours from my aunt's house.

When I called Peter and told him about my decision to spend the rest of the summer in Colorado, he was ecstatic. Every week for six weeks, I drove from Fort Collins to the dude ranch southwest of Denver for Peter's day off.

Social status paused for the summer. I was free to spend one day each week hiking or mountain biking in the beautiful Rocky Mountains with a handsome, fit guy who accepted all of my many facets: the girl who liked fashion and dressing up, the smart student with a full-ride scholarship, the cheerleader, the beach baby, the outdoorsy girl in hiking boots, and all the rest. He was always interested in what I thought about things, and he respected me. Peter made me feel cherished and special, but I was careful to keep it casual and fun between us.

We laughed, talked, and even camped under the stars without any romantic gestures until the last night when his arm moved around me while we sat in front of the campfire. Surprisingly, his arm felt natural and his closeness felt good. By the end of the night, I desired his lips on mine. It was well into the early hours of the morning when he finally leaned in for the kiss. It felt inevitable and organic. We had spent all summer together and had grown close.

But when I returned to college, I found I had an unusually large number of date requests. It seemed everyone I had wanted to date was suddenly interested in dating me. In my black-and-white world, I had a boyfriend. I had kissed Peter, and that meant we were exclusive.

I declined dates, saying, "I'm dating Peter Smith," but no one had any idea who I was talking about. By the end of the first week, after explaining over and over who Peter was, I panicked about the fact that I was dating someone considered a nobody. And then I caught myself in the panic and realized that Julie had been right. In my attempt to keep my heart safely buried, I had become socially superficial. I was too shallow and insecure to be with Peter. As soon as Peter returned to school, I told him that we should just be friends.

The dates with the surfers and soccer studs included doing what was cool, even if I was bored to death. I had no interest in hockey, but that didn't matter to the guys I dated. I was the pretty girl on their arm at the game. The date wasn't about me. It was about the game and what they wanted to do. I was using them and they were using me. After the summer with Peter, it felt empty. For months, I spent my time going to sporting events I had no desire to attend, surf contests I didn't understand, and parties where I ended up driving everyone home because I was the only sober person. No one took me to Dunkin' Donuts or considered my interests the way Peter had, and I missed him.

During the Thanksgiving break, the college campus became eerily quiet. I had no family to go home to, and I had declined invitations with friends to visit their families with the intention of using the quiet time to get ahead instead of wasting precious hours watching stupid movies and playing games and puzzles. But in truth, just the thought of seeing my friends with their family left me unable to breath. Being an outsider in someone else's family when I wanted the love and warmth of a family of my own was just too hard. I didn't want to witness what I didn't have or feel the pain of being an orphan.

Yet studying wasn't strong enough to shut out the loneliness engulfing me. There was an immediate solution: Peter had stayed on campus because his aunt and uncle worked at the school. Peter already felt like family, so I wouldn't feel like an outsider, and I was pretty sure his aunt and uncle would welcome me. I needed Peter like a daughter needs a dad, though I didn't realize it. And it wasn't only Peter I needed. I needed his family. I longed for an anchor. I longed for something stable.

To Peter, I was charismatic, sophisticated, fun, and full of life. My charisma was not only developed during twelve years of studying classical ballet but also through fashioning myself after my mother, who had modeled professionally before I was born. Mom had commanded the attention of both men and women the moment she entered a room. I had mesmerized Peter with my charm, neatly covering my sense of unworthiness, as well as the depth of angst and unresolved grief that lay deeply buried under my well maintained armor.

Before I came along, Peter had practically lived in the library, studying. He had a quiet, orderly life. I pulled him out of the library and got him studying at places where there was life in the form of people, stories, and entertainment.

Over the next year and a half of college, we continued to study together, as well as dream of our future. There were moments of questioning, but Peter's adoration never faltered. He was steady and true. I had made a commitment to myself to date him for six months. By the end of six months, everyone knew him, and once they got to know him, they loved his dry humor and wit as much as I did.

After graduation, Peter and I headed out to Colorado to enjoy some backpacking near the dude ranch where he had worked. When we rounded the corner of the trail that led to the rock where we'd had our first kiss two years earlier, I was surprised to see a table set with flowers, candles, and champagne sitting on a rock ten thousand feet above sea level. Peter feigned surprise but could not suppress the smile beginning to spread across his face. He knelt down on one knee, extending a box with a big, beautiful diamond ring. Bursting with excitement, I hardly let him get the words out before I plowed into him with such gusto that the ring flew out of his hand and sailed through the air. Luckily, it stayed in the box and was easily retrieved.

We decided to get married in Atlanta, Georgia, the following spring. Peter was from Atlanta and had the best chance of getting into medical school in his home state. I had decided not to apply for medical school. At the end of my junior year, I had realized that I wanted to make money. I didn't want to go to school for another four years and then work through internship and residency. I wanted to get a job and start living like an adult. Using my mom's contacts at JD Edwards, I secured an internship and ended up becoming one of their first college hires. The plan was all set. I would work for JD Edwards and Peter would go to medical school.

The night before our wedding, Peter and I had a beautiful rehearsal dinner at an old mansion in Roswell, a suburb outside of Atlanta. After the dinner, Cathie, my adopted godmother, asked if we could talk.

"Sure," I replied while keeping my attention on the guests. I wanted to make sure my rehearsal dinner was going to be remembered by all as one of the best parties they'd ever attended. I scanned the room and was shocked when I brought my attention back to Cathie. There were tears in her eyes and concern etched in her face.

"Do you love Peter?" she asked.

Her question immediately shifted my attention from my guests, the music, and my dress. "Of course I love him," I replied.

"Karmen," she said, "you know we think the world of Peter. He's a great guy. But what I am asking is if Peter makes your heart leap and gives you butterflies in your stomach."

What was happening? My logical mind tried to comprehend her question, but I was unable to. I was being smart about my marriage. I was marrying a man who was on his way to becoming a doctor. I didn't understand Cathie's question because she wasn't asking whether I had made a logical choice. She was asking what my heart felt for Peter, and I didn't have enough access to what my heart felt beneath the wounding from death and abandonment to be able to answer her with real insight.

Standing in the fairy-tale-like house with nearly a hundred friends and family gathered around me, I could smell the dream of having a family again. I wasn't going to engage in a discussion that had any possibility of ruining my dream. I wasn't going to admit to Cathie or even to myself that Peter hadn't swept me off my feet. It was his adoration and affection that had left me wanting to run down the aisle to marry him.

Cathie saw through it all. She didn't see me in love with Peter because I wasn't in love with Peter. He was a good, logical choice for a husband. He was smart, disciplined, handsome in a conservative sort of way, and responsible. Peter provided stability and family, and above all, he worshiped me.

Cathie patiently waited for my answer. As her eyes gushed with emotion, the wall around my heart thickened. "Cathie, that kind of love doesn't exist." I thought I knew better. My head had it all figured out. Peter was going to make me happy and replace my father's rejection with unconditional love.

Cathie lowered her eyes to the floor and shook her head so gently that it was almost imperceptible. She looked defeated and heartbroken. After a few moments, she looked up again and made one last attempt to get through to me. "Please don't walk down that aisle tomorrow."

Unfortunately, Cathie's heartfelt advice didn't faze me. I was headstrong and determined. The next morning, I was the beautiful bride and Peter was the handsome groom. It was the wedding of my dreams with flowers, toile, and the perfect dress. I felt like a princess. Our honeymoon in Hawaii was filled with hikes, romantic dinners . . . and sex!

We were both virgins on our wedding night. Why? Because we were living in a black-and-white world. We saw sex before marriage as taboo, forbidden. It wasn't something natural and beautiful. It wasn't an expression or experience to be shared between consenting adults. The church had taught us that it was prohibited, danger-ous, and destructive. In Hawaii, I realized that I loved sex. I loved Peter's touch and affection. I loved being desired and aroused. I fancied loving someone back. I delighted in the notion that I could make Peter happier than he had ever been. The world was blissful and idyllic.

We returned from Hawaii, and I returned to the of-fice. I was excited to come home to my new husband after my first day back at work. I found Peter in the kitchen cooking, stirring a delicious smelling sauce. Kicking off my heels, I threw my arms around him. But instead of hugging me back, he turned and coldly told me to go change clothes before dinner.

I froze. I wondered what could have happened, but I did-n't ask. I just turned around and headed to the bedroom. As I changed my clothes, my initial hurt turned to excitement. This was an opportunity to be the perfect wife. Whatever had caused his mood, I could make it a great night for him.

"I need to talk to you about a few things," Peter said as we sat down to dinner.

Wide-eyed, I nodded with a big smile, ready to do whatever I could to make him happy.

Peter began to describe what he thought needed to change in me. He told me that he no longer wanted me to have acrylic nails. He liked the look of short, clean, natural nails. He also didn't want me to wear makeup, and he didn't want me to color my hair anymore.

The man who had liked all of my facets suddenly wanted me to become dull and one-dimensional. He still looked like my husband, but it was as if I were suddenly a character in the movie *Mission Impossible* with some stranger wearing a mask and impersonating my husband sitting in front of me—not Peter. I had dated Peter for three years, and we had just returned from a magical honeymoon. I thought I knew him, and I thought he loved the woman I was. But my husband was now coldly, calmly *ordering* me to morph from a faceted gem into a plain, bland piece of roadside gravel. I was stunned and confused.

I thought Peter loved how I looked, and I thought he was proud of his eye-catching wife. He had never given me reason to think otherwise. In fact, it had always seemed that he viewed me as the woman of his dreams. And now it appeared that his dream woman was someone stripped of everything girly and fashionable—a woman who was granola plain.

But he was my husband, and I wanted to please him. So as I sat at the kitchen table watching Peter calmly eat his dinner, I nodded, and quietly said, "Okay."

I didn't understand him, but it didn't matter. Ever since my father left when I was nearly five, I had wanted a man to love me unconditionally. And I had wanted to be part of a family ever since my mother's death. Now I was married and had a new family. If Peter didn't quite love me unconditionally, I would make it okay. He had adored me before our marriage, and I believed I could make him adore me again. I could give up a few external trappings for affection and connection.

Over the next six years, our marriage became a set of agreements and compromises. I never did regain Peter's adoration. Much of the time, I didn't even feel that he approved of me. I tried to be quiet and plain, but that wasn't me. My gregarious spirit was suffocated by Peter's need for order and simplicity. Peter no longer enjoyed my energy. Instead, he saw me as a tornado in his life causing havoc.

We tried marriage counseling with a succession of counselors. All of them focused on relationship skills like communication and conflict resolution, but we had bigger problems than communication. Everyone around me thought Peter was a good guy and wanted me to pray for him. Peter *was* a good guy, but he was also a horrible husband. He became punishingly parental, behaving as if he knew what was best for me, and he set expectations that were impossible to meet. In essence, I had somehow married a copy of the father who had rejected me.

The truth was that I had made my own hell by doing what I thought would get me a family and babies. I hadn't been honest. I hadn't told Peter that my acrylic nails made me feel polished and increased my confidence in a professional setting where I was at least ten years younger than everyone else. At some level, I knew I found my self-confidence in the outward trappings, not in what was inside me. But I couldn't snap my fingers and feel good about myself. It didn't work that way. And I wasn't going to admit to my husband that I needed the security that feeling attractive and fashionable gave me.

I was worn down. I wanted happiness now, not just in the next life. I searched for an answer in the Bible. As I read the gospels, I saw a distinct pattern. Jesus had healed people. He hadn't simply told people that suffering was good. I failed to understand why churches preached so much about suffering and held it up as something good. That had not been what Jesus preached.

I wanted to be fully alive. I didn't want to suppress my spirit, nor did I want it to be suppressed by anyone else— least of all my husband. But I was quietly wilting away. I had morphed into everything I thought would please Peter and restore the picture of marriage and family I so desperately wanted. Nothing had worked. I felt that any personal power I'd once had was gone, and I needed to get it back. For the first time in a very long time, I asked myself what I *dreamed* of doing. Even asking felt like a sin.

The simple questioning process brought a big gulp of air to my lungs. I felt as if I had just surfaced after holding my breath underwater for so long that I was near death. I couldn't make Peter love me. I couldn't make our marriage blissful. But I could begin to dream again. The little girl who used to climb up to the top log in the front yard, close her eyes, and dream of soaring across the yard was sneaking back to the surface.

CHAPTER 11

From Employee to Part Owner

Many of the problems in large companies were less about
a lack of brilliance and more about losing simplicity and focus.

WHILE WORKING AT JD EDWARDS, I had found a natural talent in training. Every software company has to offer training on their software. JD Edwards' offerings for clients and consultants implementing the software left much to be desired.

The opportunity to manage the design of business partner training offered a chance to move to Denver. Peter loved mountain biking, hiking, and other outdoor activities, and he had been working at REI as a bike mechanic while applying to medical schools. But after two years, he had received nothing but rejections. We had no reason to stay in Atlanta, and we were both ready to move back West. He would look for suitable work and revel in nature. I would further my career.

In Denver, I threw myself into my job, and my efforts paid off. I was given opportunities to open training centers in Paris, Rio de Janeiro, Cape Town, and London. I was twenty-four, and while I had expertise, I did not have age on my side to establish credibility when I was away on business trips. I needed to look polished and professional, so I returned to sharp suits and expertly applied makeup.

Being twenty-four was also an impediment when it came to promotions. Passing by my boss's office one day, I overhead my name one step before walking in front of the open door. I froze and began to listen.

"You know, Karmen could do Nancy's job in her sleep," my boss said.

"Karmen is twenty-four. There is no way we are giving her a manager's title. I paid my dues. She will pay hers," the director of training replied.

I had hit a glass ceiling. It didn't matter how hard I worked. For months, I tried to figure out a way around the training director, but I loved training, and he was the director. Going over his head would get me nowhere. I wanted to stay in training, but I didn't want to atrophy in the same position until I became old enough to satisfy everyone else's notion of an appropriate age to be promoted. It was time to leave and find a new company that appreciated my energy, youth, expertise, and ambition.

Peter hated the idea of my leaving a stable company. My salary had doubled while I was at JD Edwards, and Peter loved how robustly I was being paid. I thought it was ridiculous because I was doing a job equivalent to that of the managers who made nearly twice as much as me. Peter was employed as a paramedic-firefighter at half my salary. Even so, between my salary and his, we were saving thousands of dollars a month. We had bought our house in Colorado based on my salary alone. Our cars were paid off and neither of us had student loans.

I hated fighting with Peter, but his position was that I should simply stay put, even if that meant stagnating for the rest of my career instead of doing what I was capable of. The battle continued for months. Then one night when Peter rolled his eyes, I began to silently cry about the stalemate in my career and marriage. His easy dismissal of me as he headed to bed might have been what triggered the simple realization that I didn't need my husband's approval to quit my job. Perhaps it was my own internal wisdom surfacing. As I sat on the couch, snuggled with a blanket, I realized I had known what I wanted to do for over nine months.

My tears stopped with the insight. I stood up and folded the blanket, placing it in exactly the correct place. I fluffed the couch pillows, did one last check to make sure the house was in perfect order, walked up the stairs, brushed my teeth, and crawled in bed next to Peter. He had no idea that someone other than the compliant wife he was used to had just crawled into bed with him.

My newfound sense of self-respect awoke with me the next morning. I showered, put on my most impressive suit, and handed my boss the resignation letter I had typed early that morning. Bewildered, she begged me to stay. I remained strong. After a scurry of meetings, I was asked to pack up my desk and leave. Shortly before noon, I drove home happily unemployed.

Even though I was certain I had done the right thing, I had no idea where I was headed. I didn't have another job or even a plan. I had used all my strength to simply leap. Quitting felt liberating, but I knew that Peter was not going to agree with my decision. For years, I had seen Peter as the means to safety and the man I would sacrifice anything for. But I had misled myself. I wanted love and a family. Instead, marriage had given me rejection and conditional love. And that had left me feeling abandoned and alone. I had foolishly looked outside myself for fulfillment. It was time to stop depending on Peter and the mirage that marriage meant happiness, at whatever cost, and rely on the only person who could give me the life I wanted: me.

Peter was furious with me for resigning and interrogated me until he ran out of questions. But there was nothing he could do. I didn't care if he was upset. I had tried to be the wife he expected and the woman he wanted. I had thought that looking more natural and becoming quieter would regain his affection. When that didn't work, I was sure that female enticement would. But that only seemed to make him withdraw further. Standing before him in a black lace nightie from Victoria's Secret had elicited no positive response. If anything, it had made him uncomfortable. Finally, I had tried engaging with him in mountain biking, backpacking, healthy eating, and living in an environmentally responsible way. This final attempt was the most successful, but Peter's response had been that of a proud father, not a lover.

I needed to use my brain and my creativity. I needed the fulfillment that working hard and getting results gave me. Peter did not understand why I had those needs any more than he understood why it was so difficult for me to be nothing more than a mousey, compliant wife. When we were in college, he seemed mesmerized by my passion and energy. Now those qualities annoyed him. He seemed to want me to mirror his mother: kind but also quiet and simple. He wanted me to be neutral beige like his mom instead of vivid technicolor, which was what I was. He'd liked technicolor until we married. I still liked it, and I needed to reclaim my full-color palate.

I looked for a job designing innovative training programs among JD Edwards' business partners. Unfortunately, no one was interested in building a robust training solution. One by one, potential employers politely told me, "There is no money to be made in training."

I seriously disagreed.

Although they didn't want to invest in a training practice, all the JDE business partners had clients needing training services and asked me if I would be interested in subcontracting. Overnight, my income skyrocketed because I was earning an hourly rate that made my JD Edwards salary looked like a pittance. Life had turned around.

Peter's disgust over my leap from a stable company quickly subsided as I started depositing hefty checks from my subcontracting. The affection didn't return, but it seemed we had struck an agreement. I could do what I wanted professionally if I brought in huge sums of money. The criticism and control from him ceased where my professional life was concerned. I had proven my worth.

The contracts grew and came in faster than I could execute them alone. I began subcontracting other trainers who had left JD Edwards. Everyone was telling me to form my own company. I didn't know the first thing about companies. I had been a bio-chem major who started with a software firm, saw an opportunity for training, and was now bushwhacking her way through new territory.

And then I met Brad Blackwell. Brad was the director for a couple of hundred JDE consultants at Whittman-Hart. JDE had a new software release that no longer operated exclusively on IBM's traditional hardware. This was a huge change, and JDE had designed over five weeks of training to cover all the new aspects. The problem was that if Brad took his four hundred consultants and put them in training for five weeks, the lost revenue from consulting would amount to millions of dollars. He needed another solution.

Brad contacted me and asked what I could do. I told him I could get his team of consultants up to speed on the new release in five days of training. The reason for the vast difference between five weeks and five days was simple: I was designing a custom training program specifically for his consultants. It included only what they needed to know.

I got the gig.

I developed the class, and on the fourth day of delivering the training, Brad asked me to join Whittman-Hart and offered me the job of national training manager. I was ecstatic. I had finally found a partner who appreciated my focus on training and would provide the business infrastructure, thereby freeing me up to focus solely on training solutions. The only problem was that he lived in Michigan with his family while I lived in Colorado. It wasn't ideal, but I became a virtual employee.

The job was short-lived. Three weeks later, Whittman-Hart was acquired by another company, and within eight months, the new company declared bankruptcy. Yet, training was profitable until the day they closed their doors.

With the closing, Brad approached me about starting our own company. He had witnessed, firsthand, my ability to blend the principles of adult learning with software expertise. There were documentation firms and change management firms, but no one had blended the true learning experience with deep software expertise and packaged it.

I knew nothing about accounting, economics, or cash flow. My liberal arts college only required one business class. What I did know was that there was a huge opportunity to do training right.

Implementation after implementation failed due to the lack of effective training. Most companies documented their processes and configuration, but documentation was not training. Documentation never resulted in self-sufficient, confident users. JD Edwards and all the partners focused on either the business or the processes. No one focused on the people. No one put any effort in understanding what users really did or what they currently knew. No one had spent time defining the gap between their current state and what they needed to know, let alone the skills they needed to have for the company to be successful. It wasn't rocket science, it was adult learning theory, instructional design, and ERP experience combined.

I was impressed to see that Brad had begun to think about how my instructional offerings could be parlayed into a business proposition, and it felt good to be validated and seen. He had detailed business plans with cash flow spreadsheets, revenue and expense lines, risks, and competitive analysis. But what was most eye-catching was the bottom line he showed me. This *could* be a business, and a very profitable one. The problem was that I struggled with the idea of asking colleagues to leave stable companies to come work for Brad and me.

I quietly returned to independent consulting, and six months passed before Brad called and asked to meet with me. He was flying to Denver for a client meeting and wanted to discuss my dream job. I met him at Starbucks.

"I've done it," he said. "I've incorporated a new company with three divisions. One division is training. I want you to run it."

Brad had secured the financial backing. All I had to do was begin hiring staff. He detailed out my budget, which included office space in Denver, computers, a training coordinator/administrator, and everything else needed to run the operation. The proposed salary was six figures. In addition to that, he offered five percent ownership in the company—including the two other divisions I had nothing to do with—and a ten percent share of training revenue, which potentially could be in the millions.

Brad and I were the perfect professional team. He gave me the confidence I needed to express the creative genius contained within me, and I gave him something to act on. Brad would be CEO; I would be the director of training. I didn't want to run the company. I merely wanted to build a training division that proved my brilliance to everyone—especially my father. It did not occur to me at the time that the primary person I needed to prove myself to was me.

My gut knew there was a need for creative training in software implementations. I had been doing it in small doses as an independent consultant. I knew my approach could be applied to a large project and result in thousands of end users actually knowing how to do their jobs with simple cheat sheets at their fingertips—and all before the switch was flipped to go live on the new software.

The concept was simple and powerful. People were used to entering transactions into a computer. They merely needed to know the new clicks. But the trick was not handing them a manual with *all* the clicks for *all* transactions. Instead, they would be handed five to twenty laminated step-by-step job aids listing the *exact steps* for the transactions *they* performed. It was so simple, yet it had been completely missed.

The consultants concentrated on the business processes and configuring the software to handle each business's unique set of requirements. Everyone forgot about the people who would be using the software. It had been assumed that they would figure it out, be given a manual, or receive some generic training, and all would be okay. But it could be more than okay. It could be exciting, and it would certainly be better if everyone knew how to do their job and had the cheat sheets for reference when they needed them. Even better, through simple workflows with pictures, they could understand where they fit in the process, probably for the first time in their entire career at that company, or maybe at *any* company.

What I knew about people was that everyone wanted to feel that they mattered. One easy way to accomplish that was to let them see their specific tasks as documented parts of the process. It was a simple thought, but somewhere in my soul, I knew that ninety-five percent of the American population had a job to pay bills, not one they were in love with. If I could create a company that made money and was successful while impacting people and making them feel seen and an important part of that success, what could be better?

For the first time since I was little, a spark of imagination arose within me. The time and effort I put into my work were not simply a means to make money and achieve status. There was something from my heart brewing, and it felt magical and dreamy. But even though it was heart-centered, I could explore it and embrace it because it had nothing to do with love. It was business. This was my chance to dream and create, keeping my heart perfectly stashed away, because I was in the business world—a world I had decided was calculating, safe, and logical.

The name we gave the company, GBSynergy, made us sound established and credible. The very first person employed was Emma Sawyer, whom I spirited away from Pottery Barn, where she was assistant manager. Years earlier, I had taken a part-time job at Pottery Barn for the employee discount. I thought that would gain Peter's approval for us to buy Pottery Barn furniture over the cheaper and less appealing things offered by Peter's choice, a big retailer with furniture I considered tacky. Since I only had to work a couple of days a month to garner the discount, I still hadn't quit my job at Pottery Barn. Emma was a tiny woman, standing five foot one and weighing less than a hundred pounds. She looked roughly my age, was impressively organized and articulate, and really understood customer service.

Pottery Barn was notorious for having Saturday 8:00 a.m. sales trainings, and Emma was charged with teaching the sixty part-time sales representatives the importance of how you *look* when you come into work. Emma was ordinarily neat and simple, but one day she walked into sales training with one pant leg hiked up, hair pulled into crazy braids, and a fake nose ring in her nose. She chomped away on multiple pieces of chewing gum as she role-played greeting a customer entering the store. In one creative gesture, Emma had clearly communicated the importance of appearance. No further words or lecture were needed. Her point was crystal clear—and it was crystal clear to me that I had just found my first employee.

I looked for an opportunity to approach her in the store, but she moved too fast to ever give me the chance. When she was in the store, it ran like a beautifully programmed piece of software. Employees were motivated and customers were attended to, which all resulted in good revenue. The problem was that she was too engaged for me to get the chance to talk to her privately. Following her around only resulted in her turning on her heels to ask me what I needed. Her piercing look clearly communicated her frustration with my being at the back of the store, following her like a rock star groupie, when I was supposed to be at the front of the store enthusiastically greeting customers.

I needed to reach her at home, so one day, I sneaked into the office, found her number, and made a plan to call her later that evening. The sound of my voice on the other side of the line was not what she expected at 9:00 p.m.

"I know my call is unexpected, but I wanted to talk to you about a position at a new company I'm starting." I spoke quickly to ensure that she had no chance to cut me off before I had completed my sales pitch. I told her how impressed I was with her ability to train, multitask, and manage. I wanted her to come on board as a training co-ordinator and was curious to know if she was interested.

To my surprise, she had been actively trying to get a job as a corporate trainer and was extremely interested in the position, especially if there was any chance for her to become a trainer one day.

The next employees, Pete and Jaime, came quickly. JD Edwards trainers and consultants were ripe for the picking from JDE and other consulting companies. The company was off and running with small training projects mostly coming from JDE business partners.

About six months into the company, Brad learned that there was a JDE implementation at Mary Kay. He got me a meeting to present our training program. They loved our job aid cards for end users and they liked our board games resembling The Game of Life and Trivial Pursuit that were designed for plant managers and financial controllers who performed few transactions in the system but needed to understand ramifications and concepts.

There were only four of us in the training division, and until then, my role in running the company had primarily consisted of selling and teaching the others in my division what I knew. That all changed with Mary Kay. For the first time, a problem was presented to us for which I had no immediate answer. In fact, I didn't have an answer even after a few days.

Upon my return to Denver, I announced to the team that I was buying dinner and we weren't leaving the office until we came up with a solution. The four of us sat around the table in my office, and I recapped the challenge. As the hours passed, we white-boarded potential solutions, all of which fell apart as we dove into the details. Then, a little after 1:00 a.m., we came up with a viable solution. I rechecked the assumptions and realized that the four of us had created something that none of us were capable of creating independently. As Emma, Jaime, and Pete left my office, I knew we had reached a milestone. We were truly a company with something valuable to offer.

Growing up, I had believed that CEOs and VPs were a special breed of brilliant people. But as the company grew and I hired and trained people, sold contracts to clients, executed projects, and took on one challenge at a time, I realized that I was learning the skills possessed by executives. In fact, I realized that many of the problems in large companies were less about a lack of brilliance and more about losing simplicity and focus.

I didn't want to simply be the boss, I wanted to be the coach who recognized raw talent and provided the leadership, training, and opportunities that resulted in champions. Unlike my bosses at JD Edwards, I wasn't intimidated by my employees' ambition and success. Their success was sweeter than mine because their success *was* my success. Life was a rush, and I was having the time of my life.

Peter had become a roommate I rarely saw due to my travel schedule. And even when I was home, he was often on duty at the fire station. Alone in the quiet house, the highs of the day melted away, and I had moments of feeling that my victories were hollow. Even though I had great work relationships, I had a lifeless marriage.

Late summer of 2002, I was leaving the office and had a craving for ice cream. It was a simple human hankering. The problem was that I was not allowed to go to the grocery store. After hundreds of fights over impulsive buys at the grocery store, Peter had set up a system requiring me to make a list of what I wanted. He would then buy items on my list during his weekly shopping trip *if* they were on sale *and* if he had coupons for the items. It was demeaning and ridiculous, but it wasn't worth fighting about.

I had made a game of it by imagining Peter as my personal butler who ran my errands, including going to the grocery store. The fantasy fell apart when I added things like raspberries or ice cream to the grocery list. Raspberries were expensive. It didn't matter that I was making a six-figure income. Peter believed that one established a budget and did not increase that budget or standard of living when the income increased.

Ice cream got vetoed from the list because it wasn't "healthy." Peter valued "right living." He always did the right thing. He was environmentally conscious: He turned off lights. He didn't waste water by letting it run while washing dishes or brushing his teeth. He definitely didn't turn on the shower for ten minutes to let the bathroom get deliciously hot and steamy. He had a system for everything, including grocery shopping. Right living was his true love, not me.

As I left the office, I realized I was craving ice cream. It was exactly the kind of reward I wanted for a long day of effort. But I had to ask myself if a pint of ice cream was really worth the lecture I was going to hear when I walked into the house with a grocery bag containing Ben & Jerry's. I was an executive building an incredibly successful training division. Surely I should be allowed to stop and get a pint of ice cream. Weight wasn't a problem. I was a triathlete. I ran three nights a week and managed a long run over the weekend. I swam with the tri-team three mornings a week and managed a sixty- to eighty-mile bike ride each weekend. I should be allowed ice cream.

I was weary of being controlled by Peter, and buying ice cream became a symbol of rebellion. Righteous indignation made me resolute as I pulled into the Safeway parking lot. I decided to buy one pint of chocolate ice cream, despite the fact that I loved the Ben & Jerry's vanilla. Peter didn't like chocolate ice cream. I walked out of the grocery store less than five minutes later with one small plastic bag. The fresh strawberries looked mouthwatering, but I had refrained from picking up anything other than ice cream because I didn't want to be scolded for impulsive shopping. I had one bag with one pint of Ben & Jerry's Phish Food flavor—chocolate ice cream with gooey marshmallows, caramel, and chocolate chips shaped like fish. I smiled at my solution. I had respected my husband's request not to buy impulsively and had not bought something that would be a temptation to him. Maybe, just maybe, we wouldn't have a fight.

When I arrived home, Peter's eyes immediately went to the grocery bag in my hand. I rapidly explained in one breath. "I had a craving for ice cream, and I know that I'm not supposed to go to the grocery store because I get things that aren't on the list, *but* I walked straight in, went straight to the freezer, got one pint of chocolate ice cream because I know you don't like chocolate ice cream, and immediately went to the checkout without picking up anything else. And I have the receipt."

"I had a coupon," Peter replied.

I was immediately deflated. I couldn't win! "And what would you like me to do now?" I asked. He couldn't possibly ask me to get back in the car, drive to the grocery store, and ask for a one-dollar refund after working ten hours at the office. It was inconceivable. It was impossible.

He did.

Where had the man gone who drove twenty-five miles to get me a Bavarian Kreme donut? How had he moved from cherishing me to shaming me?

For six years I had tried to become the wife he wanted me to be, a wife he could love and want to romance. I had tried living the lifestyle and adopting the habits that gave him comfort. But his control and disapproval had left me feeling diminished and insecure. I didn't understand how we had gotten to where we were, but one thing was crystal clear: I was done. I was rising up and standing up for myself.

I couldn't do it a second longer: the lectures on how to flush a toilet so water wouldn't splash on the seat; the incessant requests for receipts so he could reconcile the cash in our wallets to Quicken; the countless times he'd wiped the bottom of the milk carton after I'd put it back in the fridge. It was over. I was filing for divorce. I was done being controlled.

CHAPTER 12

Loss and Freedom

*I had allowed myself to become domesticated
to a level that left me stripped of my personal power
anywhere outside the business world.*

I KNEW MY MARRIAGE WAS OVER but couldn't find the courage to end it formally. Peter wasn't a bad person, and I didn't want to hurt him. I didn't really even want a divorce. I just wanted to be loved and appreciated.

Brad and I had taken many business trips. I had always portrayed my marriage as a happy one. But after the ice cream incident, I was done pretending and started spewing stories on a business trip to Washington, DC. Brad was sympathetic, and he didn't seem happy either. We commiserated. Our spouses didn't get or appreciate us.

I didn't think I was in danger of having an affair. Brad was married and lived in Michigan. Besides, I wasn't that *type* of person. I looked down on people who had affairs. I was an intelligent, self-confident businesswoman, and Brad was my business partner. I simply was not susceptible, I thought. Except that I was.

I might have been brilliant in business, but I was still a rookie when it came to relationships, and not a particularly precocious one at that. I was a woman who had neither healed nor transcended the issues of abandonment and rejection tied to her relationship with her father. And I had married a man who was as exacting as my father, though in different ways and with different things.

I had inadvertently married my father.

At the base of it, I was the archetypal Wild Woman: intuitive, creative, sensual, and a warrior. And like so many women who had gone before me, I had allowed myself to become domesticated to a level that left me stripped of my personal power anywhere outside the business world. I was like an Alaskan Malamute, born with ample strength and endurance and closely connected to the wolf in her DNA but domesticated to pull heavy loads instead of living life through her wolf instincts, intuition, and intelligence. The Wild Woman in me had been suppressed long enough that my bindings were coming loose. And because I carried within me a deep cauldron of uncooked soup in the form of issues, the antithesis of domestication was beginning to erupt.

Brad and I needed to meet with a prospective client located on the East Coast, and we had not seen each other since our trip to Washington, DC. Our approach was to visit a client, work late into the night writing a proposal, and then present the proposal to the client the next morning. This approach allowed us to accomplish the entire sales cycle in one trip and demonstrate to the client that we could provide immediate results.

We worked late to finish the proposal and made a plan to meet in the lobby before our meeting. Brad suggested that instead of checking out at 7:00 a.m., we return to the hotel after our early morning presentation to take a short nap before our late afternoon flights.

It seemed innocent enough, though the closeness of working with him until the early hours of the morning had left me fantasizing a nap together. The meeting with the prospective customer went fabulously. We returned to the hotel, stepped into the elevator, and punched in our floor numbers. As the doors opened on the eighth floor, where Brad was to get off, he turned and pulled my body against his. The doors shut and the elevator continued on to my floor.

The Wild Woman in me rose up, teased, encouraged on, and was ultimately sated by an equally wild man. Afterward, Brad napped while I lay there wide awake. I had just had sex with someone who wasn't my husband. Heavy regret began to set in. How could I have just committed adultery? Who was I?

I slid out of bed, quietly escaped to the bathroom, and sobbed in the shower as the water flowed over me. I hated myself and wanted the water to wash it all away. Peter and I had restrained ourselves through three and a half years of dating and engagement. Even after we were married, sex was polite and restrained. Sex with Brad was different. There was no thinking involved and there were no rules. It was raw passion, an expression of desire and pure pleasure. All my senses had been heightened.

Sitting in the bathroom wrapped in a towel after my shower, my remorse decreased as renewed desire crept in. I had just swung the pendulum of emotions. Thirty minutes earlier, I had been naked and blissful. Ten minutes after that, I was sobbing in the shower and hating myself.

Now I desired Brad again. I was a certified mess. Somehow, I pulled myself together, and we made our flights.

With each mile the plane traveled west, it felt harder and harder to breathe. I didn't want to return to the world of coupons and systems. I didn't want to live in Peter's neat, organized, perfectly ordered world anymore. I wanted to feel. For the first time in my life, I didn't care if it was right or wrong. I was tired of living the way I thought I *should* live. I had lived that way my whole life, and it was killing me.

I still couldn't breathe when I arrived home. I had felt suffocated for years, but now my suffocation existed on a whole new level. I hadn't known or felt passion before that day. I needed to keep feeling. I couldn't return to the antiseptic, joyless shell of a life I'd been living in. As Peter and I sat down for a late night dinner, I told him that I wanted to separate and get my own apartment. I needed space. Space felt like nourishment. I couldn't look at him. I felt dirty and full of shame, and yet, I also felt more alive than I had in a long time.

I found an apartment, moved out, and gave myself the freedom to engage in all the sex I could handle. I went from novice to expert in a few months. Meanwhile, Peter and I were still going to marriage counseling.

The irony was that Peter and I had finally found a helpful therapist who wouldn't allow us to focus on the content—the symptoms of the disease—but who used the symptoms to correctly diagnose the real issues, the real virus killing our marriage. Peter was finally listening to Lara, our therapist, and was starting to get that he made me feel caged and dead. In fact, Peter admitted that he had adored me when we dated, and he had loved that I was eye-catching and coveted by other men. But after we got married, he didn't want his wife to be stunning. He didn't want any competition because he was afraid he would lose me. As a result, he demanded that I shrink so he would feel adequate instead of insecure.

I couldn't believe it. It was his insecurity that drove him to minimize me. It was sad because all I had wanted was to get married, build a life and family together, and stay married forever. I wanted to be with one man—my husband—but he didn't want the full-throttle version of me. He wanted a lesser version. He didn't want the genuine article, he wanted a pale shadow of the genuine article because he wasn't secure enough to handle the full version.

I had not been honest. In my desperation for family and security, I had placated Peter because I didn't want to be alone. I had complied with his requirements as a daughter would comply with her father's rules instead of relating to him as a woman. That left no opportunity for true intimacy.

Lara knew instinctively that I was having an affair. The story was too classic and the symptoms too familiar. She asked to meet with me privately, and when we met, she asked me if I was seeing someone else. I had not told a soul about the affair, but I trusted Lara. She was safe, and she wasn't going to shame me. Because of that, I was honest with her, and saying it out loud made it real.

I poured out my feelings, answered her questions, and felt understood. Lara told me that I had emotionally divorced Peter, which gave me a sense of freedom and the permission to move on. That helped me understand how

I could sleep with Brad while I was married to Peter. As we wrapped up our session, Lara told me I had a decision to make. She pointed out that I *did* love and respect Peter and that it wasn't fair for him to sit in therapy exposing his secrets with a woman he trusted when that woman was already gone. I needed to choose.

I wanted both. I wanted the passionate affection of Brad and the stability of Peter. With compassion in her eyes, Lara shook her head and restated that I needed to make a decision and call her before our next session, the following Saturday morning. I felt sick as I left the session.

The week was long and depressing. I wrote in my journal, prayed, and searched for a way that Peter and I could remain married and both be happy. It seemed impossible. As I tried to find one shred of hope to latch on to, all I kept seeing was Brad's arms around me, adoring me, loving me. Why would I walk away from that to return to my soulless marriage?

Peter had no idea what was coming when we met with Lara on Saturday morning. The air in the room felt thick and heavy, and my body felt tired and sad. Peter seemed so innocent. I was the one with the sin, the dirty one. As we sat in the heavy silence, I tried one more time to picture a way, a path, for Peter and me to heal and reconcile. But all was black and void of hope. With one big breath, I looked at the floor and said, "I'm seeing someone else, and I want a divorce." The words seemed foreign as they came out of my mouth, and I questioned what I was doing, but I sat in silence.

Finally, Lara asked Peter if he wanted to say anything.

"No," he replied softly.

I would have understood and appreciated an angry response from him or even a rageful one because there might have been desire and love beneath the anger. But his lack of any response at all left me feeling hopeless about any possibility of saving the marriage. The marriage was a corpse, and no defibrillation—administered by the shock of an affair or anything else—could revive it. I suddenly felt incredibly stupid for having spent more than six years trying to win back the love and acceptance Peter had shown me before our marriage.

But as soon as I left Lara's office alone, the air began to feel lighter, the heaviness started to lift, and I could breathe. I was free. No more being fathered. No more control. As moments turned into minutes, my excitement grew. Why had I waited so long to do this?

I returned to my apartment—small and sparsely furnished, but all mine. Standing there, taking in the freedom, I remembered the sleek, metropolitan leather couch at Crate & Barrel that I had wanted for years. Peter thought leather furniture was environmentally wrong. A smile began to spread across my face as I realized I could buy it. I wasn't moving back into the house with Peter. We weren't going to reconcile. I decided that a trip to Crate & Barrel was the perfect way to mark my freedom. I bought the couch, and swiping my credit card felt liberating. I was a free woman!

CHAPTER 13

Marriage Go-Round

All I knew was running.
The thought of stopping and feeling terrified me.

I KNEW THAT WHEN RELATIONSHIPS START AS AFFAIRS, they usually did not work out, and I knew that I was using Brad to run from Peter, but Brad and I continued to see each other. Brad was a means, a fatal blow to my marriage. I knew that Peter could never get over infidelity. Subconsciously, my affair was a pathetic way to end my marriage without having to feel that the decision to do so was unilateral.

I wasn't running toward Brad, I was running away from Peter. All I knew was running. The thought of stopping and *feeling* terrified me. What I needed was a deeper sense of self-love and self-validation. My mother had loved me deeply, but she had died when I was a teenager. Her counsel and support were unavailable to me. She had, thankfully, played a big part in shaping who I was. So much of my strength and ability to care deeply had come from her, and what self-love I did have was my inheritance from her.

But a girl's relationship with her father also shapes her. Among other things, it teaches her, subconsciously as well as consciously, what she can expect from a relationship with a man. What I had learned to expect from a man was judgment and abandonment. What I desperately needed from a man was love and acceptance. But stripped of my father's love before I had a chance to internalize and integrate it, I had never become an emotionally mature woman where men were concerned. Instead, I had sought the adoration of men to shore up the holes in my ability to love and validate myself.

My gut knew I was going about seeking love the wrong way, but it was the best that I could do. I hadn't excavated enough of myself to know that what I needed to do was run home—to myself.

Peter and I divorced without attorneys. We separated everything, agreeing that Peter got the house and everything in it and I got the business. We split our savings fifty-fifty. I was able to put a substantial down payment on a million-dollar home located on the golf course a half-mile from the office. Maybe saving thousands of dollars a year and living like poor college kids held some redemption. Our divorce was logistically easy, but it was an emotional death. I lost my dog and my friends. I lost Peter's parents and the rest of his family. And I lost the hope of starting my own family and having a baby.

I successfully muted all the emotions associated with the divorce by channeling my energy into my affair. Brad proved to be a great distraction, ensuring that I processed nothing. I felt no loneliness. I had leaped into a new, exciting relationship. Brad and I gushed over each other. Outside of work, my days were filled with decorating a gorgeous home, throwing extravagant parties, and indulging in pure gluttony. I had a million-dollar home, a six-figure income, a boyfriend who adored me, and a booming company. Once again, life seemed perfect.

Brad divorced his second wife, and he assured me that it had nothing to do with me. His marriage had been over before we began our affair. As the weeks turned into months, Brad began talking about marriage. The mention of the "m" word made me shiver. I had just gained my freedom. Marriage was the last thing I wanted. Besides, Brad had two kids who were out of control. They weren't bad-spirited human beings, just insanely spoiled ones. Brad was the stereotypical good-time weekend dad. He never disciplined them, but he did manage them with bribes and gifts.

The mention of marriage seemed to increase exponentially. I had to put a stop to it and decided to speak to Brad. I told him that I had been married for seven years and needed time to heal. I admitted that we might end up together, but added that I needed to take some time and be alone.

Without a moment of hesitation, Brad replied, "We need to start working on liquidating the business then."

I was floored! Why? Why couldn't we be adults about this and return to what was working. He lived in Michigan, and I lived in Colorado. I lived in a different state than his family. It wasn't a real relationship, but simply physical pleasure and an escape from reality. There was no reason to destroy a company and put fifteen employees out of work. I tried to reason with him, but I was met with the firm opinion that if we weren't going to marry, the business had to go.

I was not going to give up my business. I had left JD Edwards against the warnings of everyone around me. My colleagues thought I was crazy to leave a growing company to begin a startup company. I couldn't prove them right. I needed GBSynergy. Karmen by herself had no value, I thought. My worth was held in GBSynergy. If I lost the company, I would die. The decision was simple: I had to marry Brad. I didn't believe in love, soul mates, or real marriages. In fact, I didn't know of one marriage that I wanted to emulate. Marriage was a contract, just like business. If I had to get married to save my company, so be it. Brad wasn't going to control me or father me. Professional failure was not an option.

We decided to get married on Valentine's Day on the beach on Grand Cayman. It had only been six months since my divorce from Peter, and a destination wedding was ideal for us. I had always wanted to go on vacation with other couples, and I had no desire to waste months planning a huge, expensive wedding like my first one in Atlanta. A wedding was the perfect excuse to go down to the beach and have a blast jet skiing, sunbathing, spa indulging, and drinking with friends. We planned to get married at sunset with our friends around us, then have an intimate dinner on the beach with our own DJ.

I fell asleep comfortably in Brad's arms the night before the wedding, satisfied with the way things had worked out. At 5:00 a.m. my eyes opened. The sun was pouring into our room, but that wasn't what had awakened me. What had awakened me was a vivid dream in which I was getting married. But instead of being on the beach in a strapless sundress, I was wearing a beautiful silk haute couture dress, walking down the aisle of a lovely stone church. The church was too old to be in America, so it had to be European. Its stone arches with gold vines towering over the wooden pews and stone floor were spectacular. I tried to figure out which church I was recalling. I had visited Europe dozens of times. But as I recalled church after church, I realized it wasn't a church I had been in.

I closed my eyes to recall more of the enchanting dream. In my dream, I was swept away by love, but there was no groom in sight. Who was the groom? I opened my eyes and looked over at the man snoring next to me. I knew that it had not been Brad standing at the front of the church because I felt differently in the dream than I did toward him. My waking self was going to get married for the second time because of logic. But my dreaming self was getting married for love, not business, and I felt exactly as I had always imagined feeling at my wedding. I wasn't marrying a man to save a company or gain a family, I was marrying a man I wanted to wake up next to every morning and grow old with. It wasn't about anything but him.

As I processed all of this, I wanted to know who the groom was. I closed my eyes again, quieted my mind, and tried to remember more of the dream. I went back to the point where I was walking down the aisle toward my groom. He stood in front of the altar, waiting for me. I looked at him with love . . . and realized that my groom was faceless. What a disappointment!

Just as I was about to write it off as a little girl's dream of her fairy tale wedding, I remembered that there was more to the dream. After we were pronounced man and wife by the pastor, we kissed and turned to walk down the aisle and out the front of the church. But about halfway down the aisle, we turned left and exited the church through side doors into a gorgeous courtyard. It was typical European, clean and simple. It had tiny pebble stones like the gardens at the Palais-Royal in Paris and perfectly pruned trees, ten feet apart, with spring blooms. It was simple and elegant, beautiful and breathtaking. I saw myself standing in this elegant courtyard in a gorgeous gown, blissfully happy.

As I turned to greet the guests flowing out of the church, I realized that everyone was speaking a foreign language. My eyes flew open. What? That made no sense.

I lay there completely confused. I'd just had the sweetest dream. It had encapsulated everything my wedding should be. I wanted to know its meaning. I wanted to know who the groom was. But the answers seemed galaxies away. I finally concluded that my subconscious mind had merely played out my childhood fantasy of being married in an old European church in a gorgeous gown. I stretched and closed my eyes to enjoy a few more hours of sleep.

My real wedding began at sunset and ended with us enjoying a beautiful dinner on the beach with friends. Our DJ encouraged a little boogying on the beach between courses. When Brad picked me up and started walking toward the ocean, I pasted a smile on my face. Surely, he wasn't thinking about throwing me in the ocean . . . was he? Half laughing, I said, "Ha, ha. You're funny." I thought Brad would put me down, and we would return to enjoying our beautiful evening with friends. Joking around was one thing; being dumped into the ocean in my wedding gown was quite another. And I trusted Brad to understand the difference.

As Brad kept walking toward the water, I began to squirm in his arms, trying to fight him off. But I soon realized that he could easily overpower me. I had witnessed Brad enjoying being a big kid when he got into a water, egg, and flour fight at our last company party, but he had to understand the difference between an afternoon picnic and our wedding. I had spent hours getting ready and was wearing a beautiful linen designer dress that would be ruined by the salt water. Not to mention the fact that if he dumped me in the ocean, I would end up being wet and uncomfortable, while the rest of our party would be dry, comfortable, and appropriately dressed for the occasion.

Brad's feet hit the water. As I resigned myself to going in, my heart sank. I had been married less than two hours, and disillusionment seemed to pick up exactly where it had left off with my last marriage. This was an act of utter disregard and disrespect. But there was nothing I could do. Brad was a forty-three-year-old adolescent trying to upstage his bride, and he was completely willing to humiliate me in the process. I stopped squirming and prepared for the cold water.

With the same abruptness he had applied in picking me up, Brad stopped taunting me and yielded to our friends' pleas to bring me back to dry ground. I was safe. The evening was not going to be ruined. Brad had been the jokester, but the adult sensibility had kicked in and the evening would continue unblemished. I smiled, and looking him straight in the eyes, a thank-you seeped out of my lips. I began to breathe, and with my sigh of relief, my body was hurled through the air. Brad had done it. He had thrown me into the ocean at our wedding!

CHAPTER 14

Learning Vulnerability

*Being perfect did not equal being loved, and I desperately
wanted to have someone know me with all my flaws.*

I RECOVERED FROM OUR WEDDING NIGHT but knew that
I was faced with being married to a big kid who needed
to either be the clown or the hero. It was exhausting but
manageable.

GBSynergy was growing exponentially. No longer was I
the passionate but unsure professional that Brad had believed
in and given a training division to. I had become a confident
leader of not just the training division, but the entire company. Training had grown while the other divisions had
dwindled. My management team was now running sales,
accounting, and operations. Brad celebrated our achievements and enjoyed being CEO of a successful company.

I continued to listen to my instincts when it came to
business opportunities. I was reflective about deals won
and lost. I paid attention to employees who were engaged
fully and those who seemed constantly annoyed with their
job. I didn't have the MBA knowledge to leverage, but I
had my gut, and I used it.

I continued to see my therapist, Lara, and started to
process how I had gotten to where I was, what had happened

in my marriage to Peter, and what was going on inside me. Lara's office became a safe place for me to be myself—including the part of me that was vulnerable. I'd always felt I had to strive, achieve, and work toward being the best at everything, which left little room for relaxation. I pictured myself like a beautiful, big, powerful dragon with strong wings and protective scales that easily deflected arrows. I thought that if I ever exposed my weaknesses to anyone, they would eventually use them against me and penetrate that secret soft spot.

Lara said I had the uncanny ability to make everyone around me feel like they knew me when in truth, no one knew me. I did it by sharing private things with people, like my mom's death, my dad's rejection, and even simple childhood embarrassments. I shared personal stories with people to encourage them, always being the one helping someone else, never coming to friends with unresolved issues. I disclosed intimate things that could be all wrapped up in a neat package, but I never revealed what I didn't understand or hadn't figured out. I showed no weakness. In and out of the office, I was articulate, poised, and self-possessed.

During one session, Lara encapsulated the essence of why I lived the way I did. "For you, average really *is* the death of you. You were rejected by your father when you were above average but not perfect. That felt like death. You were loved unconditionally by your mother, but she never revealed her own imperfections to you, so you had no model from her for anything but perfection, right up to the point when she became ill, which belied the persona of perfection. And then she died."

Lara's words began to sink in, and a weight began to lift. I realized that being average *had* been death to me in many ways, including how I related to others, both personally and in business. I felt I had to be poised every second of every day. I sat on Lara's couch and cried, mourning the years I had spent striving, settling for nothing but the best because I had believed the lie that if I was average it would be the death of me.

For the first time, I began to be angry with my dad for robbing me of the innocence and the freedom to simply be. None of my friends had to be at the top of their class to be wanted by their father. The freedom to mindlessly play, knowing that I was loved without accomplishing anything, had eluded me.

The woman sitting on Lara's couch with snot running down her face and mascara running down her cheeks was far from being the envy of every woman and definitely not ready for a magazine shoot. I was just a woman sitting on a couch, angry, brokenhearted, and confused. I felt incredibly average and vulnerable.

"You have never been more beautiful than you are right now," Lara observed.

With a grunt and smug laugh I rolled my eyes.

"You are *truly* beautiful when you are vulnerable," she added in response.

Even though I hated feeling transparent, I knew she was right. I loved when a colleague shared their struggles. That honesty invited me into their life. My heart and my life were well safeguarded from scrutiny. In the safety of Lara's office, I began to dream of letting friends into my heart. I felt the warmth of surrendering my aloneness. I longed to be free and vulnerable. If I closed my eyes, I could almost taste the freedom I had embodied standing on the back of my Shetland pony, practicing my ballet with one leg lifted in an arabesque while trying to ride at the same time. Falling off wasn't devastating or discouraging, it was part of the experience and part of the fun.

But as soon as I found myself lost in the lightness of the memory, my current reality permeated the picture and my mouth opened, protesting loudly to Lara. "I can't. No!" Tears gushed and the words choked out of me. "I will *never* hurt again. No one will ever invade my heart and leave a hole like my mom did. No." Being free and open was childish and naïve.

It was one thing to be vulnerable with Lara. I was paying her, it was on my terms, and I could always cancel an appointment. And although I was incredibly thankful to her for the safe haven she offered me to experience awareness without self-recrimination, I never saw Lara outside her safe, confidential, and private office. I saw things for what they were in her office and experienced appropriate levels of remorse instead of crucifying myself for developing survival mechanisms that had genuinely served me. I was vulnerable with Lara and thankful for the awareness, but I was also damned determined to contain that vulnerability within her office.

My head knew it wasn't the right approach. I knew that if I chose to be invulnerable and allow no one access to my heart, I would lead a life that was successful in many ways, but that life would also be empty and lonely. I didn't want that, but I couldn't imagine allowing someone to see all the silly, dorky, and naïve thoughts, words, and actions that I had fiercely kept from the world since my mother's death.

My mom had celebrated my achievements, but she had also managed to bring out the silly, fully human side of me. I didn't need to be perfect with my mom. I was free to be my whole self. After her death, no one knew me well enough and no one was strong enough to peel back the many layers of my persona to reveal and love the unedited, unmasked, real me. My older sister lived in the black-and-white world of fundamentalist religion where anything less than compliance to right behavior was sin. My father's world was ruthlessly competitive, and he'd made it crystal clear that if I wasn't first at everything, then I was nothing. I feared that my sister would not accept me with my imperfections, and I was certain that my father wouldn't.

I knew Lara was right. I was coming to the realization that being perfect did not equal being loved, and I desperately wanted to have someone know me with all my flaws. But deep within my gut, I knew that if I allowed my deepest feelings to surface, I would be unable to juggle the demands of a growing business in the world of Fortune 500 clients. I had a company to run, employees to mentor, and clients to impress. I had no idea what would happen to me if I felt everything that had been buried in me for years, but I knew one thing: It would not be something I could fit in between managing employees and winning clients.

When my hour was up, I had no more time to be unkempt. I had a conference call with a billion-dollar corporation to negotiate a multimillion-dollar contract in an hour. I zipped up my soul, rolled back my shoulders, and headed to the ladies' room. I fixed my makeup, readjusted my black Versace skirt, and fluffed my Valentino sweater. I was back, polished and ready for the world.

But the dream of being known and fully loved had been planted in my heart, and over the next few weeks, I kept returning to the picture of it that I had created in my mind. Until that day with Lara, I hadn't known what I was searching for, and without a picture, it is really hard to put a puzzle together. I didn't realize that all my actions had been based on a bullshit philosophy. Being average was not the death of me. Articulating the belief that I had accepted when I was a child and being given the opportunity to reevaluate it at the age of thirty was empowering!

I hadn't known where my crazy reactions came from. For instance, a couple of weeks earlier, Brad and I had been in the kitchen discussing the marketing company we had chosen to design a new company website. I had been sitting on the counter eating some grapes while Brad stood near the microwave. We noticed that the microwave clock was wrong, and Brad turned around to reprogram it. As I talked, he continued to fiddle with the microwave. After a few minutes of talking while watching him try to program the time, I jumped off the counter, shoved him out of the way with a nasty look and a roll of the eyes, set the time, and jumped back up on the counter before completing the point I was making about the marketing company.

"I would have figured it out," Brad said after I finished talking.

With a disgusted sigh I replied, "There was nothing to figure out," making quotation mark gestures with my hands, and then screamed, "It's a clock . . . on a microwave!"

Brad turned and left the kitchen while I shook my head, disgusted with myself. Sometimes it felt like my body was possessed by a scary bitch. I asked myself why I hadn't been able to just sit still and let him figure it out.

Of course, Lara's gift of enlightenment had given me the answer. I rejected "average" vehemently. Even reprogramming the microwave was a test of intelligence to me. I had to do everything impressively—*everything*. That included reprogramming the microwave. Furthermore, everyone around me who had any reflection on my life had to do things perfectly.

Maybe that was what attracted me to Peter. He did everything right. He was frugal, disciplined, environmentally conscious, and educated. In so many ways, he was the textbook template of right living. It was a godsend that I hadn't had a child with him. If there had been babies with Peter, I would have unconsciously passed on the sins of my father to them. I would have taught them that they had to be perfect to be loved because their failure would have been a reflection on me. The message would have been felt by them loud and clear with my immediate and vehement reaction to any misbehaver. I would have been the mom screaming at her kid for having a tantrum when she was three and at that developmental stage where she was figuring out that she was a person, separate unto herself. I wouldn't have been able to let her tantrum be *her* tantrum, having no reflection on me, because I had no confidence or belief in myself. Everything and everyone around me proved my worth. I would have selfishly needed my children to constantly show the world my brilliant mothering skills through their perfect behavior.

I had no children, but I did have a husband. And I was wired to see him as someone whose behavior, accomplishments, and appearance reflected on me. My husband needed to be impressive, right along with my company, my employees, and my house.

Of course, I had to be perfect too. My dad had penetrated every corner of my soul with the message that I would never be loved if I wasn't perfect in every way. And when I was a child, it wasn't just a threat, it was my reality. My dad *did* leave and my mom *did* die. And in my naïveté, I concluded that the only way I would be loved and not left alone was to be enchanting, dazzling, brilliant, and superlatively attractive. Now, at age thirty, I was seeing the world through an entirely new lens. Not only was I seeing how misguided that thinking was, I was also plum tired. The persona of being perfect, constantly inspired, and faultless was exhausting. The armor I had built around my heart and soul was heavy.

For years, I had tried to address the symptoms, but managing them was like trying to hold a beach ball under water in a swimming pool. I expended a great deal of effort to suppress my emotions, but they would fly up just like that damn beach ball the minute I forgot to focus on their suppression. Lara had given me the power to pull the beach ball out of the water, hold it up, take a good look at it, decide it was bullshit, and pop it. I could deal with the root problem instead of just the symptoms.

When I thought about my reaction to Brad over the microwave clock, I was relieved that a mean bitch didn't possess me. I just had deep-seated beliefs and philosophies that resulted in bitch-like actions. I apologized to Brad

and secretly decided that I was going to try to be vulnerable with him and not reserve my vulnerability for my
time with Lara and her controlled, confined office. For
the first time since my mother's death, I longed to share
my heart and soul with someone other than my therapist.
I wanted to be vulnerable to real people in my life. I
wanted to be fully known and fully loved.

A few days later, I decided to share something with
Brad that I had begun to explore with Lara. Inadvertently
choosing what might have been one of the worst issues to
start with, I began to talk to Brad about the confusion and
regret I felt about my divorce from Peter. I didn't want to
be married to Peter, but at the same time, I missed him.
With Lara, it had been safe to untangle the feelings of loss
surrounding a divorce. Peter and I had built a life together
that included friends, family, and traditions. The pain of
losing all of that felt confusing when paired with the freedom and joy of not being married to him.

What I didn't account for was that Lara was neutral
and not emotionally connected to my struggle while Brad
was intimately tied to it. He felt threatened and became
defensive. My open, vulnerable heart was met with attack.
Brad shamed me for being so inconsiderate of his feelings
and instantly turned the conversation to focus on his
childhood and the wounds he had been dealing with in
his own counseling with Lara. My attempt to share my
heart and soul failed because of my ineptness and Brad's
own dysfunction.

Opening myself and being real was just too new for
me to be anything but inept. Since leaving Peter, I had
mastered the art of garnering what I thought was love by

being exactly what others wanted or needed, not by allowing others to really know me. I knew exactly how to
make myself indispensable. After all, I had given a job to
my best friend, Ashley, who had been a stay-at-home
mom on the brink of losing her mind before knowing me.
And my team at work loved me for providing them a plat-
form on which to achieve the professional success they
were capable of.

I even suspected that my own sister and her family put
up with me because of the generous amount of money I
sent them. My affair, divorce, and remarriage drama were
far from the Christian model they strived to uphold, so I
wondered what my sister really thought of me. But this
was about me, not about my sister. Deep within me was
the doubt that anyone could love the unvarnished, un-
adorned me, so I tried to buy people. Because of that, I
believed that everyone in my life who behaved as if they
loved me had been bought. I had set out to need no one
and be known by no one, to be loved by all because they
needed me. And now that I had succeeded, I simply
wanted to know if anyone really liked me.

I needed to talk to Brad about my divorce and my
fault in it. I needed Brad to tell me that he'd heard my
part in it and still saw something in me worth knowing. I
needed to know that his love for me was about more than
the sex I gave him and the money I brought into the firm.
I wanted to expose the ugly side of Karmen and hear
from him the wonderful things he still saw in me. I didn't
like myself, and I needed someone close to me to sincerely
like me for being *me*, not for being someone who could do
things for them.

It was weird to think that I really didn't like myself. I liked all of my accomplishments, but when I was quiet, the truth was that I didn't see any beauty within me. I needed to be validated by others. How had I become so successful on the outside while being so in need of healing on the inside? How could I be blind to the real beauty woven into my soul?

What was there to like about me? I had failed at my first marriage, had an affair, and married the guy my affair had been with not because I was wildly in love with him but because he had threatened to dissolve our business if I refused to marry him. I was aggressive and independent, and I had a veneer that was thick, shiny, polished, and impossible to penetrate.

That couldn't be all there was to me! I cared about the employees of GBSynergy. I loved my sister and her family. There had to be something good about me that had nothing to do with my accomplishments, and I needed my husband to show me what it was.

It wasn't fair to Brad. We had built a marriage on a certain set of rules, and without warning, I had tossed the board game up in the air. While the pieces were suspended in the air, I changed the board game and all the rules. I didn't want the business arrangement we had made. I wanted to grow as a person, and I wanted my marriage to be based on shared personal growth, not business growth. I was becoming obsessed with rising above my need for perfection, above my need to buy the affection of others, and above my aversion to revealing my unmasked and unarmored self. I wanted to return to the unselfconsciousness of childhood and the absolute surety that I could learn to fly.

But the more I grew and took responsibility for my life and my actions, the more Brad clung to the black-and-white teachings of religion to make sense of his world. Once again, I found myself shamed by scripture. Brad used verses out of context like a child uses a phrase they've heard their parents say as a trump card.

The irony of this was that Brad hadn't even been religious before our marriage. I had introduced him to the church and God. Brad had drunk the Kool-Aid and was now swimming in a pool of biblical one-liners. At forty-four, he was ready for the promise of hope the church held out to him. Our marriage of only a year had taken a sharp left turn with my newfound desire for growth. Before marrying me, Brad had been divorced twice. He had children from one and stepchildren from the other. It had all proved a bit much for him, and now he wanted to believe that he could learn verses, obey rules, and be full and blessed by doing so.

Everyone has the core desire to be special. That need is encoded in our DNA, and the message that God is calling you, that God has something great in store for you, speaks directly to that fundamental need. Brad wanted purpose and significance, and he found it in oceanic proportions in the church. Unfortunately, he had neither the maturity nor the discernment to ground his newfound faith. Instead, he was becoming saturated with the same passionate devotion I had felt when I was introduced to the church in my childhood.

While Brad was becoming entranced by the church, I was finally allowing myself to feel emotions instead of maintaining a perpetual plastic smile. I was proud of myself for finally getting mad at my dad in a therapy session with Lara. This unnerved Brad. He needed everything to remain neat. Instead of empathizing with my anger, Brad attempted to wrap it all up with, "Let's pray together and lay your anger at the cross." I didn't want to lay it down. I wanted to *feel* it. I wanted to scream and be shit-faced mad until I didn't have any more anger.

I was awakening. I couldn't go back to the small world where everything fit neatly in a box. There *was* a power greater than myself, but I no longer saw the numinous as being confined to the Christian mythological stance that perfection was solely embodied by God and his son. I had known magic as a child, and it had disappeared. I thought I found magic again in the church, but when I didn't play by the rules and divorced Peter, I had been shunned and condemned by my friends in the church, friends who met weekly for a small group Bible study. Sitting in silence and listening to your soul was rejected as New Age. What you "wanted" was equated with your sinful side. The Bible was your guide, and it clearly said that divorce was wrong.

Of course, *I* hadn't accepted who I was either. I hid everything that I found distasteful about myself and created a persona I thought would bring me love. I was far from meeting my true self. I had made a mistake in marrying Brad, and I wasn't going to pay for my sin by staying in the marriage. I had already gotten one divorce. What was a second? My Christian friends who were praying for me would have more to pray about.

When we married, I hadn't realized the disparity between our financial positions. I had the million-dollar house that he insisted we refinance to put his name on. I had the savings account. I was the one with the creative training ideas. I had needed Brad to launch the business, but as the company grew, I had learned everything I could about the business end and had surpassed him in leadership. Brad knew divorce meant that I would buy him out of the business. He might get a nice lump sum, but the company hadn't achieved enough financial success for the buyout to be big enough to live off of.

I brought up the topic of divorce, and the drama began. Brad was not going to let me go without a fight. I was both the idea person and the implementer of ideas in our business. The division I directed made money; those he directed didn't. In fact, Brad's divisions had folded. GBSynergy was now exclusively a training company. Our company success was based on my expertise, and Brad was not going to just let that slip away.

Brad had gone from pride in finding a young professional with raw talent—me—to surprise at my ability to grow and take over the business. From surprise, he spiraled down to confusion about his role in the company. He was intimidated by my skill and independence, and ultimately, he became fearful when he began to lose his sense of control over me. All of this left Brad in a fluster, and his fluster was vented in expressions of anger against me.

As I became more confident in my decision to divorce, Brad's anger became more intense and scary. His rage wasn't confined to the privacy of our home, either. Anger came flying out of him at a restaurant, and when he screamed, "You fucking, cold-hearted bitch!" I failed to see the panic behind his anger. Nor did I expose my own uncertainty, vulnerability, and fears. Instead, I visualized his spiteful and piercing words as arrows hitting my imaginary dragon scales. My coolness and detachment only increased his anger. He wanted me to engage. Screaming back at him would at least assure him of some connection. My iciness and aloofness were too much for him to handle, and without warning, he flew across the table at me. The staff had to pull his hands off my neck.

It was that ability to remain perfectly calm and emotionally sterile that continued to infuriate him the most. The small window of vulnerability Lara had opened up had been shut with an additional steel wall added for reinforcement. I remained impervious to his anger, which only undermined the marriage further.

We were like a Molotov cocktail. Brad's anger was the fuel and I was the source of ignition. After one frightening episode, I applied for a restraining order. It was easily granted. Brad didn't even show up to court. He dialed in via conference call. His testimony didn't dispute my story. Under oath, he defended his actions with the Bible verse that admonished wives to submit to their husbands. The judge saw Brad as a religious fanatic who would justify anything under the "rules of God."

The restraining order was equivalent to punching a playground bully in the face. Brad had bullied me into marrying him. He had bullied me into staying married. A bully will strut around doing anything he wants until someone puts him in his place. And then, for a short time, he will be reasonable. The restraining order was the punch in the face that allowed us to sit down, get reasonable about what was a fair buyout for the company, and end the marriage.

The divorce was expensive and messy, but it was over. I bought out Brad's half of the company, and for the second time, I was free. I vowed to spend two years without a boyfriend. I needed to learn how to be okay without a man by my side. I needed to learn to like myself. I needed to figure out who I was.

CHAPTER 15

Horse as Teacher

Horses were teaching me sensitivity to the spirit
I had only heard about in church.

WALLACE WAS BIG, BLACK, AND STUNNING. He stood at seventeen hands and held a remarkable resemblance to Black Beauty. Lara, my therapist, was my guide in unearthing the falsehoods that had governed my life for years. Riding Wallace was my opportunity to practice my new truths in a physical way.

Leaving my office and work behind and sitting on top of an animal that weighed two thousand pounds and had moods, fears, and impulses was exactly what my soul needed. Since childhood, I hadn't felt the freedom to express feelings without constraint or mental calculation. But navigating a course of jumps with Wallace blew the noise of my life away.

Wallace reminded me of the natural flow of things. My trainer often commanded me to shut my eyes after we had turned the corner and the jump was straight in front of us. It was a good exercise for not only improving my riding skills—especially the skill of not getting ahead of a horse in a jump—but a priceless reclamation of my soul.

Horses know how to jump. It sounds so simple, but as a novice, I thought my job was to *make* the horse jump. In actuality, when a horse is in a self-calibrated, forward-moving canter (or trot, for that matter), any jumpable obstacle in front of them is going to be naturally and intuitively jumped. It was an elementary but powerful realization for me. I could simply *be*, and the horse would organically compress and spring over a jump. I got to just enjoy the ride, something I had not done for an exceptionally long time. In every way, it was the extreme opposite of mustering troops, as I did in the workplace. I was a master of marshaling and arranging, rationalizing and ordering. Wallace could not be marshaled.

Wallace was not only reminding my soul how to breathe, he was oxygen to my soul. I didn't leave the barn with new intellectual enlightenments the way I left Lara's office. I left it with a feeling that was somehow spiritually enlightening instead of intellectually enlightening, and that was precious to me. Leaving the barn was different from anything else in my life. During the course of a normal day, my head and intellect governed my actions. The physical and spiritual sides of me were cordoned off, completely separated. At the barn, my spirit and gut governed and ruled.

Great riders connect with their horse's energy, and that connection is not through logic and reasoning, but through feeling and intuition. No other activity demanded my emotional acuteness. Yoga had started to tie my body and mind together, but the failure of achievement in yoga wasn't as painful as crashing through a jump. When I crashed through a jump, it was the result of being oblivious to the fact that Wallace was not "in front of my leg" or "forward moving"—things that were felt, sensed, and detected by my spirit, not by my head.

Horses were teaching me sensitivity to the spirit I had only heard about in church. The barn had nothing to do with God or Jesus Christ, heaven or hell. But it did have to do with sensitizing me to those parts of myself and other living things that transcend persona and get right down to what is real.

Lara proposed what felt like an enormous challenge one day in therapy. She dared me to be average at riding. She knew that my modus operandi was to conquer every-thing and that doing something I was only average at—*and* enjoying it—would open a door to a whole new world. Lara was challenging me to just *be* and not use Wallace as another notch on my belt or accomplishment on my résumé. Lara was giving me the permission I needed to simply enjoy my horse and the time on his back.

Wallace became my teacher and my champion, help-ing me to at least risk jumping a few internal hurdles, as well as those on the jumping course. At the barn and on my horse, I could relax, be myself, and literally soar over hurdles. It was learning to fly all over again, but by this time, I'd crashed and burned in my life a time or two and valued it in a way I could not have as a child. I was com-bining my intellect and experience with my intuition and energy. I was stepping into a deeper and richer life I had half-forgotten existed.

CHAPTER 16

Markus

He was one hundred percent in the present.
That was exactly where I was too.

LIKE ANYONE WHO HAS JUST BEEN THROUGH the maelstrom called divorce, my internal equilibrium was off, but I was beginning to unearth what was real within me, and there was at least a part of me that was ready to celebrate being free to be myself. Seventeen days after my divorce agreement was finalized, I joined a group celebrating a friend's thirty-fifth birthday at the sleek club in the Jet Hotel, located in Denver's lower downtown, known as LoDo.

All night, I was on the receiving end of awful pickup lines. I was exhausted and would have left hours earlier if it hadn't been my girlfriend's birthday. By 1:00 a.m. I had danced off all my alcohol and was now people watching to entertain myself. The Jet lounge was a popular hangout spot for Denver sports stars and millionaire businessmen. Scanning the crowd, I couldn't find a soul who interested me in the least . . . until one did. He seemed to have appeared out of thin air, and I wondered how I had missed him.

A few feet to my left was a tall man casually leaning against a brick beam. He was wearing a crisp white shirt, plum velvet sport coat, dark jeans, and polished black loafers. I watched him out of the corner of my eye for a few minutes and realized he was alone. Impressive.

I had just finished my initial assessment when a girl who didn't look a day over seventeen stumbled over to him. She was dressed in a cheap, short, sleazy skirt, and it appeared that she was going to ask him to dance with her. This was the perfect opportunity to evaluate his personality. If he danced with her, he was out. If he was rude to her, he was also out. I directed my full attention to the scene. As she approached, he smiled and watched her dance flirtatiously in front of him for a few moments before bowing his head and saying, "Thank you." Then, holding up one hand, he gently shook his head, indicating that he was flattered but not interested.

Perfectly done.

She twirled on.

I was in full approval, and he caught me looking right at him. I had to think fast. I wasn't going to turn away as if I hadn't been watching, but I couldn't appear smitten either. I leaned toward him with raised eyebrows. "There are a lot of scary people here tonight."

"Yes there are," he replied simply.

I hadn't realized until he spoke that he was European. His English was perfect but spoken in a thick German accent. I was taking all of it in, remaining completely cool on the outside.

He took a step toward me. "But I don't find *you* scary."

"Well, that's because I have a brain."

The acrimonious words had escaped my mouth before I could control the bitter ghost inside of me. I was sure I had successfully scared him away. Mortified, I decided to wait a few seconds before calmly walking away.

Just as I was about to fade into the crowd, he asked me to dance. I smiled and said yes.

He held out his hand and we began to dance, but he abruptly stopped. "First rule: the guy leads."

He was strong and unintimidated by me. I liked that. I gave him an acquiescent smile and we continued to dance. A few minutes later, my girlfriend joined us on the dance floor. Immediately, he broke free from me and allowed my girlfriend to dance with us. Again, I was impressed. He was both a good dancer and a perfect gentleman. Staying up past 1:00 a.m. might have been worth it after all.

The lights came up at 1:45 a.m. sharp. "Sushi sometime?" he asked, suggesting that I put his number in my phone. His name was Markus. As I finished typing his phone number, he said, "Call it to make sure you got it right." Naively, I pressed the call button. Moments later, his phone lit up. "Great. Now I have your number." He had done this before. I reminded myself that I had vowed to spend two years post-divorce without a boyfriend. But that didn't mean I couldn't date. I just needed to keep it casual and not get serious about anyone.

A week went by without a call. Then, while I was at a Broncos game with a date, he called and left a message. We met the next evening. I arrived for sushi right on time in my Dolce & Gabbana black pencil skirt, Jimmy Choo stilettos, and simple Rebecca Taylor top. My hair was pulled into a long ponytail. I was in self-confident warrior woman mode.

Markus seemed unlike either Peter or Brad. He did not live in a black-and-white world, but one containing all the hues. Markus had traveled and lived all over the globe, experiencing many faiths, cultures, and people. He had two MBAs and spoke four languages: German, English, Russian, and Thai. He had come to the United States without speaking a word of English and enrolled in his second MBA program to learn English. He was comfortable with who he was, and he wasn't trying to save or fix anyone.

I didn't feel judged by Markus when I told him I had been married twice. He didn't appear to be thinking about my past or figuring out our future. He was one hundred percent in the present. That was exactly where I was too. I was simply enjoying the moment, the dinner, and the date. I decided that he would be the perfect person to date casually. He was sexy, and the way his mind worked was intriguing to me. He didn't need everything to fit neatly into one overarching philosophy. He had his own beliefs and principles, but he seemed to have no investment in whether or not anyone else agreed with him.

The date ended with a European kiss on the cheek.

Two nights after our sushi date, I saw him again. That date was as good as the first, and just before we parted, he kissed me in a way that made my head spin, my stomach drop, and my legs weak. I saw him again the next night, for dinner. I knew I shouldn't be spending so much time with him, but I just couldn't help myself. He was addictive. After dinner, we went to his loft downtown. I was not ready to have sex with anyone, and to his credit, he didn't want to have sex with a woman who didn't want to have sex with him.

On the drive home, I remembered something Teddy, my VP of business development, had said to me. "Kid, once you figure out you can have sex with a man without marrying him, you might stop getting married."

Teddy was sixty years old and more a business advisor than an employee. Having sold his company years earlier, he had become a millionaire who worked for pleasure. He was the closest thing I had to a father, and until Teddy had said those words, I had not realized how ingrained Christian teaching about sex was in my mind and heart. The church had rules about when you could have sex, with whom you could have sex, and what sexual positions were acceptable. I decided to stop worrying about what the church thought about sex. Instead, I wanted to ask myself what I, Karmen Berentsen, thought about sex.

In that moment, driving back from my date with Markus, I realized that I was growing up. I wasn't rebelling, I was taking in all the data points I had collected, including those from the Bible, life, friends, books, stories, and my own life experience. And I was finally asking my own heart what *I* thought about sex. I began to smile. The answer was right there. All was quiet as the battle between my heart and my head vanished. I wasn't going to have sex with Markus because I was needy for masculine attention and affection or to ensure that the relationship continued. It was so much simpler than that. I wanted to have sex. In that moment, there was but one thing in my head: the astounding fact that I'd been carrying a huge load of guilt for years simply because I was a sexual human being.

The next night, I proceeded to enjoy my sexual side with no hesitation.

CHAPTER 17

Selling My Business

I would be a multimillionaire on my thirty-third birthday.

A FEW MONTHS EARLIER, I had met the CEO of Titan Technology Partners in San Francisco at Oracle's annual trade show. The convention center was filled with over forty thousand people, and hundreds of companies had set up temporary booths where they hawked their services to prospective customers. The CEO and founder of Titan Technology had sauntered into our booth while I was at a client meeting, loudly announcing that he was looking for a training company to buy and asking if GBSynergy was for sale.

I returned to the booth to collect materials for the presentation I was about to make with a Fortune 500 client and knew something was wrong. I could feel the tension in my team. I had always listened to my gut in business. Many times, the facts and numbers did not support what my gut was telling me, but I had learned to trust my gut, and it had served me well. Ironically, I never thought about listening to it in my personal life.

I asked a senior project manager working the booth what was wrong. Slowly, she reached into her laptop case and pulled out Mr. Bruno's business card. "Are we for sale?" she asked with anxiety in her voice.

"No," I replied as I studied the card. I didn't recognize the company, but I recognized fear when I saw it in one of my team members. If I didn't deal with this in roughly the same way I would deal with a rampant computer virus, my best employees, all of them working the booth, would be handing out their résumés to the two hundred other firms at the conference. And they might even secure interviews before the week was over.

One by one, I looked at each directly in the eye and firmly told them, "GBSynergy is not for sale. Companies are constantly shopping for other companies at trade shows. We are not for sale. It would be stupid to sell GB-Synergy right now. We're on the brink of exploding into multiple software venues. Give me his card, and I will stop by his booth later." This was the truth. I had no interest in selling GBSynergy. I loved the company and I loved running it.

While I wanted to give my team more reassurance, I knew I would be late for my presentation if I stayed at my booth any longer. I had to trust the power of my sincerity, and I had to trust my employees. My first order of business after the presentation would be to stop by Titan Technology's booth and meet the arrogant idiot who obviously did not understand business.

The presentation was a success. It didn't hurt that the pharmaceutical company presenting with me had practically given us a dozen new clients by telling of GBSynergy's revolutionary and effective approach to end user training. Next on the list was stopping by Titan Technology's booth and politely but firmly letting them know that GBSynergy was not for sale and, more importantly, that it was absolutely unacceptable to come to my booth and ask my employees if the company was for sale.

On my way to his booth, I stopped by the ladies' room and freshened up. I needed a little beauty confidence. After reapplying liner and lipstick, I added a fresh coat of mascara. Then I lifted my Armani skirt, grabbed the tails of my white, starched shirt, and pulled my shirt tight before pulling my skirt back down. I didn't know what Muhammad Ali did to prepare for meeting his opponent in the ring, but I was girding my loins every bit as much as any challenger to the heavyweight champion would. I was ready to face the CEO of Titan Technology. Rolling my shoulders back, I stared into the mirror and told myself that I didn't care how big Titan Technology was. GB-Synergy was my company, and it was unprofessional and egotistical for Mr. Bruno to walk into my booth and alarm my employees.

At the last minute, I grabbed Teddy from the booth for "gray hair" support. I needed a visual picture that GB-Synergy wasn't a young, inexperienced band of independents but a true company with employees, goals, and an impressive Fortune 500 client list. Teddy and I found Titan Technology's booth and promptly asked for Mr. Bruno. We were pointed to a man in an expensive suit who stood six foot three and had thick, curly, dark brown hair. Projecting energy like a force of nature, he was impossible to miss.

I introduced us and handed him a business card. "I understand you stopped by my booth today and met my employees," I said. "I was surprised to hear you were so direct in asking if GBSynergy is for sale."

"I'm looking for a training company to acquire. Titan Technology is a full service information technology firm that is missing a training division, and I've decided to acquire that piece versus growing it organically."

"I appreciate Titan Technology's interest in GBSynergy, but my company is not for sale."

"Everything is for sale for the right price." Those words smoothly rolled off Nicholas Bruno's lips as the corners of his mouth began to turn upward.

I was amused. Obviously, he was arrogant and weighed heavily on his charm as a means of negotiation. I, too, could play that game.

"Well, in *that* you are correct, Mr. Bruno. I must warn you, though, that it would be a strategic sale."

Strategic in the acquisition dictionary is synonymous with over-priced.

Mr. Bruno smiled, tipped his head, and said, "I will pass your card along to my mergers and acquisitions team. They will contact you in a few weeks."

I was sure that I would never hear from Titan Technology again. I returned to our booth and reassured my team that Teddy and I had stopped by Titan Technology's booth and met with Mr. Bruno. Nothing was going to change.

Six weeks later, I got a call from Titan Technology's head of mergers and acquisitions. I had dismissed my encounter with Titan Technology's CEO as soon as Teddy and I left his booth. I couldn't believe he was actually serious about the acquisition.

"It's good to hear from you. Nicholas and I had a nice exchange at the trade show," I replied coolly. "How may I be of assistance?"

He explained their process for acquiring companies and asked if I would sign a noncompete agreement, allowing us to begin the process of speaking openly.

After a few verbal gymnastics, I hung up the phone and stared out my window at the beautiful Rocky Mountains. Life had just taken an interesting turn. I daydreamed about what it would mean if I could actually sell GBSynergy for millions.

It was the challenge that was enticing. I wondered if I was actually good enough to get Nicholas to pay a strategic price for GBSynergy. I knew enough about boutique firms to know that I wasn't just selling the company's financial statement and client list, I was selling myself. In fact, there was no distinction between the company's value and my personal value. In my mind, the two were synonymous. If GBSynergy was attractive and had value, I was attractive and had value. This also meant that I was indispensable. Titan Technology would never buy GBSynergy without me. The sale felt like the first definitive affirmation of *my* value. If GBSynergy did sell for an impressive price, maybe it would supersede my father's assessment of me.

This was the ultimate sales challenge. Could I intoxicate Nicholas with my company? Could I make GBSynergy something Nicholas had to have? I knew the only way to make my company something Nicholas had to have was to make myself something Nicholas had to have. This wasn't about sex but about enticement, desire, and an absolute need to be around me, to have me as part of his circle. The challenge was to make Nicholas believe I was his oxygen and that he couldn't breathe without me.

This was obviously easier to fantasize about than accomplish. The game of acquisitions is all foreplay. I had made the mistake of mixing business and pleasure once already and was not about to do that again. But the idea of playing with a worthy adversary was succulent. Nicholas was no beginner at charm and getting his way, but neither was I.

The game of acquisitions was also the ultimate cat-and-mouse game. Perfectly played, you kept them intrigued and wanting you, but you never made it so hard that they walked away. I was serious about the purchase price needing to be high. The reality was that I had a great company and wasn't about to give it away, but the process of seeing what I could sell it for excited me because I saw it as a true evaluation of Karmen Berentsen.

Besides, the acquisition game would keep me from getting serious with Markus. I adored Markus. In fact, I was coming to enjoy him a little too much. I was single for the first time in my adult life. I needed to keep it that way. Focusing on work would be good for me.

I had to eat some serious crow with my team. I had sworn that GBSynergy was not for sale. I had been passionate about that fact. When selling became the obvious strategic thing to do, I knew I owed it to my team to get them involved up front. And once it became clear that Titan Technology wanted to not just buy and control GBSynergy but invest in the company and give us the money to expand to other ERP markets, the team not only bought in but got excited about the idea.

As the acquisition heated up, I became seriously busy and desperately needed a week away. Running a company while proving its worth in the due diligence phase of the acquisition was all-consuming. I needed peace to decide what I *really* wanted out of the acquisition. I contemplated a week or more in the British Virgin Islands and admitted to Teddy that I didn't want to go to the beach alone for the week. I was clueless to the fact that my need for constant entertainment and stimulation had everything to do with my lack of self-love.

"Invite Markus to go with you," he replied without hesitation.

Markus and I had only been dating a few months at this point, and we were trying to keep it casual. But when I explained this to Teddy, he just reiterated that I should ask Markus.

Knowing that debating Teddy never worked because he always won, I invited Markus to come with me to Little Dix Bay on Virgin Gorda Island. He seemed happy to be asked and agreed to go as long as we went Dutch. I had planned to pay for the trip if he agreed to it, but this was even better. The cost of the trip would be cut in half *and* I would have his company.

We were perfect travel companions. We were together, but we didn't suffocate one another. We read. He would find a lounge chair under a tree or umbrella and I would lie on a floating raft, soaking up just as much sun as my skin could absorb. We played tennis, mercilessly trying to kill each other.

The next to last day, we realized that all the water toys—boats, Hobie Cats, kayaks—were free to use by resort guests. Markus lit up like a little kid on Christmas morning. He was excited to take out a Hobie and sail for the first time in his life. As I watched him take one out into the bay, I was blown away by his ability to let down his guard and try something he was sure to fail at miserably. He could hold his own at any red-carpet event and be cool as a cat, truly confident and chic. The next minute, he was willing to be a little boy, playing in the water and looking geeky in his rash guard shirt, shorts, and Boston Red Sox cap.

He was unreservedly willing to be less than perfect at something, and that made him an excellent model for me because I was a beginner at that. I could allow myself to be average at horseback riding, but I was still struggling with expanding that to other areas of my life. Markus's willingness to be a beginner at something made him almost irresistible to me.

As I watched him sail, I felt a tug within me to allow myself to be as playful and unselfconscious as Markus. But almost as quickly as I felt that tug, I got in check. My heart was running away from me, and my heart was not allowed to do that. I controlled my heart. I had to get ahold of it. My heart was like an innocent child who did not understand she would get hurt if she ever tried to fly. I would not do that to my poor heart. I would protect it. I carried that determination back to Denver with me when my brief vacation came to a close. Markus needed to be nothing more than an entertaining date, not some-one who could tug at my heart.

The acquisition was on schedule to close April 30, which happened to be my birthday. I would be a multi-millionaire on my thirty-third birthday.

All the while, everything was going too perfectly with Markus. One night in bed, I looked over and asked, "Do you just love me because I have money?" My question categorized his love as shallow. I could handle that kind of love because it was based on money and had no power to penetrate the steel wall around my heart. My heart would be safe.

But my question was not solely asked to put Markus back in his place. I didn't know how to differentiate the people in my life who genuinely liked me from those who were just along for the ride. I had the universal need to be validated. That need had not been met by my father and therefore was a constant itch that needed scratching. I was all too willing to buy my friends. I had surrounded myself with people who benefited from knowing me. Ashley, my best friend, had received a golden opportunity to get back into the workforce as a top paid sales executive, and all she had to do was follow my lead. Teddy had gently warned me to question the sincerity of her allegiance, and he suggested that I separate what she did for reward from what she did out of sincere friendship. But since our relationship had mostly been one between boss and subordinate, it felt impossible to flesh out what was sincere from what she did for the ride.

Did Markus like *me* or did he merely like the high profile life we had experienced at the resort in the Virgin Islands and were sure to repeat once I was a multimillionaire? Except for my sister, there was no one in my life I had known prior to being a business success. Even the man I thought adored my gregarious spirit and enthusiasm for life in college had been threatened by it after our marriage, and he had continually attempted to reel it in until our divorce. Both my dad and Peter had rejected me, and I had been a meal ticket to Brad as much as anything else. Perhaps I had dealt with that pain by unconsciously deciding to buy people's love.

But how could I be mad at Markus for being attracted to a life lived on my coattails? At some core level, I knew that I had gotten exactly what I wanted, but now that I was so close to feeling worth something, I wanted to be liked for who I was inside and not for my accomplishments. I had felt the stirrings of this desire during my marriage to Brad, and now those stirrings had become a serious rumbling within me. I wanted Markus to assure me that he saw the big heart I fiercely protected. I wanted him to convince me that he was attracted to it more than he was attracted to what my ambitious personality had produced.

Markus had left East Germany once the wall came down. There was something in him that resonated with the idea of the self-made man. Was I the female poster child of the American Dream? There didn't seem to be anything transparent or vulnerable about our relationship. I wanted to see if we could move in that direction, so I asked Markus if he loved me irrespective of my money.

His response was slow and seemed to come out of his mouth carefully. "I understand why you would ask that question after your own father threatened to not attend your sister's wedding unless you invested in his company. But over time, I will show you that my love is real."

He was referring to something that had happened many years earlier. My father had disappeared during my first year of college, only to reappear the following year once he learned of a settlement I had accepted after breaking an ankle when I'd fallen into an unmarked construction ditch on campus. One week after I received the check, my dad reappeared in my life, making no apology for his yearlong absence. My sister was engaged and getting married in less than a month, and he said he was excited to be the father of the bride.

A few weeks after visiting my sister and me, he presented me with a business opportunity and told me that he needed my settlement money as seed money. For years I had watched the tension over money between my dad and his father, and my parents had divorced over money. I was not going to become a business partner with my dad. I told him that I could not bring money into our relationship.

He called the next day and told me that if I did not give him the money, he would not walk my sister down the aisle. "You will forever know that it was because of you that your sister didn't have her own father at her wedding," he said.

I was devastated. I went to my sister thinking she would ask me to give him the money. Instead, I was met with a strength I had never seen in her before—or maybe it was the righteous anger of a young woman protecting her baby sister. Moments after I entered her dorm room and recounted Dad's threat, she picked up her phone, dialed his number, and told him that if he didn't want to be at her wedding without payment for doing so, she didn't want him at her wedding. He never came.

My father's attempt to extort money from me had made me fear that other people in my life were there only because they saw me as a money tree. But Markus gave me exactly what I needed, and he didn't shame me for my question. He just reassured me of his love. Maybe someone *did* love me for being me.

CHAPTER 18

Joining the Old Boys' Club

*Was it a double standard to roll my eyes at men
who disrespected women but, at the same time,
use my feminine charms as a business tool?*

IT BECAME OBVIOUS that I was going to be needed in
Titan Technology's Charlotte, North Carolina, office as
the merger progressed. Titan Technology had no clue
how to integrate training into their software consulting
divisions. The only way to realize the benefits of the acquisition would be for me to work out of the corporate
office in Charlotte.

But moving to Charlotte had another advantage, and
that had to do with Markus. One moment I was feeling I
had finally found someone to share my heart with, and
the very next moment I felt antsy. The need for me to
move to Charlotte was the perfect excuse to remove my
heart from the physical proximity of Markus.

I never expected him to suggest moving to Charlotte
with me, but he did. It was the ideal moment for me to
be transparent and tell him about my fluctuating feelings.
Instead, I told him it was a great idea.

If I had been honest with Markus and myself, I would
have said, "Actually, the thought of you moving with me

to Charlotte feels suffocating. I don't mean to hurt you. I like dating you, but something in me is not ready to have you move across the county to live with me." I wasn't honest because having Markus in my life was nice, and I didn't want to risk losing him. Talking about it required a level of self-love that I had not developed. It was much easier to simply agree to live together.

As part of the acquisition, Titan Technology had scheduled an offsite strategy session at the Ritz Carlton in Key Biscayne, Florida. I flew in with my team and had a little under an hour to get unpacked and prepare for our first meeting. I was surprised when Nicholas called and asked me to meet him in the lobby in five minutes. I grabbed my portfolio and used the five minutes to collect my thoughts about the issues I had seen come up in the last month during the due diligence phase of the acquisition.

When Nicholas met me in the lobby, he asked me to follow him up to his suite. I assumed he just wanted a few private minutes with me to go over some things, so I followed him to the elevator. His suite had a gorgeous full-sized grand piano. I had a baby grand in my house, which I loved to play when I was alone. The piano calmed me. My days often ended with a glass of red wine and playing Pachelbel's *Canon in D Major*. As I sat down at the piano, Nicholas returned from the other room with a Neiman Marcus bag.

He had bought me a pair of nine-hundred-dollar heels instead of the Mont Blanc pen he normally gave *men* whose companies he acquired. Had he been paying attention to the fact that I clearly loved designer shoes and was just trying to give me something I valued, or was he treating me like a call girl who could be bought with a pair of expensive shoes? I wasn't sure.

I slipped on the new Christian Louboutin heels, walked the length of the suite, and made a dramatic twirl. Do they work? I asked.

The two-day strategy session kicked off a few minutes later with a meeting in a conference room overlooking the water. I hadn't met Nicholas's executive team, but I knew I was the first woman to join them. I had heard about company culture in the South and the good old boys' clubs, but I thought those notions were just myths. I was sure that a thriving global consulting firm like Titan Technology wasn't filled with patronizing men who saw women as arm candy and entertainment. I felt confident that they would respect me as a colleague.

Still, there was no harm in smiling prettily, laughing heartily at their jokes, and stroking their egos as I got to know who was who and what was really happening under the covers at Titan Technology. Then, just when they didn't feel defensive or guarded with the inner workings of the business, I would engage as much more than a beautiful piece of ass with legs and high heels. I would be responsible for the business improvements that increased stockholder equity, and everyone would win. I wanted to avoid the more than a year it usually took to gain the team's trust and get in the club because I needed to understand what was going on as soon as possible if I was actually going to be able to accomplish something substantial.

Over the next few days, I realized that while Titan Technology was a company with a great business vision, it was horribly run. Nicholas's management team was filled with men who agreed with whatever Nicholas said. Half of them were unqualified professionals who had their jobs because they shared the same background and, in many cases, the same blood as Nicholas. Nicholas had surrounded himself with cousins and college buddies, along with a brother-in-law and even a soon to be son-in-law. No one told Nicholas anything other than, "Great idea."

When the acquisition was first suggested, I honestly thought I might be out of my league. In reality, GBSynergy was a much better run company that Titan Technology. Titan Technology was a mom-and-pop company that fed Nicholas's ego. Titan Technology could double in size practically overnight if a competent leader actually put the right people in the right positions, drafted new players, and made a game plan they then followed. I had found my next goal: CEO of Titan Technology. It was the perfect challenge and would be financially rewarding. I could easily reach my goal of ten million dollars in the bank by the age of forty.

In the previous thirteen years, I had learned to use my good looks to get prospective clients to extend a ten-minute meet and greet into a two-hour lunch. But I never won a deal on good looks and charm alone. I might have gotten appointments and the opportunity to make my sales pitch, but no one was going to commit their company's software implementation, not to mention their job, because I was cute. Companies signed contracts with GB-Synergy because there was a brain—and a damn good one—behind that pretty face. I worked hard and never depended on anything as superficial as appearance to win a deal. I never kissed, slept with, or exchanged sexual favors to close a deal. By the time contracts were being written up, it didn't matter if I had moles on my face.

I had the same strategy with Titan Technology's thirteen male members of the leadership team I now sat on. I decided that I would get them to invite me to golf because they like watching me putting a tee in the ground in a short golf skirt. They would invite me to dinner because they liked having me at the bar. I didn't resent it. I was going to use it to discover the real politics of Titan Technology and become CEO.

I returned to Denver on a high, but as I started talking to Markus, I realized I couldn't tell him about the shoes. That meant I also couldn't tell him about the fact that the team I was about to join was little more than a southern boys' club. And I couldn't tell him about my plan to become CEO. It quickly sunk in that there was actually little I could tell him.

In my experience, no man would understand and be okay with using innocent flirting in business. I wasn't sure *I* was okay with it. For that matter, I wasn't sure it was all that innocent. I knew it worked, but I never talked about it with friends or business mentors like Teddy. Talking about it would have led to all kinds of questions. Was it a double standard to roll my eyes at men who disrespected women but, at the same time, use my feminine charms as a business tool? Being honest with Markus would mean revealing too much and admitting to myself that my plan was somewhat devious.

What was certain was that my plan to be CEO of Titan Technology was not going to work if I had to keep spinning things for Markus, fearing that his eyes were looking straight into my heart. So while we were busy making dinner, I calmly announced that I was moving to Charlotte. I didn't say "alone," but there was no invitation being extended. I didn't look up, I just continued to chop away at the red peppers I was preparing, acting like I had just announced something as insignificant as who was going to be on Jay Leno's show that night.

It was simple: I wasn't sure my actions were going to be justifiable and I didn't want to defend myself. I did not want to be chastised or, worse, abandoned. My head defended it with extremely rational explanations, including the fact that I had only been divorced a very short time and needed to heal, coupled with the fact that this was the career opportunity of a lifetime. I needed to convince myself that I wasn't being coldhearted, just logical.

I chopped with my head down, knowing that if I looked at Markus, he would see right into my soul. I feared that I might feel his love and become soft. The only way to stop my heart from being swept away and destroyed—this time, maybe for good—was to become the ruthless, work crazed, success driven bitch that Markus's heart would never be attracted to. I talked about my move like nothing had just happened. I was sure Markus would retreat and my heart would soon be safe.

I seriously underestimated love.

CHAPTER 19

Business Success, Personal Mess

I felt like a walking, talking missile of self-destruction.

THE DEAL WAS SET TO CLOSE. I was getting ready to move to Charlotte and Markus was still around. Distance had grown between us, but there were moments when my guard came down. It proved to be just enough to keep Markus from retreating and writing me off as another typical, overachieving American female.

I flew out to Charlotte to close the deal. Meetings ran long, and it was highly unlikely that I would catch my 5:50 p.m. direct flight from Charlotte to Denver. As I sat next to Nicholas at the conference table, surrounded by the team of lawyers needed to close a multimillion dollar acquisition, he calmly said, "If you miss your flight, I'll take you to dinner to celebrate. It's a big day for you. We should celebrate."

And with that, his executive assistant excused herself to change my flight to Saturday morning.

As the last papers were signed and I received the wire confirmation, I realized that I had done it. I was a multimillionaire. I wanted to call my dad and tell him that I had just sold my company for millions of dollars at the age of thirty-three. I wanted to ask him if that put me in the top five percent and if I was finally worthy of his love.

All those years of sacrifice had paid off. Maybe I could finally relax and start living. Was it possible? At the moment, I didn't know, but what I did know was that I wanted to celebrate by heading straight to Neiman Marcus. I wanted to buy a fabulous new outfit, enjoy a couple of cosmopolitans at the Westin, go to dinner, and celebrate my success.

I made a quick call to Markus to let him know that I would fly home in the morning and then walked into Nicholas's office. We made plans to meet in the lobby of the Westin in an hour. All was set, and I was off to Neiman Marcus. I had seen a pair of Dior shoes in the spring catalog that were silver with a strap across the toes and an eye-catching buckle. The exact same strap and buckle were replicated on a slightly elevated ankle strap. I went directly to the shoe department and bought the shoes before riding the escalator up to the designer area.

As I stepped off the escalator, I stood perfectly still and observed. With only an hour to shop, I needed a talented stylist, someone who could take one look at me and know what I needed, know what would work well. Men had that. When they walked into any high-end men's clothing store, a clerk would approach and immediately say something like, "Forty regular, right?" That clerk would assess the man and steer him to exactly the right thing in sixty seconds flat. That's what I needed.

I knew I would be greeted by a sales person if I entered an area with clothes, and I didn't want just any sales person. I wanted someone who could take one look at my five-four, size two, no hips, boyish frame and translate the words, "I just became a multimillionaire. I'm going

to dinner with my new boss, and I want to feel gorgeous."
And I wanted that translation in Prada, Dior . . . something high fashion.

This was my night, and I was going to celebrate by owning it.

I observed the Neiman Marcus sales staff and ruled out the shop girl talking on her cell phone, twirling her hair. She only had the job for the discount. I also ruled out the girl straightening the racks who was dressed in a gorgeous Chanel suit but was still in her twenties. She obviously loved labels and hadn't a clue how to use clothes as an expression of her mood, personality, or soul. She would have filled my dressing room with St. John knits or swung the pendulum the other direction to the Dolce & Gabbana sexier-than-hell line that truly should only be worn in Miami on South Beach.

I continued to scan and caught a glimpse of him. I knew I had found my man. I watched as he moved around the store as if he were magically hovering a foot above the ground. He moved quickly but as gracefully as Rudolph Nureyev. He was perfectly dressed and had that determined "I'm saving the world" kind of look on his face. Without wasting another second, I walked directly to him, ignoring the Chanel girl when she asked if she could help me.

In ninety seconds flat, I was in a dressing room and his assistant was fetching me a San Pellegrino. I observed a moment of adoration for the gorgeous Dior sandals before buckling them on my feet. Then I saw my sales guy's shoes on the other side of the dressing room door beside the wheels of a garment bar containing his finds. He rolled in eight items. With one look at the selection, I knew I'd be out of there in twenty minutes flat.

Exactly eighteen minutes later, I left the dressing room wearing my new Dior sandals, a black silk Dries Van Noten skirt with a black patent leather Prada belt, and a simple cotton crew neck, drop back tee shirt with three-quarter sleeves. From the front, my legs were the focal point and from the back, I sealed the deal. My sales guy had run to the lingerie department and brought me a NuBra (the stick-on bra) allowing the full exposure of my back. All I needed now was to be escorted downstairs to his favorite makeup artist and have a few people freshen me up. That would allow me to walk out in thirty minutes flat and be nicely seated in the lobby nursing a martini in a new outfit before Nicholas arrived.

The Westin lobby was filled with business professionals, more men than women. Nicholas arrived after me and began to lay it on thick. He suggested we consummate the deal . . . in the biblical sense! Was he kidding me? Was that the best he had? He continued to come on to me in a very direct way, and I couldn't have cared less. The contract had been inked. I had sold my company for a strategic price.

My second martini disappeared, and because I hadn't eaten lunch, I was quickly passing tipsy. I needed to eat something and was thrilled when the driver of the town car Nicholas had ordered appeared in the lounge, ready to take us to dinner. However unwise, some people seem to have mastered the art of driving home drunk. I had mastered the art of walking in five-inch heels while being legally drunk.

I made it into the town car and was happy to have a little time to recuperate on the way to the restaurant. Once there, I merely needed to maul some bread and water. In twenty minutes I would be sober and back in complete control. To my surprise, Nicholas slid in on my side, and before I could move much to let him in, the door had closed and his mouth was on mine. I wanted to hit him, but I was too drunk to trust myself. He was my boss, and I had teased him mercilessly over the past few months. I conceded, even though his kiss held no tenderness. Nicholas was conquering me, groping me and having his prize, and I not only let it happen, I engaged a little to give myself time to get everything back under control.

I had seen Nicholas whispering to the driver before getting into the car, but I hadn't realized that what he was doing was handing him a hundred-dollar bill and instructing him to get lost for a while on his way to the restaurant to extend his command-and-control session with me.

Surprisingly, despite the fact that we had made out in the town car for twenty minutes before arriving at the restaurant, dinner was not awkward. And I learned a lot about Nicholas during that dinner. He wasn't the idiot I had first thought him to be when I met him at the trade show. He had sold his first company at thirty-five for fifteen million dollars. He was recently divorced, had two homes, and was so bored with Titan Technology that he was secretly spending most of his time making a movie.

Now I was interested. My plan was more realistic than I could have ever dreamed possible. If I played my cards right, I could be the CEO of Titan Technology in less than six months.

When we returned to the Westin, I quickly exited the town car and came around to Nicholas's side, extended my hand, and thanked him for a great night. We were now in public. Charlotte was a small town, and Nicholas was well known. He knew as well as I did that any public display of affection could be costly to the deal, as well as compromise my ability to be effective in the company. No one respected the owner's mistress. He had no choice but to accept my hand and say good night.

I rode the elevator up to the twenty-fourth floor, relieved. I regretted kissing him, but I hadn't done any irreparable damage to either my relationship with Markus or to my career. My relationship with Markus was safe because I planned to tell him nothing about it; my career was safe because, unlike sex, a kiss was not professional suicide.

I had begun to undress and had dropped my skirt, still wearing my heels, panties, and top when I heard a knock on my door, followed by the sound of a key in the lock. I panicked, wondering what I would do if it was Nicholas. Then I realized that was impossible because I had paid for my own room when I checked in to the Westin. The Westin would never give my room number to a stranger, let alone a key. Nevertheless, the door began to open and Nicholas walked in.

He had bribed the girl at the desk to give him a key, telling her that he had forgotten his wallet at the restaurant and, therefore, could not prove that he was Mr. Berentsen. He had told her my name, the name of the company I worked for, my mobile number, and the dates of our arrival and departure. All of this proved to be compelling enough to get a key to my room. A part of me was impressed by his determination to get what he wanted. I had never expected or desired for the night to continue, but as I stood there, I felt powerful in my sexuality. My mind quickly transported me into a Bond girl—hot and sexy enough to drive a man to scandalous acts.

I knew I had been playing close to the fire. I had not been an innocent. I had enticed Nicholas and felt a certain amount of responsibility. But I had no idea that Nicholas would make such a bold move. I thought he had been amused with the game of cat and mouse, and I had expected it to be over with the acquisition. But he was as intent on closing the deal personally as he had been on closing the deal professionally. He had acquired GBSynergy, and now he was intent on acquiring its owner. I had played too close to the fire, and I was about to get burned.

I felt like a walking, talking missile of self-destruction. I wanted professional validation and thought I had developed enough savvy to use my feminine wiles, as well as my brains, without doing damage to myself or others. I was a fool.

My body was toned and tanned, and my style was impeccable. I was capable of being taken anywhere, including home to meet the parents, because I had mastered the behavior of teachers' pets everywhere. My demeanor oozed I-have-so-much-to-learn-from-you. I was equally presentable at business dinners where colleagues discussed strategic company goals because I was an expert at strategy. I knew how to be charming, but I also knew how to use that charm to seduce. And I was about to pay the price.

Once Nicholas left, I sat in the bathroom sobbing while trying to come up with a plan to end things with Markus without revealing anything. Then real sadness began to permeate my heart. I knew I wouldn't be able to sleep. In fact, I knew I couldn't even stay in that guilt-permeated room. I jumped in the shower, cleaned up, got ready, packed my suitcase, and checked out of the hotel at 4:45 a.m. I didn't understand how I could be so successful professionally and such a mess personally. Maybe I was doomed to be wealthy and incredibly lonely.

CHAPTER 20

Listening to My Gut

Why was it so hard to get beyond what I thought
I should do to what I wanted to do?

MARKUS KNEW SOMETHING WAS UP. I was distant, and he was good at reading me. One night at my house, I began to explain to him that I had decided I needed to give my full attention and energy to my career. I explained the unique opportunity before me: I could be CEO of Titan Technology in a few years. "It wouldn't be fair to you for me to keep dating you because I will be fully engaged in pursuing my career."

He just sat there, studying me. It felt as if his eyes were looking *through* me.

Taking a deep breath, I decided I needed to say it more dramatically, even if it meant lying. "Any man who is going to be with me needs to realize that my first love is and will always be my success. If you aren't comfortable with that, then we just aren't meant for each other."

Markus still didn't react. He just continued to study me. He finally stood up and said, "I will get my stuff. I guess this means we're finished."

I watched him walk away and wanted to scream, "No! This isn't what I want. I want to build a life with someone who knows me fully and loves me. I want to stop striving and rest. I want to stay home and have babies. I want to stop carrying the weight of the world on my shoulders." Instead of saying any of that, I remained expressionless. "I guess so," I replied.

After Markus left, I cried myself to sleep on the couch.

But with the morning came renewed focus and determination. I started packing and directed all my energy to my professional success. I was going to be CEO of Titan Technology.

The move to Charlotte was easy. I justified flying out my interior designer from Denver to make my move to Charlotte turnkey. I was in the office by 8:30 a.m. each morning and usually left sometime between 9:30 and 11:00 p.m. I had absolutely no time to unpack boxes or make my apartment presentable. My real estate agent had found me a new personal assistant in Charlotte. Between my assistant and my decorator, I had a beautifully furnished, decorated, organized, personalized apartment in two weeks.

But I was lonely in Charlotte, and Nicholas and I were having booty calls. It was unfulfilling and self-destructive, but I allowed it anyway. I knew no one in Charlotte, and working twelve to fifteen hours a day allowed no time to make friends. Besides, I didn't want friends, I wanted professional success.

I was focused on being CEO of Titan Technology, and my efforts were paying off. In the first month, I sold a two million dollar training contract to an SAP client. GBSynergy had never trained on SAP software. Our breadth of clients was limited to the Oracle software space. This was a huge win. Essentially, I had doubled GBSynergy's revenue capability in the first month following the acquisition. Along with the SAP win, Nicholas and other members of the executive team had witnessed my sales ability with clients. They had also watched me seamlessly incorporate my entire team into Titan Technology. Companies usually lost a significant percentage of people when a larger corporation bought them, but I had managed to lose no one.

I was thrilled when Nicholas asked me if I wanted to run sales for the entire company. Without hesitation, I said yes.

The next day he announced my new position on the weekly company conference call. "I have promoted Karmen to executive vice president of sales, the second highest position in the company. This means that everyone in the company works for Karmen. A company that sells services is run by sales, and she is the person running sales. She understands what our clients, the industry, and the future demands. She will set our strategic direction. That is why I'm letting everyone know that as of this moment, you all just got a new boss."

I had done it. In five weeks, I'd won major clients, leaving no room for anyone to challenge the promotion. Nicholas was literally handing me the company to run. And he had no problem with that because he knew I would work my ass off, and he would not only have more money as a result, he would also have the freedom to work on his movie.

I returned to my office more determined than ever to always be the last person to leave the office each night. I worked until my eyes hurt. I didn't pack up my laptop until 11:30 p.m. As I walked out into the warm summer night air, I couldn't help but look at the lone car in the parking lot. It was a beautiful car, a brand new Lexus SC430 hardtop convertible. I had a great apartment, a career that was spiraling upward, a closet full of designer clothes, and a car that turned heads. But I had no one to share any of it with. I appeared to have it all, yet it felt like I had nothing.

I remained totally focused on work. My work required a great deal of travel, and when I was in the office, I worked long hours. I also worked weekends, sometimes in the office, but as often at a local Starbucks or at home. Business plans and sales proposals often got attention on weekends, but I also used weekends to keep up with cutting-edge business books and periodicals. As June approached, I decided to take a break from work for one weekend. My mind certainly needed a break. I scheduled it and decided I would do only what I *felt* like doing that weekend. If I felt like sleeping until 11:00 a.m., I would. And I would not beat myself up about it.

Even with the permission I had given myself to sleep in, I awoke at 7:45 a.m. on Saturday morning. I lay in bed and asked myself what I *wanted* to do. Immediately, my mind raced to my "should" list. I should . . . read that magazine article . . . go to the gym . . . find a gift for my friend's birthday. Why was it so hard to get beyond what I thought I should do to what I wanted to do?

Internally, I asked again. *What do I want to do?*

Quietly, my gut spoke. *I want to roll out of bed, put on sweats, pull my hair into a ponytail, and hobble to the Starbucks at the bottom*

of the building. Once there, I want to sit in the sun and enjoy a tall,
whole milk, triple shot latte while I read an entertaining novel.

I did have desires! Who knew?

I did exactly that. Sitting at Starbucks, I felt happy.

After two hours, my butt had fully fallen asleep and
the caffeine was racing through my body. When my
"should" list started formulating in my mind again, I
stopped and closed my eyes. Again, I asked myself what
I wanted to do, but this time I added *now*. *What do I want
to do now?*

To my surprise, once again, an answer came. *I want to
go to yoga.*

As I opened my eyes, I realized that I wanted to go to
yoga. This was not me feeling that I should go to yoga so
I could fit into a dress or maintain my body. I wanted to
go. It wasn't a means to an end. It was an end in itself. I
jumped up, ran upstairs, and found that my favorite class
started in twenty minutes. I couldn't have planned it better
if I had tried.

As I sat on my mat in the heated room, the instructor
began by asking us to sit with our eyes closed. She told us
that she was going to challenge us. An internal smile
began to appear. I was good at this game.

"I want you to *try* less today," she said.

What? How was I supposed to balance all of my
weight on my forearms as I used my stomach muscles to
lift my legs to the sky and then continue to drop them with
perfect control to touch the top of my forehead while trying less? I thought she had misspoken.

But just as I was about to open my eyes and give her
a roll of the eyes, she said, "I challenge you to stop striving

for one hour and feel your body, allowing it to do what feels good."

The mantra of "try less" resonated with the theme of the weekend. I decided it wouldn't hurt to follow her suggestion. When the class ended, I couldn't believe the positions I had achieved. I had never been able to extend my legs before in side crow position. But when I let go of expectations and simply did what felt good, I had been able to execute the position. It was magical. I didn't quite understand why it had worked, but I was delighted.

I returned to my apartment and realized that I had no idea what I wanted to do next, but regardless of what I wanted, I needed a shower. I stood in the shower with my heart more open than it had been in months and asked myself what I wanted to do that evening.

The answer came as easily as the question. *I want to go on a date with Markus.*

The words had barely left my gut before my head pounced on them. *That is ridiculous. He's in Chicago this weekend. He probably won't even answer the phone. You're in Charlotte. How do you expect that to work?* As my head continued to fire questions like a courtroom litigator, I ignored them. For the first time, I didn't bother fighting them. I simply ignored them.

I finished my shower, opened my laptop, and checked flights. There was a flight at 3:38 p.m., and I realized that I could be at the airport by 2:20 p.m. I could make the flight. The flight landed at 5:00 p.m. I would be in the city by 5:45.

Now all I had to do was call Markus. I had not spoken to Markus in months. I only knew he was in Chicago through a friend. *What will he think? He's going to think I'm crazy.* I stared at the computer screen, which was waiting for me to click "purchase" on the United website. This was ridiculous. It was one thing to wake up and sit at Starbucks for two hours instead of doing errands or laundry. It was a completely different thing to call a man I hadn't spoken to in months and ask him if it would be okay for me to jump on a plane in less than an hour and come to Chicago for the night. As I was about to put my phone down and close my laptop, I stopped. I had committed to *feeling* that weekend. I had committed to doing what I felt. I wanted to call Markus.

I closed my eyes, hit the key on my BlackBerry dedicated to his number, and held my breath as my phone dialed Markus Klein. With each ring, I started to breathe again, realizing that he probably wouldn't answer his phone. If he didn't answer, I would be off the hook.

"Hello there, stranger," he said when he answered.

The sound of his voice was like the sound of gentle rain after months of drought. I knew I didn't have much time, so I cut right to the chase. "Do you have any plans tonight?"

He paused. "Not really," he finally said, "but I'm not in Denver. I'm in Chicago."

I had to admit that I knew he was in Chicago because I had been keeping tabs on him. I had come this far, why stop now? "I know. I was wondering if you would go out to dinner with me if I flew to Chicago for the night."

The phone was silent for a long moment. "Sure."

That was enough. I told him that I'd see him at his friend's apartment around 5:45 p.m. and hung up.

I hurried to the airport, grabbed the first parking spot I saw, and literally ran all the way to the ticket counter kiosk. I swiped my credit card, got my boarding pass, ran through security, and was at the gate moments before they closed the door. I had made it. I was on a plane heading to Chicago. I laughed at my own impetuosity. I was happy. I might also be crazy, but I was happy. Listening to my heart was kind of fun.

Markus and I started the night with a glass of champagne at Pops before heading to dinner at Avec. After dinner, we had drinks at a couple of clubs and enjoyed a little dancing before deciding to go back to his friend's apartment. We had reconnected without skipping a beat. It was easy and comfortable. We climbed into bed and made wonderful love. Later, we decided to meet back in Chicago two weekends later for the Fourth of July.

I must have had that freshly fucked glow at the office the following day because it didn't take Nicholas but a few minutes before he entered my office and shut the door.

"Good morning. Did you have a good weekend?" I asked.

"Yes, but more importantly, how was your weekend?" Nicholas replied.

Did the man have cameras on me? Not wanting to arouse any more suspicion or answer any more questions, I replied, "Fine." I said it with a smile and a confident look that told him this was all the information he was going to get, no matter how long he stood in my office and stared me down.

He did exactly that.

"Is there something I can help you with?" I finally said.

Without a reply, he turned and walked out of my office.

The morning was filled with conference calls. I left the office to grab my favorite lunch at Dean & DeLuca and returned to the office parking lot at the exact same moment as Nicholas.

"So, what are you doing for the Fourth of July?" he asked casually.

How did the guy do it? Was he bugging me?

"Oh, I think I'm going to go to Chicago for the weekend," I said, trying to sound casual. I turned to walk into the office, but Nicholas's stopped me. It wasn't difficult for him to do. He was tall and had the frame of a football player. All he had to do was step in front of me.

He squinted his eyes. "Markus is in Chicago, isn't he?"

I couldn't guess how he knew that.

"Yes, as a matter of fact he is," I replied, looking him directly in the eyes. Then I walked around him and headed into the office.

He allowed me to continue just enough ahead of him for us to take separate elevators up to the fifth floor. He followed me into my office, closed the door, and sat down in one of the chairs across from me.

Now I was perturbed. "How can I help you?" I asked.

"I don't want you to go to Chicago," he replied after a dramatic pause.

He was being ridiculous. Only a week earlier, he had told me that his wife had tried to commit suicide. Yes, his wife. At our post-acquisition dinner, he'd told me that he was recently divorced. What he'd actually been was recently separated—and not even legally separated. Once his wife attempted suicide, he had gone back to her. He reported having no desire to be with her, but he felt it was his duty to do so. If she committed suicide, his children would be without their mother, and he didn't want to be responsible for that.

"Other than the fact that you lied to me about being married, I don't care," I had replied. "I wasn't planning to marry you. We were two adults exchanging sexual favors." I told him to go back to his wife and enjoy his life but couldn't resist adding, "Oh, by the way, she won." He looked confused. "It's not hard to kill yourself if you really want to. Your wife didn't want to kill herself, she merely knew how to get you back exactly where she wanted you." It had been blunt, but I'd felt he deserved it. He was a master manipulator. How had he not seen his wife's manipulation?

The affair was over.

I was dumbfounded by Nicholas's audacity. He had told me he didn't want me to go to Chicago with the authority usually wielded by a dictator. He wasn't my husband. He hadn't even been a serious lover. He was my boss. The problem was that I knew arguing with him would get me nowhere. He could sit in my office the rest of the day, harassing me. I, on the other hand, had his company to run. I knew arguing with him would do no good, so with all the southern charm I could assemble, I said, "I'll think about it." I looked at the door, communicating that it was now time for him to leave my office.

The afternoon included three additional visits from Nicholas. As the day ended, I realized that I simply couldn't go to Chicago for the Fourth of July. I was in a real pickle. Markus knew nothing about the affair with

Nicholas. I couldn't reveal the truth about him now because we were just reconnecting.

I decided to tell Markus that I had wanted to go to Paris ever since I'd sold the company, that the Fourth of July week was a great time for me to do that, and that I would love him to come too. I expected him to be excited. He was nothing of the kind. I thought about telling him the truth—the whole truth—but I couldn't bring myself to do that. The conversation ended with him being mad and hanging up. Markus called a few days later and agreed to meet me in Paris, and I wondered what had made him change his mind.

When I told Nicholas I was going to Paris for the week of the Fourth of July, he was so thrilled that he bought me a first-class ticket. I loved that he had no idea I was meeting Markus in Paris. It served him right. For months, we had been sleeping together while he was going to marriage counseling with his wife. They had separated in the spring, and it turned out that I was only his latest conquest. They had been married for twenty-three years. Missy, Nicholas's wife, clearly had it all figured out, as proven by her suicide act.

I adored Paris. I'd been there many times, and I loved everything from the intimate restaurants to the fact that people kept to their own business. I loved the cafés that stayed open until the early morning hours. When I worked for JD Edwards, I had opened a training center in Paris and had fallen in love with the city during my three weeks there.

July was the perfect time to visit. All the spring and summer clothes would be on sale as they made room for the fall arrivals. I asked my best friend, Ashley, to come with me

and promised to pay for her ticket if she did. She was excited about going and flew over with me on Saturday. We
had until Wednesday before Markus arrived. My reward for
selling the company wasn't buying a boat or a bigger house.
It was an unrestrained shopping spree. I decided that I
wouldn't look at any price tags and would allow myself to
buy absolutely anything I wanted during that week. We
shopped till our feet were literally bloody. We ate, smoked,
drank, and bought *Sex in the City* in French, which we
watched in the apartment I had rented. Ashley was scheduled to fly out Wednesday night, but we were invited to a
private gallery opening for Christian Louboutin, so she
changed her flight. It turned out that spending nine thousand euros for two pairs of shoes and a handbag a few days
before a party got us a couple of tickets.

Markus's taxi delivered him to the rental apartment
on Wednesday morning. I had decided to give up all expectations and let it be whatever it was. He responded
perfectly to the news of the party that evening. A man
after my own heart, he announced that we must go shopping because he had nothing appropriate to wear.

The "party" was actually the David Lynch Fetish exhibit of twenty-one photographs of women wearing
nothing but Christian Louboutin shoes. To Europeans,
the human body was beautiful, especially the female body.
It was something to be celebrated and worshiped, and the
exhibit was a celebration of both the female body and
Christian Louboutin shoes.

Ashley, Markus, and I floated around enjoying the
sensuous photography. Other than our inability to speak
French, we fit in perfectly. Of course, both Ashley and I

were wearing Christian Louboutin shoes. That certainly didn't hurt. I wore a Catherine Malandrino runway cocktail dress, Markus was dressed in black Hugo Boss from head to toe, and Ashley was dressed in red Prada socks with a black Dior baby doll dress. And then we saw her! Cécilia Sarkozy, the first lady of France, was at the party! Ashely was so glad she had changed her flight. We partied until 5:00 a.m., then returned to the apartment in time for Ashely to change into jeans and catch her flight home.

Markus and I had a wonderful time together. We wanted the exact same things. One night we wanted to go out and be seen in the scene. The next night we wanted to sit for hours in a tiny restaurant off the beaten path in jeans and then walk for hours along the Seine before collapsing in bed.

Back in the US, Markus and I emailed, texted, and talked daily. We met every weekend in Charlotte, Denver, or Chicago. It was working well until we were in the wine bar at Dean & DeLuca and I slipped on a verbal banana peel. I mentioned that things at the office were a little tense because Nicholas's wife, Missy, was jealous of me. As soon as the words came out of my mouth, I knew I was in trouble. In my panic, I tried to talk fast and change the subject.

"Does Missy have anything to be jealous of?" Markus asked quietly.

I knew better than to try and spin things for Markus but I still said, "Yes, Nicholas and I kissed once," thinking that would nicely wrap it all up.

Markus didn't buy it. "You only kissed?"

"Yes," I replied.

I couldn't tell him that we'd not only had sex, but that it had started the night the GBSynergy sale closed. My heart was finally beating again. I didn't want to lose that. I longed to have a lover who knew my soul and heart and loved them more than just my body, accomplishments, and money. The problem was that *I* didn't know my heart and soul.

I had no idea. I knew that Markus would push until he got to the heart of the matter if I told him, and I didn't want to go to the heart of the matter! I was finally starting to feel love for him. Couldn't we stay there?

He let the matter go, or at least I thought he did. But two weeks later, he was distant at dinner, then lost it in the restaurant. "I can't do this. I can't fucking do this."

"Do what?" I asked as I looked around at the patrons nearby.

"Sure, look around. That's all you really care about, isn't it?" He stood up. "We're done. It's over. You are fucking unbelievable."

He walked toward the restroom, and I calmly motioned for the waiter. I paid the bill, grabbed my coat while quietly apologizing to those at the tables around us, got in the car, and waited for him. Did I really want to be with someone who lost it in a restaurant?

A tiny little voice in my gut said, *Actually, yes!*

I wanted to be with a man who would not excuse behavior to gain a rich life. I longed for a relationship in which I was seen. I longed for a relationship like I'd had with my mom, one in which I knew that I was deeply loved. Growing up, that had included challenging me when I wasn't loving or kind. If she hadn't died, she would still be confronting me on my questionable behavior—and there was a lot of questionable behavior to confront.

Markus wanted more too. He wanted to know the real Karmen, not the image I projected. But the challenge was too big. I didn't know who I was, let alone why I had slept with Nicholas, and I was afraid to find out. What if I had a sexual addiction and would never again be able to be faithful to a partner? What if the world was as black-and-white as the church had preached and I was a sinner who needed saving? What if it *was* dangerous to think for myself and not blindly follow the Bible's rules as the church had presented them?

Markus opened the passenger seat door and slid in. I knew that it was over and I had nothing to lose. I was so tired of always having it together and spinning everything. I asked myself why I had slept with Nicholas and trusted what came to me in that moment.

Without a moment's hesitation, I let the words form. "Yes, I slept with Nicholas. I slept with Nicholas because I teased him throughout the entire acquisition. I believed that my company and me were one and the same and the sale of GBSynergy defined my value. I got caught playing with fire. I kept sleeping with him because I was lonely in Charlotte. I've only been with three men, besides you. Two of them were my husbands. The third was a multi-millionaire who wanted me, and it felt good, and I wanted to feel what it felt like to be with someone rich and successful. And that is the shallow, ugly truth."

All logic told me that the small window I had just given him into my heart would end the relationship for good.

Instead, he said, "Now *that* I can live with. I just wanted the truth, and I finally got it."

I had nothing to say. There wasn't one explanation my head could formulate. There was no logic to his reaction.

Markus brushed my arm as if to wake me up. "Are you ready to go?"

Dazed, I shook my head yes.

CHAPTER 21

Thrown Under the Bus

I knew I had been pushed out and made to fail.

MY OFFICE LIFE BECAME HELL. Nicholas was jealous, suspicious, and controlling. But I was firm in my conviction to not have sex with him.

I had an employment contract with Titan Technology. Part of the acquisition deal was that I had to stay at Titan Technology for two years, which was meant to provide protection for the company. Nicholas had to keep me around or pay out the rest of my employment contract. I knew it was torturous for him to keep me at the company and not be sleeping with me, but I could not have predicted the devious plan he would devise to deal with me.

Nicholas became suspiciously absent from the office. I usually had no problem locating him when I needed his assistance in closing a deal, approving organizational changes, or seeking his help on other business related things. I had perceived power, but in truth, nothing happened without Nicholas's direct approval and sign-off from his sidekick, Bill Gordon. Bill had been with Nicholas at his first company, and all sales contracts, organizational changes, and deal negotiations had his signature on them. Up to that point, I had worked directly with Nicholas, and Bill's signature was a mere technicality. But suddenly, my emails and voicemails to Nicholas were being answered by Bill. I wasn't used to going through Bill to get to Nicholas.

At first, aside from the extra step of bringing Bill up to speed on a few items, it was nice to get work accomplished without dealing directly with Nicholas. But when the answers coming back from Bill became nonsensical, it moved to maddening. I tried to explain to Bill why Nicholas was critically needed at a new billion-dollar prospect only to hear in reply, "Nicholas clearly communicated to me that you need to close the deal on your own."

I couldn't close the deal on my own. A Fortune 500 company was not going to sign a contract for millions of dollars a year to outsource their department without meeting the CEO. Nicholas knew this. The entire history of sales at Titan Technology proved this.

I wished I could handle it by myself, but the company wasn't IBM. Prospects expected to meet the top executive if they were going to entrust their success to a mid-size company. Nevertheless, what other option did I have? I began to develop a new sales approach—one that didn't require the CEO's participation. I worked through the weekend to put together polished case studies containing all the evidence a prospect would need to gain the confidence traditionally secured by meeting the CEO.

Then, in a weekly sales meeting a few days later, I learned that Nicholas was joining a sales person who reported to me on a visit to a much smaller client. As soon as Nicholas's pronouncement of his plans to travel with one of my sales guys came across the Polycom speaker phone, I looked directly at Bill for an explanation. Bill stared back at me confidently while the corners of his mouth turned upward.

Nicholas was trying to make me fail. I got that Nicholas didn't want me around, but I couldn't comprehend that he would purposely lose a multimillion-dollar contract just to make me look incompetent. It didn't compute. I understood that Nicholas might want to sabotage me so he could demote me and get rid of me, but why not just lay me off and pay out my employment contract? Financially, that made more sense than losing a multi-year contract. I had to be missing something.

Over the rest of the summer and into the fall, Nicholas communicated directly with everyone but me, effectively undermining my authority, power, and ability to be effective as the VP of Sales. It was awkward for my entire sales team to be engaged directly by the CEO when he would not engage directly with me, their immediate supervisor. On a daily basis, I suppressed shock upon hearing news that should not have been news to me.

I was determined to sit tall in my chair with a plastered smile on my face. Over and over again, I learned things I was being kept in the dark about from one of my direct reports: the hiring of new sales executives I had no idea were even being interviewed; services I didn't know we offered. I felt like a baby elephant that had been separated from the herd. So far, I had eluded the lions, but the end was inevitable. It was just a matter of time. With each day that passed, my exhaustion grew, along with the inevitability of my leaving Titan Technology.

By October, I was resigned to the fact that he had won. I couldn't be successful in Charlotte when he didn't want me there. Just when my exhaustion was palpable, Nicholas appeared in my office. I hadn't seen him in months. He behaved as if we had been seeing one another every day, and he left no room for discussing his absence and nonsupport. Over the past few months I had sent him emails and left voicemails in an attempt to address the issue directly. His response had been consistent. "You are the VP of sales. You need to manage it yourself." He stood there as still and stoic as my father had when I'd ask him where he'd been the years between visits. Both men had dismissed me, leaving me feeling invalidated and depreciated.

He sat down and looked straight into my eyes. With the best display of feigned concern I had ever witnessed, he asked me if I was happy. He suggested that moving to Charlotte maybe hadn't been the best idea and proposed that I might be happier in Denver.

I was speechless! He was clearly the master, and I was clearly the apprentice. For months he had undermined me in every way and now, without a hint of guilt, he sat in my office faking concern for my happiness. He was good! I was out of my league. What else could I do but concede? I couldn't find the words to question or challenge Nicholas. Instead, I agreed that returning to Denver might be a good idea.

I was tired. I resigned myself to moving back to Denver and functionally disappearing for the remainder of my two-year employment contract, just running sales for the small division of training. Moving back to Denver was professional suicide. As soon as I accepted the demotion, announcing to colleagues that I missed Denver too much and needed better work/life balance, Nicholas began throwing me under the bus on conference calls and emails every chance he got, in every way. He had begun his full-court press to make my life miserable in an attempt to get me to quit. I knew something had to be done, but I gave myself some breathing space for a while.

Markus asked me to go to Germany with him for Christmas. He planned to spend Christmas with his parents, then go to Cologne for a friend's wedding. I accepted and was excited about it.

As Christmas approached, I realized I could not continue working at Titan Technology. But if I quit, I stood to lose a lot, and not just the cash from the employment agreement. The purchase price of four million was half stock, half cash, and the stock was tied to my employment contract. If I left before the two years, it could literally cost me millions. I knew I had a case for a lawsuit. I knew I had been pushed out and made to fail after Nicholas couldn't have me sexually, but a lawsuit was the last thing I wanted. I decided to enjoy Christmas and then fly to Charlotte at the beginning of the year to have it out with Nicholas.

I put Titan Technology out of mind when Markus and I boarded the plane for Germany. Markus had never brought a girlfriend home to meet his family. I was nervous about meeting them, but once I did, it helped me understand what made him the man he had become. I envied the stability he had grown up with. His parents had been married for forty years, and each still lit up when the other came into the room. Markus and his sister were very different, but in this family, there was no expectation for them to be alike in personality or temperament. They were accepted for who they were. No wonder Markus allowed everyone to be who they wanted to be.

Markus's family was not religious, but it was a family tradition to attend church on Christmas Eve, so on Christmas Eve we walked to the small local church that had been built in 1271. The stone church had a clock tower, and the church bell was ringing. We entered and slid into a pew about six rows from the back of the church. I was thankful that it was packed because that meant free body heat in the otherwise unheated church. I wouldn't understand a word of the service, but it didn't matter.

I soaked it all in. There were vines on the pillars, and the church arches were lined in gold. Slowly, it sunk in. I had been in this church before. But that was impossible! My heart began to pound. I had never been to Germany before. How could I have been in this church before? It didn't make sense, but there was something very familiar about the place. I felt it.

Then it came to me: This was the church I'd dreamed of the night before my wedding to Brad, three years earlier. That didn't make any sense! More than that, it was impossible.

Markus looked over at me and whispered, "Everything okay?"

I remembered the detail of the side door exiting to a courtyard in my dream, but we were sitting behind a pillar that blocked the view to the right side of the church.

Whispering back, I pointed to the right. "There aren't doors on that side of the church that exit into a courtyard are there?"

He looked surprised by the question. "Yes. How did you know that?"

I thought my head was going to spin around ten times and pop off the top of my body. "Just wondering," I replied, knowing I hadn't really answered his question.

I couldn't believe I had never connected Markus to my dream. He was German, and everyone in my dream wedding was speaking German, but I had never made that connection. My head looked for a rational explanation. Had I already lived that life and it was all just a past life memory? I tried to put Markus in my dream to see if the groom's face had actually been his, but it was still blank. I had seen the church and the courtyard in that dream but not Markus.

I couldn't talk to Markus about it because my mind couldn't explain it. There was still an essential need in me for a black-and-white world. I had not learned how to sit in a feeling that I didn't understand and let it unfold without knowing where it would take me. And I had no model for openly sharing the déjà vu experience with Markus and examining it together. I could find only one explanation for the strange experience: It was a sign that I was supposed to marry Markus. But the thought of marriage made me physically ill.

When we returned to Denver, I felt lost. Markus was wonderful; his family was wonderful. I had dreamed of the church in his small German village two years before meeting the man and yet, I couldn't breathe when I thought of marrying him. Why couldn't I just be happy? Why couldn't I simply enjoy the love around me?

I decided it had everything to do with my predicament at Titan Technology. I had to take care of that once and for all. I decided to fly out to Charlotte and confront Nicholas.

I felt sick as I prepared for my meeting with him. I wanted to avoid a sexual harassment lawsuit. In an effort to quietly move on with my life, I believed that I had come up with a mutually beneficial proposal. I went to Nicholas's office and shut the door behind me.

"Nicholas, you and I both know this isn't working. You practically shoved me back to Denver, and I know you would be absolutely delighted if I resigned from the company."

I laid out the two options I was prepared to live with. Option one was to leave my stock in the company until Titan Technology was sold or went public and he would lay me off, pay out the remainder of my employment contract, which amounted to fifteen months of salary, and pay my yearly bonus. Option two was to give me liquidity for my stock, and I would waive my employment agreement, minus the remaining bonus for the first year.

My proposal was exceedingly fair. The truth was that he had committed sexual harassment. The case law described our relationship perfectly. Nicholas wanted a sexual relationship with me, couldn't have that, and had made the working conditions intolerable. Not only had he made my working conditions miserable, he had demoted me without cause. It took a few minutes for the reality to sink in for him. He could clearly tell I was aware of the law and my rights. He probably also suspected that I had already talked to a lawyer.

And I *had* met with a lawyer. I had been informed that sexual harassment lawsuits got ugly fast, and if there was any way to settle this without a formal lawsuit, I should do so.

It took a few hours of negotiating, but we finally agreed that I would resign. In return, he would pay my salary through April and pay the remainder of my bonus. He would also liquidate my stock over the next few months, acting as a broker with other investors. I had not gotten immediate liquidity, but I was sure that liquidity would come.

Nicholas and I met at Starbucks the next morning to finalize the agreement. Nothing was written. It was a simple verbal agreement between two adults. I left Charlotte feeling relief, but it was all a chimera.

PART TWO
Awakening

CHAPTER 22

Finally Facing My Grief

I was about to be alone with myself, and it petrified me.

THE TRANSITION OUT OF TITAN TECHNOLOGY was quicker than I expected. By the following Monday I had been excused from all emails, conference calls, and meetings. In the course of a few days, my inbox went from averaging 150 emails a day to less than ten. It was obvious that Nicholas had been waiting for me to resign. With no job to rush off to each morning, I began to plan my next company.

Women needed help shopping. I couldn't count the number of times I had heard intelligent, accomplished, professional women recount the horrors of shopping, of trying on clothes for hours and finding nothing that fit them right. I had been one of them. I drafted a business plan that eliminated all clothing pieces that wouldn't work under any circumstance for a particular woman's body. My plan was to create a virtual store that only presented clothes that actually fit *their* body type, as well as being age, climate, and price appropriate. It wasn't difficult to accomplish using computer algorithms. Using the design specifications they created about each item, along with information on their body type, age, and other demographics, it was possible to create a virtual shopping experience that would feel like walking into Nordstrom and being presented only with items that worked. Once I had the algorithms figured out, all I had to do was figure out if I was going to stock the inventory myself or simply be a distributor who served as the link between the customer and the manufacturer.

This new business adventure was much more feminine in focus and vastly different than the IT industry I had been living in, but the basic business principles were the same, and the entrepreneurial expertise I had honed over the past several years was completely applicable. This new venture combined my business acumen with my long-held passion around fashion and my growing appreciation for my own sex. I didn't know if I was just worn out trying to fight with the good old boys or somehow connecting to a feeling that women ought to be able to look good in business without being harassed.

I seamlessly went from overworking at Titan Technology to overworking on my new plan. All the while, Markus was telling me that I needed to stop. He had been encouraging me to take a trip by myself, but taking a trip by myself was the last thing I wanted. In fact, the thought of being by myself made me want to jump out of my skin. I wanted to leap right into my next company. I wanted it to consume every minute of every day, allowing zero time to feel anything.

The simple truth was that when my mom had become sick eighteen years earlier, I had survived it by staying busy. It had proven to be an effective means of survival and had yielded extreme professional success. I knew how to conquer the world at a speed of Mach 2. I didn't know how to do anything else.

Unfortunately, Markus wasn't the only person telling me to stop. When I was married to Brad, my therapist had used the exact same words. During one session, she'd said, "Karmen, you need to just stop!"

What was I supposed to do? Was I supposed to sit on the couch all day and stare at the walls? What was the point? The idea of getting still and feeling everything inside me was scary. But a voice inside me quietly whispered, *It's okay. It's not as dark as you fear.*

Tears welled up in my eyes. Markus could see that I had just had a moment of insight. "I will start looking for a house for you to rent on the north shore of Oahu," he said.

With a shrug of my shoulders and tears in my eyes, I agreed. We found the perfect cottage located right on the beach. Before I could change my mind, I emailed the management company and gave them my credit card for five weeks and four nights. It was done. I was committed. I bought an airline ticket and added myself to the upgrade list. While I knew I should be exhilarated, I was actually terrified. For almost six weeks I would be alone with no team and no clients depending on me. I wouldn't even have the distraction of friends or a lover to help me fill every second of every day. I was about to be alone with myself, and it petrified me.

My mind raced the night before I left. Even though I was all packed with two huge suitcases containing everything needed for snorkeling, hiking, trail running, cycling, and swimming, I lay in bed thinking of every reason not to go. I tried to quiet my mind, but it was relentless. *What are you doing? Why are you going to Hawaii when you have a brilliant company to launch?*

None of my relaxation methods had worked. Ignoring my mind had proven ineffective, so with utter exhaustion, I decided to determine an objective for the trip. I asked myself a simple question to focus my mind: What is the goal of the trip? I felt ashamed for needing an objective before I left for paradise, but I did. I sat in bed, frozen with fear.

My gut answered. *Fall in love with Karmen.*

I laughed. That was ridiculous.

Shaking my head, I heard it again, slower, with each word clearly enunciated. *Fall...in...love...with...Karmen.*

Tears formed in my eyes, and I realized that my gut wasn't telling me to logically assess my strengths and weaknesses, it was telling me to reclaim the carefree, adventurous, joyful, dreamy little girl who believed she could fly and believed that the world was not only good, it was magical.

I stopped mocking my gut for a few seconds and heard something else. *You might actually like what you see.*

Before I knew it, I was fast asleep.

I had a first-class seat on a 757. I watched movies and read a new Robert Parker novel. But as the airplane wheels touched the ground, trepidation came flying in. Everyone around me jumped up to disembark when we came to a stop, but I sat frozen. I wondered what would happen if I didn't get up. Would they physically force me off the plane? The plane was probably heading back to Denver. If I just stayed in my seat, I would be back in Denver in a few hours.

"Ms. Berentsen, are you okay?"

Looking up, I saw the flight attendant peering at me with concern and realized I was moments away from being deemed a crazy woman. I quickly collected myself. "Yes. Sorry, I was just daydreaming about the beach. Have we landed?"

"Yes, the plane is almost empty," she replied.

Feigning surprise, I jumped up and grabbed my things. If I was miserable, I could change my flight and be back on a plane the following day. I collected my two huge suitcases and my bike carrier and loaded them onto a luggage cart. Everyone around me was with someone. I was the only person alone trying to manage way too much luggage. I hit a bump crossing the street to the Hertz rental center and my entire cart tipped over in the road. I reloaded it as cars stopped and waited for the lone female with baggage to clear the road so they could continue driving away with their friends and families.

I managed to drive to the other side of the island and find my little cottage. It was beautiful, and I was miserable. Trying to be positive, I stepped outside. There was a couple walking down the beach, hand in hand. Farther down, children were playing. And I was all by myself.

I went inside and phoned Markus. I lost it when he answered, sobbing too hard to be understood. He asked if I was hurt, clearly concerned. I must have sounded as panicked and distraught as someone who had just survived a head-on car collision. Taking a few deep breaths, I managed get out words that were comprehensible. "No, I'm not hurt, I'm just *alone*." Then I started sobbing again.

He chuckled. "Your assignment for tonight is to head to a bar and get a drink." I was about to protest, but he cut me off. "I love you. Talk to you in the morning."

Before I could reply, he hung up. I just held the phone and sobbed.

Without a better idea of my own, I accepted his and rummaged through my suitcases to find a brush, hair-spray, mascara, and sundress. Fifteen minutes later, I was out the door, looking for the nearest bar.

I walked into Haleiwa Joe's to find it packed with locals. I looked at the full bar and almost walked right back out the door until I remembered that only suitcases and tears awaited me at my cottage. I ordered a drink and waited for a stool to open. In a few minutes, a seat at the bar opened and I grabbed it. Sitting at the bar usually gave me time to catch up on the dozens of unread emails, but that night, my BlackBerry had zero unread emails. No one needed me.

I ordered tuna and vegetables, and thankfully, it was soon in front of me. The guy next to me, a local, was talking to the bartender about his swim that morning. I joined their conversation and learned that the local man was a triathlete. He and his wife had moved to the North Shore after visiting from New York ten years earlier. After spending one week there with their son, they flew home, sold their apartment, and moved to Hawaii. They had been in Hawaii ever since and now had two more kids. Hearing the former New Yorker, I somehow knew that it was all going to be okay. He felt like an angel sent to encourage me to slow down and just breathe.

At sunrise the next morning I headed off to enjoy a thirty-mile bike ride, relishing the fact that I was in bike shorts and a jersey while all my friends were freezing in Denver. I wondered why I had fought coming to Hawaii and realized that I had surrendered. I was settling in to the idea of being with myself and doing whatever struck me as fun in the moment. The week flew by with long bike rides, gorgeous trail runs to waterfalls, swims with sea turtles, and delicious fresh fish dinners with talkative bartenders. I was thoroughly enjoying myself.

Markus came on Saturday afternoon to spend a week with me in paradise. He had planned on coming later in my trip, but after the first day and the sobbing phone call, he promised to come see me if I would stay for six days by myself. We hiked, snorkeled, jumped off the rock in Waimea Bay, and made love under the stars.

When he kissed me good-bye at the airport, I could feel the loneliness coming on. I drove from Honolulu back to my cottage on the North Shore, blasting the music in my Jeep as I tried to convince myself that it was just another beautiful day in paradise. It didn't work. The loneliness was closing in on me as I returned to my cottage on the beach. I knew the feeling well. For almost two decades, I had escaped it with hard workouts, intense work deadlines, fashion, and friends. I was sick of running from this faceless ghost. I decided to try something new and *feel* it.

I walked to the middle of the room and sat down on the floor. I had run from this feeling forever, and I was tired of running. I could see the ocean from where I sat on the floor, cross-legged and still. I watched the waves crash on the shore. "Bring it on," I said aloud, and then my mind kicked in with a bit of consolation. *What's the worst that could happen?*

Within seconds, I was sobbing, and while my mind had no clue why, something in me gave it words. "I'm sad. I feel *so* sad." And right behind that came, "I miss my mom!" The mourning had begun. Seventeen years after her death, I was finally crying, *really* crying.

When my mom died, I feared that if I felt the depth of her loss and started to cry deeply and fully, I would either become a homeless drunk on a park bench or go insane. To be human is to have and know connection. Without it, we have insanity. My soul knew this truth long before taking Psychology 101. At seventeen I didn't trust that anyone was big enough in my life to protect me from being destroyed by the depth of my loss. At my mother's funeral I decided that she was gone and in heaven and that crying about it wasn't going to do a bit of good.

Over a decade later, I sat still for the first time and began to really cry. I missed my mom! My tears turned into violent sobs as I allowed myself to feel the depth of my sadness. When the sun began to set, I realized that I had sat on the floor and cried all day. And now I wanted to sleep.

The next day I didn't feel like riding my bike or running. The tears were still coming, and I wanted only coffee and tissues. The timing was almost spooky. My mom had died when I was seventeen, and I was a little over a month away from turning thirty-four. Seventeen years had passed since her death. My life was evenly split between the number of years she had been alive in my life and the number of years she had been gone.

I sat on the beach completely incapable of accomplishing anything other than producing massive amounts of tears and mucus. I had needed to grieve for years, but I had told myself that if I took my eye off my work for one moment, it would bankrupt me. That left no time for grieving. Besides, I had made the decision to be a strong woman with an impenetrable heart when my mother died. My impenetrable heart had to crack open, at least a little, for grieving to happen.

But nothing now stood between me and my grief, neither work nor hardness of heart. I had loosened the ropes around my heart enough to feel. Again, I cried until the sun was setting and my bed was calling. Then I slept for more than sixteen hours.

The next morning, I grabbed coffee and my journal before heading back out to my beach chair. I still had no desire to run, bike, swim, hike, or do anything else that closely resembled effort. Crying had been effort enough. My morning was filled with the full spectrum of emotions as I recorded memories about my mom in my journal. I laughed as I recalled certain things, cried when I recalled others, and cringed at the memory of more than a few things. Age provided a different perspective on a few memories. I looked up and offered a silent apology to my mom who, God knows, had put up with a lot from me.

As I wrote, my mind recalled a dream I'd had more times than I wished to admit. In my dream, my sister, my only family left, had been killed in a tragic car accident. What was most disturbing wasn't the fact that I dreamed this repeatedly but how I felt each time I awoke from the dream. I had never told my therapist about the dream because I knew she would have asked how I felt when I awoke. I had learned from her that dreams were, among other things, a window into our subconscious feelings. The real question to ask when I awoke from a dream was, "How do I feel about the events, people, and situations I just dreamed?" That was the scary part. When I woke up from dreaming that my sister had just died, I woke up *wishing* it would happen.

I hadn't ever told a soul about my dream or how I felt when I awoke. This was just one of the many things I saw as irrefutable proof that my heart was truly ugly and dark. Who wishes that their only sister would die? I had always pushed my dream away by flying out of bed and onto a treadmill or by doing anything else that allowed me to escape my horrific heart. But now, I decided to ask myself why I wanted my sister to have a fatal car crash.

The answer came immediately. If I were working for a company and announced that I was going to take a month off to mourn the loss of my mom, who had died when I was seventeen, no one would understand. But if my sister were suddenly killed, everyone would understand that I couldn't handle working for a while. Tears streamed down my face as I realized that I wasn't a monster. My heart wasn't black and evil. I simply craved permission to grieve and needed an excuse to stop and come unglued for a while.

I grabbed my beach chair as another day came to a close. My next-door neighbor, whom I had met the previous week, passed me. I hadn't looked in a mirror for days. In fact, I hadn't consumed anything but coffee and trail mix for three days. My neighbor saw my swollen eyes with dark circles underneath them and, with fierce concern, asked if I was okay.

"My mom died," I replied as big tears rolled down my face.

I didn't say that my mom had died seventeen years ago and I had just gotten around to crying. I didn't try to explain. I was sad, and it didn't matter if it had taken me half my life to stop and feel it. The compassion in his eyes made me realize that I hadn't shared my sorrow with anyone, including my best friend or my boyfriend. This stranger on the beach was the first person to see my unprotected, hurting soul.

It felt wonderful. I felt both exposed and safe at the same time.

For years I had worked so hard to feel lovable because, at my core, I didn't think there was anything to love. The only person who really knew me and loved me had gotten sick and died when I was in high school. In my juvenile mind, I had concluded that if I were über-successful, it might make my dad love me. But even if that failed, money would provide me the means to buy people. If I could provide things for friends that no one else provided, they would need me. It wasn't love, but it kind of felt like love. Who wouldn't love someone who could take them to Paris for the week? Everyone loved free trips, free food, and glorious experiences. And maybe if I "bought" their love at first, they would come to genuinely love me.

I had run away from anyone who couldn't be bought because that left me vulnerable. My soul wanted to be loved unconditionally, but I wasn't willing to risk being rejected, as I had by my father, or devastated by losing real love through death, as I had with my mother. Buying people and their affection was much safer. It was also exhausting.

Making enough money to pay for my life and all the lives around me was grueling, and filling every moment of every day with activity so there was never a moment to have to deal with the nightmares in my head was draining.

Finally, I felt free. Ironically, the Bible verse, "You shall know the truth, and the truth shall set you free," played in my mind. The simple act of finally sitting on the floor to purposefully feel the panic I had been running from for seventeen years had not only resulted in a colossal release of sorrow but had revealed that my worst reoccurring dream was nothing more than my core desire to mourn my mom's death.

I wasn't a monster!

I felt reborn. I could stand still and feel the sand under my feet. I didn't have to use every moment to create money to buy love. Love was already there for me. For the first time, I loved myself. I wasn't afraid of myself and didn't feel the need to move at Mach speed to hide what I thought was all the darkness in me. It wasn't darkness! My soul wasn't black! I knew I had hurt people, but it wasn't the only thing I was capable of. I was also capable of love.

CHAPTER 23

Training to Surf Life

"Once you catch the wave, stop trying.
Have fun and ride it! Stop trying to control it."

I HAD NEVER TRIED SURFING FOR ONE REASON: sharks. I had seen *Jaws* at way too young an age, and it had made a big impression on me. Water equaled sharks. No way was I going to dangle my legs over some board to have a shark enjoy them as an afternoon snack. But my new outlook on life was birthing new desires. I was in awe of the world. It was as if I had awakened from a black-and-white dream to find that everything around me was in color.

The nonstop, high-speed life I had been living was tied to the assumption that everything was a means to an end. I had never fully taken delight in the majestic Rocky Mountains as I rode my bike because biking was about burning massive amounts of calories. In fact, every one of my hobbies had been nothing more than a means to an end. Others could stand still and enjoy a sunset, or thundering waves, or the fresh smell of the forest, but after a millisecond, I had finished appreciating it. My explanation was that I was much more complex than everyone around me. Because of that, simple things couldn't hold my attention. Of course, that couldn't have been further from the truth, and I was finally beginning to be mesmer-ized by simple things.

I wanted to get in the water and try to surf.

My local bartender pointed me to Uncle Bryan's Surf School. Bryan had been a world-ranked surfer and was now retired. He had a surf school on the North Shore, and I showed up in the morning to sign up for a lesson. Bryan's approach was to get you up on the board, riding a wave. He and his right-hand man Jake would swim be-hind the board with fins on their feet and literally catch the wave for you. Traditionally, the exhilaration of riding a wave is not felt for weeks, but because of Bryan's ap-proach, I was riding a wave on my first attempt.

The next morning I returned for my second lesson. The third morning I returned again. I was hooked. My senses were overwhelmed with the pearl-blue water, the sea turtles popping up next to my board, and the feeling of flying as I rode the wave. Uncle Bryan and Jake quickly got to know me. On the third day, they realized that I would be showing up every morning until I left Hawaii.

Unfortunately, the simple pleasure of the water didn't last long. With each wave I caught, I longed to conquer surfing. I wanted to be as good as those surfers sitting fifty yards behind the beginners catching the real waves. The simple pleasure of enjoying it was gone, and I was focused on adding another thing I'd mastered to my personal résumé.

I arranged a deal with Uncle Bryan to pay twenty bucks a day for a surfboard and go out with the class with-out being a part of the group and their lesson for the day. Each day, I studied the real surfers riding waves farther out in the ocean and tried to mimic their moves. But it seemed the more effort I marshaled, the faster I fell. I concluded that I simply needed to try harder.

After falling dozens of times, Jake paddled toward me. "What are you doing?"

"I'm trying to mimic those people," I said, pointing to the dozens of surfers catching real waves behind me.

Jake threw his head back and looked up to the sky as if to ask God how he could get through to me. "You are not stronger than the waves."

I ignored his comment and recounted the steps in my head that I had been practicing with each wave I tried to ride.

"You don't get it, do you?" he said, clearly becoming perturbed.

"I paddle. When I think I'm ready to stand up, I paddle one more big stroke, as you taught me, and then I stand up and try to replicate the maneuvers the guys behind me are doing."

Jake shook his head. "I don't know what you do for a living, but you have to be some sort of business big shot since you rented a house on the North Shore for a month and seem to have limitless funds. You may have conquered the professional world, but you will not conquer the water. You are *nothing* compared to these waves. You don't tell them what trick you are going to try. They tell you! Once you catch the wave, stop trying. Have fun and ride it! Stop trying to control it. You aren't going to win."

Jake had just summarized my life perfectly: I always tried too hard. Jake wasn't telling me to be lazy. Surfing was a combination of effort and release. It took serious effort to catch a wave. You had to paddle with all your might. Each stroke fired every muscle in your arms and back before you felt the thrust of the water as it caught your board. Then, and only then, could you stand up and ride the wave. I had mastered the first part, filled with massive effort, but the second part, the part requiring me to let go and enjoy the ride, eluded me. The harder I tried, the quicker I fell. Surfing didn't allow me the control I was accustomed to. I needed to let go and listen to the wave. I needed to feel the water under my board and let *it* move *me* versus thinking *I* could do something with *it*.

Within a few minutes, a great wave was forming. The surfers around me let me know it was my wave if I wanted it. I wanted it.

Paddle, paddle, paddle. Paddle two more strokes. Feel the thrust. Stand. *Let go.* I rode down the wave, then turned into shore, then back into the wave. *Oh . . . my . . . god! So this is surfing.*

I rode the wave all the way in and sat down on my board. It was amazing. I had to do it again. I paddled back out and passed Jake.

"It's kind of fun to just go with it, isn't it?" he said.

For most of my life I had believed I had to make everything happen. If I didn't make it happen, nothing would happen. My life had been heartache until I started taking control of my destiny and my heart. My experience fit with the biblical teaching that this world is "fallen" and belonged to the fallen angel, Lucifer.

But letting go and riding the wave was a totally different experience. It was both good and easy. I had heard people advise to go with the flow instead of trying to swim upstream, but I had always thought that doing so would take me right over a waterfall to my death. Maybe I could stop striving and the universe would provide. I had never trusted that what was supposed to come into my life would come into my life and what was supposed to go out of my life would go out of my life. I had fought hard to always be exactly where I wanted to be, whether that was a job or a specific table in a restaurant.

Surfing showed me how I could be both ambitious and go with the flow. I had always made a plan, and come hell or high water, I made that plan work. But Jake had shown me that surfing didn't work that way.

Maybe life didn't work that way either.

At twenty-two, Jake had a life I knew many surfers envied. He taught surfing, lived simply, and seemed happy. At first, I thought he was happy because he was a simple guy without much ambition or drive. But I quickly began to see that he was happy because he was doing what he loved, and as I got to know him, I came to understand that his happiness hadn't been facilitated by an easy life.

Jake and his sister had grown up surfing in Florida—living in the water. When his sister graduated from high school, she went to college on Oahu so she could surf the North Shore. One day, she disappeared at sea. A surfboard washed up on shore, and the search began. She was never found. Jake had come to Hawaii with his mom and spent weeks on Coast Guard boats searching for any sign of her, dead or alive. They were finally forced to accept her death and had a memorial for her at sea.

Jake put his surfboard away and went to college in the landlocked state of Ohio. After a few months, though, he grabbed his backpack, walked out of class, drove home, got his surfboard, and headed back to Hawaii.

"How is it that you are so happy?" I asked him one day while waiting to catch a wave.

He shook his blond head and let out a little grunt. "It's not that hard."

In a rather patronizing tone, I began to explain to him that he was mistaken, that the world was actually pretty hard for most people.

He interrupted my lecture. "What do you *want* to do?"

There it was, such a simple question.

I thought I had it all figured out. I knew what my employers wanted me to do. I knew what my family wanted me to do. I knew what the world at large wanted me to do. But I had no clue what I, Karmen Berentsen, wanted to do.

Jake wasn't living for anyone but himself. He wasn't asking what his parents, friends, or the world thought of his choice to drop out of school, move to Hawaii, live in a basement apartment, and teach surfing. I had never asked myself what I wanted to do with my life. It had only been a couple of months since I had asked myself what I wanted to do for a couple of days over a weekend. I needed to ask myself what I wanted to do next in my life.

I thought figuring out what I wanted to do would be a long process. There were whole companies built on assessing personalities, IQ, and natural talents to decipher what career one should pursue. I grabbed my journal, beach chair, and sunhat, figuring I would be out on the beach for a while. When I got settled, I closed my eyes and asked the critical question: What do I want to do? I was ready to record the millions of thoughts that were about to rush through my mind and use a "mind map" to record them all.

I want to write.

I opened my eyes and looked out at the waves, frustrated. That was the most ridiculous idea in the world. I decided to try again. I took one deep breath and filled my lungs completely, then closed my eyes and slowly exhaled, asking the same question, but with one word of clarification. What do I want to do . . . professionally?

I want to write.

Did I really want to write? I hadn't a clue how to do it. I didn't know how to break into the literary world. My résumé was full of management and leadership experience in the IT industry. How was I ever going to be a writer? On the other hand, I had done the sensible thing my entire life, and I wasn't happy. I was successful and wealthy, but I wasn't happy.

I hadn't realized that I had brought my phone with me to the beach until it rang. It was an old friend, Kendra, who now lived in Dallas. The first fifteen minutes of the conversation were filled with covering the current details of our lives. But our conversation quickly left the shallow details and took a deep dive as I began to recount the days of mourning my mother's death. I talked, she listened, and we both cried. I could feel her smile from thousands of miles away.

"Karmen, you have to write your story," Kendra said when I finished talking about my mom.

I was stunned. What had she just said? I hadn't said anything about the revelation I'd had less than thirty minutes earlier.

"Why did you say that?" I asked.

"You live in the laboratory, while most of us live in the library. Please, write your story."

It had been confirmed.

I called Markus and told him that I knew what I wanted to do. But as soon as the words, "I want to write," came out of my mouth, I found my mouth continuing with, "Of course, maybe not right now. I mean, I need to do some research and maybe go to a couple of seminars and see if I do, in fact, have any aptitude—"

"That is perfect!" Markus interrupted.

I couldn't believe it. He didn't think I was crazy.

In fact, the only thing that proved to be crazy was how it seemed to make perfect sense to everyone close to me but had completely eluded me. In the conversation I'd just had, Kendra had even said, "I've been telling you this for years."

Really? I had no memory of it because it had not been on the career trajectory I'd graphed out for myself. By the time the day ended, I had no idea how I was going to do it, but I finally knew what I wanted to do. I wanted to write.

I woke up the next morning and didn't move. I just lay there to see how I felt the morning after my big realization. I genuinely did want to write, even though I had no clue how to do it. I decided to move forward with the idea instead of killing the dream because I didn't have it all figured out.

I was about to get up and head out to surf when Markus called, bursting with excitement. "You know I have been ready to leave Denver and that I love Hawaii. What do you think of me coming out the weekend after next and us looking for a place to rent for a year? You can write, and I will get an IT contract in Honolulu."

I loved his support, but he was suggesting that we live together in Hawaii. In so many ways, this was exactly what I wanted. But the air around me was once again thinning, and I couldn't breathe. Why did I have this reaction every time Markus wanted to plan a life together? I loved him and I loved being with him. I wanted to stop working so much, build a life with someone, and have kids. He was perfect for me. What was my problem?

I hung up the phone having agreed that he would come out in two weeks and we would look for a place to live. Still unable to breathe, I paced my cottage while trying to convince myself that this was a great plan.

My gut had its own opinion. *You're not ready.*

I mentally argued with my gut. *Shut up! I am ready! Markus is wonderful. I love him.*

I had begun to feel again, and I wanted to feel love and be with someone. Markus was going to come out, and we were going to live in Hawaii. I had a plan, and now it was time to make it happen. And just like that, I cut off my gut. I dismissed the very part of me that had enlightened me about my deepest desires. I had, in effect, said to it, *Thanks for your help. I got what I needed. I'll ask for your help again when I need it.*

CHAPTER 24

Letting Go

I felt I was awakening to a whole new world.

THE MAI TAI IS A DANGEROUS DRINK, in part because the rum is nicely hidden in the sweetness of the pineapple juice. The drinks were disappearing, and Jake, his friend Sam, and I were having a blast dancing at Turtle Bay Resort. When I finally got home that night, it was no longer night, it was early morning. I decided to take the day off from surfing.

After a short nap, I headed over to Sam's apartment to check on him. We had all been drunk the night before, but I'd last seen Sam at his truck in the hotel parking lot, and I wanted to make sure he had gotten home safely.

I met Sam's roommate, Drew, at the apartment. Drew was a massage therapist and avid surfer. He was also closer to my age than Jake and Sam. Sam and I laughed about the previous night's bacchanalian shenanigans, and Drew announced that he was going for his beach run. Without thinking, I asked if I could come along. I needed a good workout. But as soon as the words left my mouth, I could feel that I had invaded Drew's space. I was about to retract my self-invitation when Drew asked if I knew how to belly breathe.

I had learned about belly breathing from a massage therapist who pointed out that when a baby breathes, their stomach rises and falls. She said that many adults have somehow lost the ability to breathe from their belly naturally, and their breathing is shallow, typically only involving their chest. I was surprised by Drew's question but responded proudly, "Actually, I do."

"Lie down and show me," he challenged.

I demonstrated belly breathing sufficiently for Drew to be satisfied that I actually knew how to do it, and he invited me to go on his not-so-typical beach run. As far as I was concerned, nothing was proving to be typical. What was one more unique experience?

We walked down to the beach in our swimsuits and flip-flops, but as soon as we got there, Drew removed his flip-flops and stashed them under a nearby bush. I followed suit. I was ready for a hard run that would clear my mind, and even though I feared I might not be able to keep up, I trusted my ability to tap in to the reserve of determination within me.

As I was mentally preparing, Drew told me to follow him as he did his "beach entrance." And with that, he began leaping forward in a side-to-side motion toward the water. He looked like a leprechaun jumping through a forest. Part of me wanted to grab my flip-flops, make an excuse, and leave, but I was intrigued. With a shrug, I muttered, "What the hell," and started my own awkward leaping toward the water.

At the water's edge, he began an easy run. I followed his lead. Then he slowed to a walk, entered the ocean, and began to walk in knee-deep water. I followed him, staying a few feet behind. When Drew stopped, I stopped. The waves were crashing close to us, and as I stood in the knee-deep water, I experienced the familiar occurrence of being pushed over by it. I was quickly getting exhausted from fighting the water.

But Drew was standing perfectly still. He was right in front of me with the same waves crashing into him, but he wasn't moving an inch. I was battling to avoid falling over while Drew stood motionless. I had to ask him how he was accomplishing being perfectly still without physical effort.

"Close your eyes and picture yourself as a five-hundred-year-old oak tree with roots that go hundreds of feet into the ground, standing brilliantly with water rushing around you."

I had already entered the water in a tribal sort of way, so I quieted my mind and began to imagine a huge, beautiful old tree with strong roots sprawling deep into the earth.

I stopped moving. The water no longer pounded against me but now moved easily around me. I opened my eyes to validate that I wasn't imagining it and confirmed that I was perfectly still, despite the water turbulence. I looked at the powerful waves moving around me and began to question the experience. I demanded an explanation. Memories, facts, and experiences rushed through my mind. And as my mind raced, the picture of the tree disappeared—and with it, my balance. My body once again began to fight the water.

Drew smiled, turned, and resumed walking. Within half a mile, the beach became covered with coral that extended far into the water. Drew began a slow, thoughtful walk on the coral. I followed. "Be careful where you step so you don't cut your feet," he cautioned.

I stopped, paralyzed with fear.

Drew began to laugh as he turned around and saw me teetering on the coral, fear-possessed and paralyzed. "Ask yourself if it is safe to step and your intuition will tell you," he said.

This was too much. I rolled my eyes. "Okay, Yoda, now you've gone too far. My intuition will tell me if it is safe?"

"Yes, it will," he replied, ignoring my attitude.

I was perturbed. I was trapped in an island of coral with a bizarre man, and I didn't want a cut foot.

Drew looked down at the scars on my knee. "When you blew out your knee, you knew you were going to get hurt before it happened, didn't you?"

Years earlier, during my first year in college, I had gone skiing with friends. I was a good skier and had spent the weekend skiing with two guys from school who had been ski instructors. We skied black diamond runs, jumping off rocks on the sides of the runs, catching ten-plus feet of air before landing and skiing down the mountain. We had flown down the mountain on Sunday afternoon, trying to catch the last lift up before they closed. We barely made it and skidded to a stop behind the last family in line. The guys at the lift laughed and let us jump on the last chair lift.

"Everyone gets hurt on the last run of the day," I said as we ascended. "I'm exhausted, so I'm going to take the blue run down and meet you guys at the bottom."

I meandered down the mountain and ran into our other friends from college before reaching the bottom. Fifteen of us had caravanned up to Utah from San Diego. I joined my novice friends and continued down the mountain.

There was a cliff on the side of the run. A friend who had played ski instructor all weekend to the newer skiers shouted, "Karmen, take that jump! It's the last one of the season."

I was tired. My legs were shot. I had no desire to take any more jumps, but his invitation seemed to be a challenge, and I had to rise to it. A feeling began to swirl in me as I side-stepped up the mountain. But as the intensity of the feeling grew, so did the strength of my mind's argument. My mind fiercely argued that the jump was smaller than many of the jumps I'd made that weekend, and the run was grossly less steep than others. What option did I have but to rise to the challenge? Besides, many of my college friends hadn't seen me ski. My ego puffed with each step up the side of the mountain, and my mind's arguments squelched the deep feeling in my gut that was warning me not to jump.

I finally reached the top. The jump was bigger than it looked. I was going to catch some serious air from this seemingly small jump. My gut screamed, "Don't jump!" My eyes saw no danger and my head calculated no threat, but my gut was screaming at me to not jump.

I was about to ski back down to the groomed run when four guys above me on a chair lift started to chant in unison, "Jump, jump, jump."

I felt I had no other choice. I had to jump. I decided to avoid anything spectacular like a helicopter jump, but merely ski, jump, land, and continue down the hill. My ego and head had won. I pushed off and hit the jump, flew through the air, and landed beautifully. But as I went to ski away, my left leg stuck as if cemented in the ground while the rest of my body continued with the powerful momentum from the jump. My upper leg and body flew forward and my anterior cruciate ligament tore off my kneecap along with my meniscus, all the way through to my posterior cruciate ligament. I collapsed in the snow.

My friends had seen me jump, land, and then collapse in the snow. There wasn't any big wipeout. It merely looked like I had buckled in the snow. As my friends started to haggle me to get up, a girlfriend caught my terrorized face. "Ski patrol! She needs ski patrol!" she screamed.

The ski patrol arrived, loaded me on a toboggan, and raced me down the hill to the clinic. When the doctor at the clinic began to cut off my ski pants, I was prepared to see a grossly swollen knee. To my surprise, my knee looked fine. The doctor announced that he was going to test the integrity of my ligaments. With one hand, he held my leg above my knee while his other hand gently pulled my calf toward him. My entire leg below my kneecap moved inches toward him. It was surreal. I felt absolutely no pain as I watched my entire lower leg dislodge from my knee and then return. A wave of nausea swept over me from the sight of watching my body contort.

"It didn't hurt. That's a good thing, right?" I said, trying to muster both composure and positivity.

"Actually, that is a very bad thing," he replied. "It means that not only did you tear all the ligaments that joined your tibia to your femur, you also severed the nerves completely."

I had ripped my leg in two. The only thing holding my leg together was skin. I was going to need my knee completely reconstructed.

☙❧

I was amazed with Drew's insight. My gut *had* told me that it wasn't safe to make that jump. I hadn't listened. My ego and my mind had overruled my intuition.

Drew smiled proudly at his enlightened student, then he turned and continued his slow, meditative walk, listening to his gut with each step. I followed, and with each step, I asked my gut if it was safe.

I had grown up trying to listen to the Holy Spirit. I had been taught that the Holy Spirit could only enter me and speak if I confessed my sins and accepted Christ as my Lord. But I had never considered that the divine was within me all along and could be tapped in to without any defined religious step. I felt I was awakening to a whole new world. I had never even thought about asking my soul something as literal as whether or not it was safe to take a step.

I knew what *no* felt like. It was the feeling I had on the top of the mountain looking at the jump. It was the feeling I had right before I made fun of someone to make myself feel superior. It was unrest.

But I had never asked myself what *yes* felt like. As I stepped on the coral, confident I was not going to be harmed, yes felt calm, warm, tranquil, and fluid. Yes felt light as a feather floating through the air. I walked slowly across the coral asking my gut if it was safe, and when I felt the yes, I stepped.

There was a tiny bay at the end of the coral, a small inlet about fifteen feet wide. The water gently lapped on the sand. About four feet out from the shore, the ocean floor dropped abruptly. It appeared to be five feet deep, but was actually close to twenty feet deep. The ocean was so clear that the bottom was easily seen. Drew began to float in the water effortlessly. The water washed him up on shore and rolled his body onto the sand, and then it rolled him back into the deep pool. I was struck by his ability to be an organic part of the water instead of an object fighting it. I wanted to try it but became acutely aware of the people up on the beach watching us. My ego had once again risen up, choking my soul. Drew encouraged me to forget about the people watching and join him, pointing out that I didn't know them and never would.

He had nailed me.

I joined him in the water, but it wasn't as easy as it looked. I struggled to float without constantly taking gulps of salt water. Drew instructed me to fear neither the power of the water nor my lack of control. Slowly, I surrendered to the water, and as I did, I became a thirty-three-year-old woman playing in the water. My body was being tossed by the water from the deep pool to the sand and back to the pool. I felt utterly weightless. Each second was filled with magical anticipation, and I had no idea what was coming next. It was the best ride in the world. This was no roller-coaster ride; my body wasn't being thrown around violently. The water was fluid and graceful, but still quick and surprising.

It reminded me of being tickled as a little kid. I had begged my dad to tickle me. The anticipation was thrilling as his hand hovered over my chest. I would begin to giggle before he ever touched my ribs. Then, just as I thought he had retreated, he would attack my neck, and I would begin to laugh uncontrollably. This was the first adult experience like that.

We left the water and broke into a good run on the beach, eventually collecting our flip-flops and arriving back at the apartment.

What an afternoon! I had learned how to stand perfectly still in crashing waves, I had practiced walking on coral while asking intuitively if it was safe, and I had finally ridden the water as if I were part of it. It had been surreal in the way that experiences are when you know you have touched something important, something almost mystical and thoroughly transcendent. I was trying to stamp all of it solidly in my memory when Drew wrapped his arms around my waist and pulled me into a kiss. My mind was perfectly still as he kissed me. Our bodies moved fluidly and freely. It was intoxicating and different.

Growing up, the sexual part of me had been fiercely hidden and shamed. As an adult, it had been opened and wildly explored. But instead of being simply enjoyed, I had learned to use my sexuality to control men—or at least convince myself that I was in the driver's seat. I used sex to further my agenda.

Kissing Drew was not about power. Instead of controlling, I was yielding. I was soft and supple, and I was following his lead instead of directing. It was different, yet it felt as natural as breathing. Something deep and pure— something spiritual—was beginning to swell. My feminine side was sprouting. The sexuality I had been strutting around in was not feminine, but masculine. My sexual power was protruding and dominating, not receiving and feminine. Sex had never been about yielding or opening but about conquering and controlling. Kissing Drew was the opposite of wielding power. I was soft, fluid, responsive, and open. And what I was experiencing with Drew was an entirely different kind of power, one that was shared instead of closely held.

It felt like awakening from a dream when we stopped kissing. I was in a state similar to that half-awake, half-asleep place before your mind turns on in the morning with its to-do lists. In that brief moment, you can still feel the softness of the sheets and the comfort of the pillow under your head. I was high—not on drugs, but on the experiences of the day. My mind was quiet and my soul was beaming.

When we made love, my soul felt open and unprotected. Another human was touching it and my exposed, vulnerable interior felt safe and open. Sex felt strangely like the high I had experienced as a young kid in church. I was connecting to something greater than myself. I wasn't alone. It was spiritual and soul-changing instead of earthly, dirty, or even sexual, for that matter. I saw that Drew's body was merely the shell holding a brilliant, beautiful, awake soul. And for the first time, I realized that my naked body was also merely a shell holding a brilliant, beautiful, awake soul.

I fell asleep at Drew's apartment, blissful. When I awoke after a few hours, so did my mind. My mind began racing, questioning what I had done.

Without a word, Drew placed his hand on my forehead and said, "Shh."

I had said nothing. I hadn't moved. I was in the exact same position I'd been in before my head kicked in. Yet, Drew somehow knew that I was panicking.

I turned, grabbing the sheet as I rolled to cover my naked body, and feigned confusion. "What?"

"I can feel your mind racing, and it's exhausting."

Now I was completely wigged. Maybe it was all a dream. Maybe I was actually dreaming right then. But as I lay there, I realized that Drew and the entire afternoon had been real. I didn't understand any of it, but I needed to understand it. I needed to leave. I needed to process all that had happened and make sense of it. I bolted.

I made it home and collapsed on the couch. I had no answers, and I could make no sense of it. But I found myself surrendering to that.

All of my life I had forced everything. I was tired of forcing. I was tired of the black-and-white world. I was tired of making everything fit into one of two categories: good or bad, moral or immoral, right or wrong, righteous or evil. Judgment as physical as clothing began to fall off and a smile began to radiate across my face.

CHAPTER 25

Men as Kryptonite

What I hadn't realized was that I was okay without a man.

I COULD PICTURE A LIFE WITH MARKUS, just not quite yet. I knew Markus couldn't come to Hawaii. He would take one look at me and know something had happened. My gut was right. I wasn't ready for a relationship. I rationalized that there was no reason to tell him anything, and I decided that it would be inconsiderate to let him fly all the way out to Hawaii only to break up.

My whole being was waking up for the first time in over twenty years. I felt full of life and dreams, and I wanted to be free and unrestricted. I needed the year after college that everyone but me seemed to have taken. I needed time to do whatever I wanted, with whomever I wanted, anytime I wanted. I wasn't ready to be committed to anyone but myself.

I called Markus. Before he could say anything, I blurted, "I can't have a boyfriend." I felt horrible. I knew what I was doing wasn't fair, but for the first time, I was discovering my true self—both the glorious side and insanely human side. I needed to learn to love all of me and display compassion for myself before trying to be with someone else.

Markus was hurt and angry. I hung up and began to sob.

I thought my big revelation in Hawaii was mourning my mom's death, but I obviously had some serious, unresolved issues with my father because men seemed to be my kryptonite. I was done with Hawaii. I packed my bags and headed home.

It turned out that kryptonite was not as easy to defeat as I thought. I changed my mind about breaking up with Markus, but it did not matter because Markus decided he needed a break from me. As soon as he distanced himself from me, I was all the more sure that I needed him in my life. My moments of enlightenment in Hawaii disappeared as quickly as a shooting star. I fell right back into my old patterns.

I decided to go to Germany and learn German. I loved Europe and had always wanted to live there. I went online and found a language school in Düsseldorf with a four-week course. No man, not even Markus, could resist a woman who flew to Germany to learn his native language.

In Germany, I quickly learned that languages did not come naturally to me. My ears heard the teacher, but when my mouth tried to repeat what I had heard, it sounded like a completely different word. My head hurt.

I was in an apartment I hated and I was lonely. To make matters worse, two weeks into the trip, Markus called to tell me that he was moving on. My attempt to manipulate Markus into dating me by flying across the world to learn his native language had backfired. The distance had only proven to be a *relief* to him, and he'd realized that he needed more than a break from me, he needed to break it off with me.

I hung up the phone and stood frozen in the middle of the apartment. The old panic began to rise in me, and I wanted to run from it. I couldn't breathe. I had been rejected and I was alone. But just as I was truly starting to panic, I heard a voice inside me telling me that I was okay. *You are okay. You are okay without a man.*

In Hawaii, I had grieved my mom's death. I had been set free from my nightmare of my sister's death, and I had realized that my soul was not evil. What I hadn't realized was that I was okay without a man.

Over and over, my gut had tried to tell me that I needed to be alone, yet here I was in Germany for the sole purpose of winning back a man. It was time to deal with what I had tried to repress, conceal, and ignore my entire adult life: my deep-seated belief that I was not okay, and especially not okay without a man.

I instinctively knew that it had to do with my father. With all my might and all my will, I had tried to convince everyone, including myself, that my dad's actions had not wounded me. I had created a persona. On the outside, I was a woman who could have sex like a man—unattached and without emotion or commitment. It was too painful to deal with my dad's rejection, so I enticed men sexually. That made me feel wanted and desired, which was exactly what I needed from my father. But when men desired me, it wasn't really me they were desiring. What they wanted was sexual fulfillment. At some level, I knew that and was left feeling rejected and alone. Because I didn't have a healthy sense of self-worth, I sought validation of my worthiness through man after man.

It was time for me to develop self-worth. It was time for me to spend time with myself, and I couldn't think of a better place to do that than in Europe because Europe felt like home to me. I decided to stay in Germany. I wanted to finish what I had started, not for Markus but for me. And Germany was proving to be rich in many ways. I called my girlfriends to let them know that I was staying in Europe indefinitely and told them they had a free place to stay if they wanted to visit me.

Over the next months, I continued to learn German and make new friends. For the first time in a really long time, I was making friends, not buying them. I wasn't gaining new friends because I offered them a job or because I was their best customer. My new friends didn't have anything to gain from me from financial, business, or social perspectives. I didn't rent a boat and invite them to dine on it. I simply hung out with them at parks, restaurants, beer gardens, and our homes. Slowly, I began to realize my own worthiness. I had shed the personas that had served as my armor and protection. Without employees, clients, status, or fancy worldly trappings, I got to know Karmen. I was getting to know my strengths and flaws and hold them both lovingly, without disregarding either. I was discovering who I was at my core and genuinely falling in love with myself.

In Hawaii, I realized that I wasn't evil. In Germany, I found the things about me that were uniquely Karmen and the reasons why I enjoyed myself and liked who I was. It didn't happen in one aha moment. It happened

one day at a time as I lived without chasing men or conquering the world in an attempt to validate my worth. I
accepted that my dad's rejection and abandonment had
wounded me. I accepted that now, as an adult, I needed
to hold that hurting little girl and tell her all the wonderful
things that existed in her with or without a father's love. I
had no parents to parent me, but I realized that I could
parent myself. I could love myself as a mother loves her
daughter. I could have the same compassion for myself
that a parent has for their precious, loved child. It took
time, but with each day, I realized, more and more, that
my soul was beautiful. I was growing up.

I turned my professional focus to fashion. I filled my
days with traveling to surrounding cities and attending
graduations from major fashion schools. Dries Van Noten
had made the fashion school in Antwerp, Belgium, famous.
It was almost 200 kilometers from Düsseldorf to Antwerp.
I rented a BMW 5 Series and drove on the Autobahn at
240 kilometers per hour. It was better than any adventure
ride at any theme park. Driving alone in a foreign country,
finding my hotel, and figuring out where to park were both
nerve-racking and exhilarating.

When I stopped trying to be everything to everyone
and just live, I began to know myself. I was an adventurous soul. I hadn't merely craved adventure as a distraction, I genuinely had an adventurous spirit. Day by day, I
learned who I was and realized I was pretty cool without
a pedigree, wealth, or fame. I was beautiful just as I was.

In Antwerp, I met with young designers about distrib-
uting their lines in America. I had no master plan for my
time in Germany. The old Karmen would have figured out

a lofty goal and wouldn't have stopped for anything or any-body until it was accomplished. But I had changed. I didn't need the affection of a man or success in my profession to define me. I didn't need my life to be overstuffed and mov-ing at hyper-speed—except, of course, when driving.

As I reflected on the men in my life, I realized that they had been a perfect reflection of what was undevel-oped in me. Instead of figuring out why I struggled with consistency, structure, and discipline—characteristics I loved in Peter—I orchestrated a "merger" through mar-riage and "acquired" the traits. Brad had not simply of-fered an out from my marriage to Peter, he had modeled what being a business owner was to me. I had not only learned how to become a successful business owner from him, I had stepped into my own power doing it. When I wanted to take it further and become a high-powered ex-ecutive, I slept with Nicholas. Even Markus reflected a desire to be a cultured, stylish, world traveler. I was learn-ing about the positive things about me that were devel-oped, some of which I wanted to develop further.

Life was good; I felt healthy. And then Markus called. He was coming to Germany and had called me to tell me of his trip, but he would not make any plans with me. Be-fore Markus's call, I felt strong, independent, and confi-dent. After his call, I found myself slouched in the corner. How was that possible? How could I feel so much passion and excitement in finally becoming an adult yet be shaken to the core so quickly by one man's decision not to make plans with me? Markus was still my kryptonite.

Markus did end up making plans with me, and he was surprised with the woman he found. I was a more adult, emotionally settled version of Karmen. I still wanted him. We reconciled, and I moved back to Denver.

Once settled, I realized that I needed to decide what I was going to do professionally. I had made all the business relationships I needed to open a clothing boutique in Denver, so the next step was to find space to rent. I started looking at storefront retail space, but when I got into the details of the new business, it wasn't coming together. For some reason, it didn't seem to be the right time to embark on this new adventure in the fashion industry. I sensed I was forcing something instead of tapping in to a plan that was already in motion.

When I was growing up, I had never believed in fate. I believed in the self-made woman who single-handedly made her destiny. But that had changed. I still believed in pursuing a passion wholeheartedly, but only if what I wanted to pursue felt like a fit versus being something I was pursuing to prove that I was in the top five percent of the human race. The outward action looked the same to me, but now I asked if I was going after the goal to feed my ego or if whatever I wanted to pursue felt supported by the universe.

Doors weren't opening as I pursued the idea of opening a clothing boutique. Instead, they seemed to be slamming shut in my face. This time, I paused instead of charging ahead. It wasn't the right time to open a boutique. My gut knew it, and I listened. I opened myself up to the possibility for something else to present itself.

Within a few weeks, the owner of a company that had created a reporting solution for Oracle clients asked me to design a training solution for him. It was a three-month contract that fit and felt good. I didn't know where it would lead, and better yet, I didn't need to know. I didn't have to design the entire map and see my entire course plotted out. Just as I had done during my walk across the coral in Hawaii, I trusted my intuition to guide me. Any path that felt good to my heart would, undoubtedly, be a good one.

Before Markus and I reconciled in Germany, he had planned an around-the-world trip using the frequent flyer miles he'd accumulated through business trips. He was going to take six weeks to fly around the world, seeing friends and exploring new countries on his own. He invited me to join him on his last stop in New Zealand. I agreed without hesitation.

New Zealand is a place so beautiful that to be there is like stepping out of ordinary life and into some mythological ideal, like the Elysian Fields. We were in paradise, but we were fighting like a grouchy, old, married couple that despised each other. We had reconciled, but we had not really resolved anything.

In so many ways, Markus seemed like the right man for me. I liked his business drive, his worldliness, his ability to play with abandon, and his sexiness. But our history had done some damage. Instead of feeling like a partner to him, I felt like I was along for the ride, accompanying him on *his* adventure, not *our* adventure. There was some energy to it that reminded me of my marriage to Peter, and even though Markus seemed nothing like Peter, I recognized the feeling. My gut was telling me to leave, but the rest of me wanted to make it work with Markus.

Things were tentative between us until our final night in New Zealand. Over dinner, Markus told me that an old colleague had moved to Singapore and needed a senior director of services. He had offered Markus the job weeks ago, and Markus had all but accepted. He wanted me to go with him.

I'd never had any desire to visit Asia, let alone live there, but I loved adventure, and the thought of moving to a new country with Markus excited me. Still, I didn't have a visa to work in Singapore, so the logistics of my getting an apartment there seemed like an impediment. When I pointed this out, it wasn't a problem as far as he was concerned. He didn't just want me to join him in Singapore, he wanted me to *live* with him in Singapore. He would pay all of the bills.

This wasn't just going on an adventure with him, it was agreeing to become a couple. We could build a new life together in a place where neither of us had lived before. It felt like a chance to erase our history and begin again.

I had a three-month commitment, but once I had fulfilled that, there was little to prevent me from going to Singapore. I agreed to go with him. I could play, write, and continue the self-discovery I had begun in Hawaii. Markus and I would have a chance to take our relationship to a deeper level. It seemed as if the universe had dropped a beautiful opportunity into my lap, and I was excited about it.

But the next day, just as I was settling into the idea of life with Markus in Singapore, all hell erupted in a taxi. I thought we had lots of details to work out including finances, expectations, and length of stay, so I began asking some questions about how it would all work. To my horror, Markus turned toward me in frustration and shushed me. I had never been shushed like that by Markus or anyone else. Unsure about what had just happened, I began to talk again. Markus shushed me again. Markus wanted me to shut up.

"Did you just shush me?" I asked.

"Yes," he replied unashamedly.

"Why?" I asked.

Markus paused, seemingly contemplating his answer, then replied, "This is not an appropriate conversation to have in front of a cab driver."

We were in New Zealand—halfway around the world. I was sure the cab driver didn't care about our conversation. I wanted to argue but knew that if I did, we would be squabbling again. With focused determination, I calmly asked when an appropriate time to discuss things would be.

"At the restaurant," Markus replied coldly.

We had plenty of time before our evening flight and had planned to get something to eat and shop a bit in Auckland before heading to the airport. I was okay with waiting until we reached the restaurant to talk about Singapore. I concluded that in the German culture, taxis were not the place to have intimate discussions. Still, we would have to discuss his shushing of me.

When we reached the restaurant, we ordered local beers with fish-and-chips and spent some time in small talk. When I thought we were sufficiently relaxed and ready to have a productive conversation about our move to Singapore, I said, "The point I was trying to make in the cab was that—"

Markus pounded his beer glass down on the table. "Damn it, Karmen, I thought I made myself clear in the cab."

I was stunned by his outburst and totally bewildered. "You asked me to wait to have this conversation at the restaurant. We are at the restaurant."

Markus threw his head back in frustration. "I just said that to shut you up."

And then it dawned on me. Markus didn't want to have *any* conversation about anything that had to do with *our* life. In so many ways, Markus had moved away from the East German rigidity, but he had retained something intrinsically German when it came to our relationship. His expectation was that we would behave like his parents and his German friends. The man made the decisions and then informed the family.

I understood this concept. I used it in business. There was a time for brainstorming sessions, but there was also a time for decisive leadership. When it came to my company's vision and mission, I never held brainstorming sessions. Markus's frustration was identical to my frustration when an employee came into my office and attempted to have a conversation about a new vision for the company.

But this was not business, it was a personal relationship. I wanted a partner. I wanted a soul mate to journey through life with me. I didn't want a leader or dictator. But this step toward building a life together meant something else to Markus. It meant that the wild woman in me would finally be domesticated. And he would be calling the shots.

This was never going to work. Markus was wired to run a household, not cooperate in its management as an equal partner with his wife. My head was beginning to catch up with what my gut already knew. Even in Hawaii, my intuition had told me that I was not what *Markus* needed, but my emotional immaturity and baggage kept me solely focused on what *I* wanted and needed. I never thought to ask myself if I was what Markus needed.

Now I could fully answer that I was not what Markus needed or wanted in a wife because I had taken the time to get to know myself, and I was beginning to live that self-knowledge. I had learned what my deal breakers were in relationships, and not being an equal partner in a marriage was one of them. I no longer needed to change who I was to be the person I thought would make me loved and accepted by others. I no longer needed my father's acceptance in the form of a husband. I had submitted to Peter's rule at home for the promise of a happy marriage and a family. I had submitted to Brad's threats to keep a company. I had even submitted to Nicholas's harassment in hopes of becoming Titan Technology's CEO. But I was finally getting it. I could not surrender who I was or my intrinsic worth as a human being and expect to have a healthy relationship with a man. As important, I was finally beginning to lovingly care what the other person needed and bravely accept that I might not be a fit with it.

Even though I couldn't begin to articulate the feelings in my heart in a way that Markus would understand or accept, I knew that the relationship was over. I stood up and looked straight into Markus's eyes. I felt compassion for him, but I also felt sure of what needed to happen. "Good-bye."

I walked out of the restaurant, trailing my suitcase behind me.

I had never realized it before, but Markus and I truly had different philosophies about marriage. I tried to console myself with the wisdom that the entire point of dating is to try people on and see if they fit. The angst came when ninety percent of a person was a fit, but you wanted that last ten percent. Everyone had virtues and vices. No one was perfect, including me.

I wondered if I could ever accept Markus's position on appropriate roles for men and women in marriage as simply one of his vices. I could accept that he used one particularly offensive swear word as a synonym for idiot. I could accept that he liked to take a nap in the afternoon and start partying at 11:00 p.m. I could accept that he smoked cigarettes when he was really drunk. But this was different. This was a deal breaker. Having a partner who didn't treat me as an equal was a deal breaker for me. Smoking cigarettes might be a deal breaker for another woman, but this was a deal breaker for me. I realized that I needed to figure out my deal breakers because no matter how long I chose to ignore them or sugarcoat them, they would always assert themselves, and I wanted that to happen before I married, not afterward.

If I ever had a daughter, I thought, this would be the advice I would give her: Date and figure out your deal breakers—not society's deal breakers or your parents' deal breakers or your friends' deal breakers, but *yours*. Grow up enough to know and embrace your unique self. Become self-confident enough to not care what everyone else thinks because you know, without a shadow of a doubt, what *you* think. And don't just ask if they are what you need, also ask if you are what they need.

As I scripted this conversation in my head for my not-yet-conceived daughter, I heard it as if my mom were saying it to me. Even though she was physically gone, I felt her arm wrapped around me as if she were with me.

"I'm growing up, Mom," I said to her. "It's painful, but I think I'm finally growing up." And with that, I took a big breath and recalibrated.

I needed to get to the airport and catch an earlier flight than originally planned because the last thing I needed was a seventeen-hour flight next to the man I had just broken up with.

I ran out the door to catch a cab to the airport.

CHAPTER 26

The Present Moment

I needed to enjoy the happiness of the moment instead of waiting for happiness in the form of a marriage and motherhood.

MADONNA—THE MOST INDEPENDENT, constantly evolving woman I could think of at the moment—was singing "Like a Virgin" as she danced on stage four rows in front of us. This was her first concert in Denver in years, and my girlfriends and I had tickets. The girls had picked me up from the airport, where I had arrived three hours ahead of Markus. I removed all of my stuff from his apartment before he landed, dumped my things in my empty house, and headed to the Madonna concert.

For me, breaking up with Markus was analogous to breaking up with your first love in high school, the one you really thought you were going to marry because you had never experienced love before. I had missed the entire concept of dating before marriage when I married Peter straight out of college.

The Madonna concert was a great way to celebrate, along with being salve for my emotional wound. But to heal, I needed to go to yoga. I needed to sweat, move, and stretch. At my first opportunity, I found a class taught by Tricia, one of the few instructors who brought chanting into the yoga studio. Following her in a chant felt strangely comfortable. I always thought it had to do with how down-to-earth she was. Tricia didn't talk slowly or softly in an attempt to artificially create a mood. She walked into class with the same hello I got from the barista at the coffee shop. It felt real to me.

The chanting around me felt like a warm blanket covering my soul. I had come to class alone and didn't know anyone else there, but I felt connected to everyone. The moment felt eerily the same as church worship, which had always elevated me out of the daily grind and created a sense of expansiveness and community.

I breathed in all the sorrow of losing Markus, letting the pain ooze into every part of my body. Nothing was off-limits. With each ujjayi breath, I breathed in the depth of our breakup and let it permeate me completely until I pushed it out as I emptied my lungs of air. In church, I had felt connected to something bigger than me, but I had never tried breathing in emotional pain. I liked standing alone on my mat, touching no one but feeling supported by everyone and everything. For so many years, I had tried to make myself invincible. Now, standing barefoot on my mat with no makeup and no designer clothes or heels, I felt stronger than ever. And my ability to breathe in pain began to expand beyond the pain of losing Markus.

I had run from the sorrow of my mom's death for years because when I felt one tiny ounce of grief, it overwhelmed and suffocated me. I couldn't have imagined purposely breathing in the grief of losing her. And yet, now I could breathe in the depth of my mom's love and the pain of my dad's rejection. I could let it fill me completely without fearing that it would destroy me.

Standing in mountain pose with my hands at my heart, chanting, I had connected with the divine, and it was the same God I had grown up worshiping in the church. But instead of being only the God of the church, he was the God of the universe. I felt I'd come full circle in a healthy and complete way. As a small child, I had an innate understanding of God, without necessarily using the word. That understanding shrank when I adopted the God of the church. Now I was sensing God viscerally, as I had as a child.

After yoga, I returned to my new house, a 1920s bungalow in the Washington Park area of Denver, and lay before the blazing fire in my wood-burning fireplace. Save for the firelight, the house was dark. It was the crucible I needed to process all that had happened. It was hard to avoid falling back into the thinking that I needed a man to complete me. In Germany, my gut had told me that I was okay without a man, and for six months, I had listened to my gut. But once Markus came back into my life, I became obsessed with the future instead of living in the present and trusting that things would work out if it really worked between us. I forced the relationship, but the honest truth was that I had not been happy in the relationship with Markus. I was always apologizing for the crazy woman I had been the first year we dated. I was constantly being agreeable because I feared he might question getting back together with me if I wasn't accommodating. Instead of being myself, I adapted to what I thought Markus wanted, and that just made me miserable.

I needed to live in the present moment. Just as my mom had taught me to practice making good decisions about what I ate on a daily basis, I needed to practice making the good decisions to be in the present moment on a daily basis. If I was going to be truly happy in a relationship, I needed to enjoy the happiness of the moment instead of waiting for happiness in the form of a marriage and motherhood.

All of this seemed remarkably simple, but it had eluded me. My entire life, I had wanted to have a baby. I had never consciously decided to look for a man to give me a baby, but once I was in a relationship, I did think about it. I needed to stop trying to make things happen—including having a relationship with a man so I could be a mother. What would it look like if I started dating and focused solely on paying attention to whether I enjoyed the man, the date, and the present moment?-

I had been performing sleight of hand to get men to love me. I felt like a magician performing card tricks. I mesmerized my audience and seemed special, but every magic trick is really about speed and distraction. If I was skillful enough and provided enough distraction, I would remain special. For years I had tried to get my needs met in the wrong way. But now that I loved myself, I didn't have to mesmerize and fool men into loving me. I could just be myself.

After my epiphanies in New Zealand and at the yoga studio, dating became a balanced part of my life instead of a means of fulfillment. Work also became a financial means, not my total definition of self. The three-month contract I accepted before going to New Zealand resulted in creating another training company, but I wasn't building this new company as a means of self-validation, I was building it because it was fun and easy. And it felt good.

I got to know my neighbors and fell in love with a dog. Months later, I found myself back in front of the fire, this time with a fifty-pound, eight-month-old yellow Labrador retriever named Bagley who was sleeping with his head on my lap.

I'm going to grow old with you.

It came out of nowhere. It was just a thought that raced through my head. The puppy sleeping on my lap was the first living thing that had become non-disposable. It wasn't that I hadn't loved my friends, but they had always been replaceable. I had moved to Charlotte and Germany without thinking about my friends or neighbors. No one really affected the decisions I made—until now. The dog lying on my lap had somehow captured my heart, and it wasn't just about me anymore.

Was I really serious about this? If I got a job offer that took me to New York, would I really turn it down because of Bagley?

Yes. The answer was truly yes.

This slobbering Labrador on my lap had penetrated my heart. My life was no longer solely about me, and until that moment, I hadn't even realized that it actually *had* been only about me. I was kind and generous to people. I sacrificed for people. I loved people. But no one had deeply infiltrated my heart since my mother's death. I hadn't allowed it. I loved things and I enjoyed people, but they could all be replaced—until Bagley.

I had to start writing. The voice that spoke to me in Hawaii about wanting to write had not diminished or faded. The problem was simply *how* to start. I knew what I wanted to write about, but I didn't know if I should enroll in a writing class, start typing on my laptop, or draft an outline of a book in pen and paper. The task of writing a book seemed monstrous. For that reason, I had put off doing anything for almost a year.

In business, networking is key. It couldn't hurt to connect with some published authors. I would have loved to have called up Elizabeth Gilbert, the author of *Eat, Pray, Love*, but I was pretty sure I would never get through to her. I was, however, able to connect with an author who had published dozens of Christian books and spent his days speaking at conferences.

After the quick hellos were completed, I wasn't sure where to begin. Should I tell him the gist of the story? Should I ask him questions about being published? I felt as insecure as I'd been at my first day of employment at JD Edwards immediately after college. The confidence of being a successful entrepreneur didn't provide me any comfort in the new world of authorship. I babbled away, jumping from question to question with no pause for any answer.

Eventually, after I had been talking nonstop for over twenty minutes, he interrupted me.

"Just begin."

I threw my arms down and head back, much as a child who was about to begin a tantrum would. Fortunately, he couldn't see my theatrics because we weren't meeting live but over the phone.

"I don't know how to begin," I replied in frustration.

"Just write your story," he said.

His advice was so simple. I waited for him to elaborate, but the other end of the phone line was resolutely quiet. I waited a little longer. I wanted to make sure he wasn't the kind of person who took dramatic pauses between thoughts. Silence.

Finally, I said, "Thank you. I will sit down and start writing my story."

He had caught me while on a walk in my neighborhood park. We had played voicemail tag for weeks, so when I saw his number on my phone, I stopped and took his call. I had walked in circles during our thirty-minute conversation. Poor Bagley was completely confused. We were in the park and he was on his leash, but we weren't covering any new ground.

I was in front of Washington Park's south lake. The sun was high and warm and the bench called to me to sit. Pulling my feet up Indian style, I closed my eyes, tilted my head toward the sun, and breathed in the words, "Just write your story."

I grew up in a black-and-white world flowed as naturally from me as my last exhalation. I popped up off the bench, and Bagley spun around a couple of times as he felt the burst of energy. We took off on a fast run home. I had to get to my laptop.

For the next six weeks, my story gushed out of me faster than I could type. When I wasn't writing, I was reading Anne Lamott's book, *Bird by Bird*. Ten years earlier, my therapist had suggested the book to me. I had never opened it until the subtitle, *Some Instructions on Writing and Life* caught my attention. Anne Lamott was a *New York Times* best-selling author who had written a book covering the content she taught in her writing classes. I loved the chapter titled "Shitty First Drafts." It gave me permission to sit down and write without worrying about how bad the first draft was going to be. Without her encouragement I would have never made it past the first pages.

I hadn't set out to write my story as a cathartic experience, but putting myself back in the moment of seeing my mom's body convulsing amounted to reliving it. I knew readers didn't want to read an account of my life's events, they wanted a story that captivated them, just as I did when I picked up a book. For the story to be captivating, the words had to paint a three-dimensional picture for the reader, one that felt as real as their own memories but maybe with more insight. A good therapist actually recaps a story with words better than your own, and it heals because someone has finally captured the essence of the pain, fear, shock, and trauma that you lived. That is what I wanted to do in writing my story. My heart ached to encourage all the other women I knew who were incredibly successful professionally but exhausted personally from the relationships they had single-handedly sabotaged.

It was serious work reliving every memory while figuring out if that particular part of the story was even relevant. I was working as hard as I had as CEO of my company. Some days the words came easier than others, but regardless, each day I sat in my chair and stared at the computer screen until more pages were finished.

"Listen to Your Gut" could be a bumper sticker, but I didn't believe that bumper stickers changed lives. It was going to take an entire book to recap the journey from innocence to the hardening of my soul and the wake of bodies left in my pursuit of success and independence. The process of facing my shadow side and honestly seeing who I was in Hawaii was more than a footnote. Finding my true light over the years that followed and reclaiming the parts of my soul that had been lost with the abandonment of my father and death of my mother was more than a bumper sticker.

Casually, I'd share some of my insights with my close friends. Over and over, they begged me to continue to write because they wanted to absorb what I had to say in the private rooms of their own lives, not in a public restaurant or park. I ached to get it out. I felt as if I had been given a sacred gift. Not many people I knew were able to quit working, rent a house on a beach for five weeks, and begin to heal. I felt obligated to share my story and encourage others to meet themselves—their real souls, not their personalities—and get giddy about themselves.

I was amazed by the honest admission of one of my friends over martinis. "I wouldn't be getting my fourth divorce right now if I had gone to Hawaii and done what you did ten years ago," she said to the collected group.

I had to write my story for my friend and others like her. I knew the story had soul, but I also knew the writing was poor. Turning my experiences and desires into a book that actually had some legs felt impossible, but I kept at it, trusting that it would all come together in time.

And I wasn't just writing about the act of listening to my gut, I was practicing it daily. I woke up each day and channeled myself at age eight on Christmas morning. As a kid, Christmas had been magical for me. I believed in Santa because each Christmas there were presents under the tree that my mom would never have bought for me. Only Santa understood my passion for the Barbie Townhouse. Mom only saw the lack of space in my overstuffed bedroom. Gifts seemed to appear from simply radiating my soul's desires.

Now, as an adult, I made it a practice each morning to close my eyes and sit quietly on my bed until the feeling of the magic of Christmas vibrated through me. Of course, my practical mind, full of painful life experiences, often dulled the anticipation. But I committed to staying in my bed until I had achieved a glimmer of anticipation for the day that came from the divine, not my own efforts.

One day when I was working with a recruiting firm up in Boulder, the owner mentioned a brilliant editor who had worked on their marketing pieces. Her name was Melanie Mulhall. I hadn't Googled "Editors in Denver." She had truly come to me through no effort of my own—just as my Barbie Townhouse had shown up under the Christmas tree.

I sent my manuscript over to her, realizing that it would require some work on both of our parts to turn my writing into the interesting, multidimensional story of inspiration I envisioned—if she even agreed to take me on. That was okay, though, because when I had asked myself in Hawaii what I wanted to do, my gut had responded with *write*—not *write, get published, and become famous*. With

Melanie's help, I was going to learn the art and craft of writing and maybe have a piece of work worth publishing one day.

Fortunately, she saw it the same way and our work together began.

CHAPTER 27

Ending the Business Drama

*Now that I loved the real me, I was running toward what
I wanted instead of running away from what I didn't want.*

WHILE MY WRITING WAS MOVING FORWARD, the verbal
agreement between Nicholas and me was spiraling into a
nosedive. The agreement was for my Titan Technology
stock to be liquidated—and when that happened, it would
fund my writing and lifestyle for some time to come. Unfortunately, the chances of Titan Technology actually
paying out that agreement had become about as likely as
my chances of winning the lottery.

I had remained on payroll through April 30 of the year
following the acquisition. During my entire time in Hawaii,
I had been receiving a bi-weekly paycheck, and I was confident that Nicholas was working on brokering my stock. I
checked in with Nicholas before I left for Germany, and he
gave me the assurance I wanted. The summer months escaped quickly while I was experiencing life as an expatriate.
When I returned to Denver in the fall, I had been devastated when Nicholas stopped pretending to honor our
agreement and said, "Sue me if you want your stock."

I had been the fool. I filed a lawsuit, hoping that doing
so would bring Titan Technology to the table to have an

honest discussion with a fair and quiet resolution for both parties. I was severely mistaken.

Lawsuits get ugly fast. Titan Technology didn't show any signs of fear or accountability. My lawsuit was followed by a countersuit by them for my stock. They came out of the bullpen swinging with all their might and money. Within months, my monthly legal bill was over ten thousand dollars. I went into the lawsuit believing that right would conquer wrong and it didn't matter if I was a single person fighting a big corporation. My belief was both laughable and naïve. I had been playing Titan Technology's game. They had limitless funds and legal experience. They were prepared to see the game through dispassionately, treating it as little more than a chess game. The problem was that while I was very good at chess, my emotions were involved. I couldn't be dispassionate and I wasn't ruthless. Titan Technology's legal strategy was simple and clear: Fight everything and bleed Karmen out financially with false accusations.

I had to find a new strategy or I would soon be done. It was time to step away from the computer, pause conversations with my attorneys, and get quiet. It was time to stop looking at the problem and thinking more effort, a harder punch, or more guns would solve it. I needed a fresh strategy. Intuitively, I knew I needed to get into nature. It was time for a trail run. I threw on my sneakers and headed for the foothills just outside Denver. In under thirty minutes, I was pounding the dirt of the Bergen Park trail near Evergreen.

The fresh air began to shift my mindset. Maybe I could find a strategy that would work after all. Then the pine trees and wildflowers had their way with me, and I began to feel limitless. During a few miles of trail run, I moved energetically from feeling desperate, beaten, and hopeless to feeling calm, expansive, and hopeful. I had an idea.

Without a word to my attorneys, I flew out to Charlotte, tracked down Nicholas's wife, Missy, and had a very long conversation with her. I had suspected that Nicholas's representation of her as emotionally unstable might be wrong, and I also suspected that he might have represented me to her falsely. I was right.

We talked for over six hours, and we both physically squirmed in our seats as the disgust of the reality wiggled through our spines. We both felt betrayed. Nicholas had lied to me about his marital status. Missy had threatened divorce in the "fault" divorce state of North Carolina after learning of our affair, and he needed to get rid of me to keep the two of us from ever meeting. He had painted me as a seductress who had taken advantage of him and their separation to gain professional success. All the while, he had painted Missy to me as an emotionally unstable woman who might succeed at taking her life if I ever confronted her.

There was no longer any question about Nicholas's reasons for undermining me to the point of sabotaging multimillion-dollar sales deals. Had Missy and I met, she would have realized that I wasn't the seductress. That might have made her furious enough to file for divorce, and if she did that, he stood to lose tens of millions of dollars. He saw sacrificing a few million in a sales deal as more prudent than risking the entire company. Missy and

I could never meet, and that was only a threat if I stayed at Titan Technology. He couldn't simply let me go and pay out my employment contract. The act of willfully terminating me and paying out a contract would be permanent evidence of his guilt should Missy ever file for divorce. The only option was for Nicholas to get me to leave of my own free will, hoping that this would mitigate the chances of any hard evidence being presented to Missy.

As much as I wanted to confront Nicholas directly, I flew home without doing so and gave my lawyer all the information I had gained from the trip. Titan Technology agreed to both drop their lawsuit and let me keep my stock if I dropped my suit. The only cash I would receive would be enough to cover my legal fees. I didn't have liquidity for my stock or a payout for my employment contract, but I did have peace of mind.

The stress of the lawsuit was over. The Titan Technology chapter was finally closed, and I was free to move on to bigger and better things. The world felt enormously abundant and hopeful. The settlement felt like a healing that allowed me to step into the adult version of the self-confident, adventurous girl I was before my mother's death and my father's abandonment. I needed Titan Technology to purchase GBSynergy to give me the confidence that I was worth knowing. It wasn't logical, but that was what my deep wound of abandonment needed. I needed to feel worthy, and the sale of GBSynergy provided that sense of worthiness. It was an artificial sense of worthiness, coupled with a false sense of confidence, but it was what allowed me to go to Hawaii, get to know myself, and heal the wounds that had been shadowing me.

Thanks to the time in Hawaii and Germany, I could now sit with myself. I didn't demand constant entertainment or stimulation. I realized that what I had always thought was my dynamic personality had actually been a symptom of my lack of self-love. Now that I loved the real me, I was running toward what I wanted instead of running away from what I didn't want. I could finally be still and figure out what I really wanted at this phase of my life. And then, because I knew what I was looking for, I would recognize and passionately pursue it when I saw it.

I wanted to write; I *was* writing. I wanted to work and have income; I had a new training company. I wanted to spend time with friends; I was developing good relationships and wasn't buying friends but, instead, was touching and being touched by people. I wanted a partner in life; I had clearly defined what he looked like. I knew that I would recognize him when we met. But until then, I was okay being alone.

CHAPTER 28

Saying No to a Job
and Yes to Motherhood

My life had become magical.

I LONGED TO HAVE A CHILD OF MY OWN. It felt like everyone around me got pregnant by thinking about it. I had been pregnant twice when I was married to Peter, but both pregnancies ended in miscarriage. It was eventually determined that Peter's sperm had been damaged by a high temperature during his childhood at a time when his reproductive facility was in development. The fetuses were not healthy and would never have survived. I had also attempted to have children with Brad. He had gotten a vasectomy reversal in an attempt to get me pregnant. I had tried everything and still was not a mother. I had even tried accepting that I wasn't meant to be a mother, but the desire to have a child echoed through my entire body.

My massage therapist, Maggie, had a little boy who was almost two, and she was pregnant again. As Maggie massaged my back, I thought of the little life growing inside her. This baby had picked a good mother. I wondered if an unborn soul would choose me for a mother. Years earlier, I would have quickly answered yes and would have

defended my answer with facts about my financial stability or the opportunities I could offer a child. But as I lay
there on the massage table, I wasn't sure if a child would
choose me because children don't care about wealth or
professional success. They simply want to be loved.

Maggie had a heart that loved without restrictions.
What child wouldn't want all the love she had to offer?
On the other hand, my heart loved carefully. I wouldn't
choose me for a mother. I knew what I had to do. I had
to open up my heart to more than just Bagley. I needed
to begin loving in an unrestricted way. Just as the mother
I loved had died, other people I loved would die. That
fact should not stop me from loving. People would come
into my life at one point and leave at another. That fact
should not stop me from loving either. I would get hurt,
but I would also gain the world. It was just another gut
understanding, and those intuitive insights were now coming to me on a daily basis. I would begin to practice
openly loving with the full knowledge that I could and
would get brutally hurt at times.

Except for my new dedication to writing, my daily life
looked, in many ways, like it had a few years earlier. I
owned another training company, had a dog, visited my
sister's family in Santa Barbara a couple of times a year,
and still loved fashion. What had changed was *how* I lived
my life. Instead of sprinting out of bed to the treadmill
and worrying about all that needed to be done, I started
my day by reminding myself that I did nothing to get that
glorious sun to rise. And whether I accomplished great
things or stayed in bed all day, the sun would set that night
and rise again the next day. Being reminded that I didn't

have the clout to make the sun rise was comforting. For so long, I had been self-absorbed and dependent on making things happen. Now I realized that I was not the center of the universe, and I liked being just another human being. I also realized that there was very little in life that I could actually make happen, and I not only surrendered to that fact, I embraced it.

Feeling the sun's brightness was also a daily reminder of the universe's abundance. My daily mantra was love, gratitude, and forgiveness. I had found that gratitude dramatically changed every situation.

Outwardly though, I still wore my Christian Louboutin heels and designer clothes while building another company. The difference was *how* I did it. I surfed life. At certain times I exerted great effort, but my gut told me when to stop paddling and ride the wave. The universe was good and provided not only the sun each day, but also business opportunities, new friends, beautiful Colorado days, and interesting men I dated just for the sake of dating.

One of those men was Brian. Brian was fifty-four and had a twenty-year-old daughter who was in college. I was thirty-five and lived with a dog. Brian was not a means to having a family. He was pure enjoyment. He was fit, tall, athletic, and youthful. He didn't compete with me. Instead, he simply enjoyed me. And I enjoyed him.

Brian and I had actually known each other for years. We had met when Teddy brought Brian into GBSynergy. It was a unique opportunity for the company to be able to hire such an experienced executive. Brian had previously run all consulting and training services for JD Edwards, worldwide, before they were acquired by PeopleSoft. Brian got a nice exit package when PeopleSoft took over the company, which meant he could work for us because it was merely extra money on top of his multi-year exit package.

Brian and I had been catching up over lunch every three to six months, and earlier that spring, Brian told me that he and his wife of twenty-three years were getting a divorce. When he had returned from a business trip in India, the house was devoid of his wife's belongings. She had simply left a note.

What impressed me most when we met for lunch in the fall was how Brian embraced the pain, remorse, and fear brought on by the divorce. He hadn't hit the bars in an attempt to dull his feelings with alcohol or romantic experiences. He had sat in the depth of the pain until enough of it had seeped out for him to breathe normally. Six months after his wife filed for divorce, he had processed the feelings of failure, rejection, disappointment, loneliness, and fear of the future. He was balanced and truly ready to move forward in life.

Brian said that he missed the friends whose exit had accompanied the divorce. I had a great network of friends and invited him to join us for wine. That didn't work for him, but when he mentioned how lonely his second home in Winter Park seemed, I offered to join him there the following weekend. I had known him for years, and we both had dogs. A weekend up in the mountains sounded fun.

He liked the idea, and to my surprise, he sent me an email with a proposed itinerary for the weekend and an inquiry about whether I had any food allergies. He proposed cooking at the house Friday night, hiking on Saturday, and going out to dinner on Saturday night. His attention to detail and his thoughtfulness made me smile.

When we arrived at the house in Winter Park that Friday evening, we opened a couple of beers and sat down to relax. Then he handed me several sheets of paper without any explanation. The word *nondisclosure* was the title at the top of the first page.

I was confused. Brian didn't own a company. He wasn't about to reveal trade secrets with me over dinner.

"Read it," he said.

I did as he asked. "I, Karmen, agree to not disclose, use, or profit from any events, stories, or statements that happen with Brian." The document continued for two pages.

Brian had just handed me a nondisclosure document so he would not end up in any part of my book! Of course, as soon as I got the joke, he took the papers and folded them up to be deposited in the trash. But his clever playfulness stayed with me.

We had a great weekend together, and as the weekend progressed, so did our level of closeness. He was easy, intelligent, and fun. We bonded during our hike and dinners together, ultimately becoming more intimate than I had expected.

But I was not looking for a relationship and made that clear once the weekend was over. Undeterred, Brian asked if he could take me to Cabo San Lucas for a long weekend to celebrate his divorce. I agreed on the condition that I was not going as his girlfriend, but in truth, no man had ever asked to take me away for the weekend, and I felt cherished and wonderfully special. Brian wasn't sappy. In fact, he was downright sarcastic most of the time. We didn't talk about the future because we didn't have a future. He was older, had a grown child, and was preparing for retirement. I was in my professional prime and still dreaming of being a mother.

Living in the present and not using people as a means to happiness had become a habit with me. I loved Brian's wit, his humor, his experience, his body, and his mind. He wasn't a means to anything other than enjoyment. My life was richer with him in it. The confusing part was what I should do with my desire to be a mother and have a family.

Ten years earlier, my therapist had talked about holding two opposing things simultaneously, one in each hand. The natural reaction is to hide one behind your back while hoisting the other one. This only leads to constantly shifting gears, one moment running toward one thing, the next moment running in the exact opposite direction toward the other. I decided to simultaneously hold both Brian and a baby without hiding either behind my back. I wanted both. I wanted a man I connected with like Brian *and* I wanted a baby. Instead of frantically trying to convince Brian to have a baby with me or convince myself that I didn't want a baby, I held both as true desires. I didn't know what to do with them, but I resigned myself to acknowledging both of them as true.

As the months moved forward, Brian and I grew to love each other, continued to enjoy each other, and became exclusive. But because of his respect and genuine caring for me, Brian eventually decided to walk away from our relationship so I would start dating younger men who wanted families. For weeks I cried hourly, then daily. I loved spending time with Brian, and yet I knew I also longed to be a mother. I no longer wanted to be a mother so I wouldn't be alone or because that was what women were supposed to want. It was simply a soul craving. I knew being a mother was work, exhausting work, but I had love I needed to share and a deep desire to experience life through the eyes of a child.

After a few weeks apart, Brian and I got back together. He told me that he was torn. Had he been forty-five years old, he wouldn't hesitate to have four kids with me. He had always wanted a large family, but his wife had ovarian cancer when they were newly married, and they had adopted their daughter when she was three days old. His wife's continued battle with cancer had made adopting another child unsuitable. Brian loved kids and the family life.

We decided to give the family idea some time to marinate.

Out of nowhere, a huge job opportunity came along. An international company wanted me to be their vice president of marketing for America. It was a reminder that the universe brings us gifts when we just allow things to evolve on their own instead of trying so hard to make things happen. *Try less* was one of the mantras that had stayed with me since the yoga class I had gone to that first weekend I'd allowed myself to do only what I wanted to do. At the time, I thought the instructor was crazy, but the experience of surfing had confirmed the truth behind the saying. Trying less made life a lot easier. And now a job that seemed a great fit was coming to me with no effort on my part. If I succeeded, the job could lead to a similar role at companies like Google or Apple.

The company flew me to India to meet the CEO and his executive management team. I saw it as an opportunity rich with possibilities . . . until the CEO decided the position needed to be based in Atlanta because that was where the company's US headquarters were located. They had a Denver office, which we all assumed would be where I worked, but as we talked, the job moved to Atlanta. I told them I needed some time to think about it.

I returned to Denver with a heavy heart. It was the job of my dreams, but Brian was in Denver. I wanted a crystal ball. I wanted to know if Brian and I would last. I wanted to know if we would have a family one day. I wanted to know if the job was as good as I thought. How was I supposed to make this decision?

Maggie had the answer—not to the job, but to finding the answer. She told me to sit down and ask both Bagley and my unconceived child where *they* wanted to live. I was mature enough now to see this suggestion for what it was: wise advice.

I went to yoga early to mediate for a few minutes before class. I knew the wisdom was in me. I thanked my gut for the wisdom it had, sat quietly, and asked a very simple question: *Bagley, where do you want to live?* In Denver, Bagley played in Washington Park and in my backyard. In Atlanta, I had no idea where he would play, but assumed he would have some very fine places to do so. Right now, he ate Purina dog food, but if I took this job, I could buy him filets every night.

The answer came quickly: *Denver.*

I smiled. If I was a dog and was just asked that question, I would choose Denver too.

Okay, on to my unborn child, who I saw as a baby girl. *Baby girl, where do you want to live?* With my current income and lifestyle, my child would probably be attending a public school, but if I took the job, she could go to the finest schools in the world.

Denver.

I opened my eyes. There was no question in my gut about the job, but my mind began to argue the logic of the situation with so much money on the table. Turning down the job wasn't the logical choice, but I had learned that the decisions coming from my gut transcended logic. I knew my potential boss would not understand it. I couldn't even explain it to him, but my gut was crystal clear. When I turned off my head and asked Bagley and my unborn daughter where they wanted to live, it was clear that moving to Atlanta was out of the question.

The next morning, I called the company and turned down the position. Even as I turned it down, my head was racing to convince me to take the job and laugh at my gut. But listening to my gut had proven true too many times now to discard the clear impression that I was to stay in Denver. Logically, there was nothing preventing me from moving to Atlanta. Brian and I weren't married, my dearest friends would remain my friends, and I had no family in Denver. Those were all facts, but what was also true was that my heart knew I needed to stay in one place for a while and cultivate the friendships I had. I needed to put down some roots and be settled for a while. I asked the company to reconsider letting me take the position in Denver, but they had become firm on Atlanta. I thanked them for the opportunity and let the job pass through my fingers. Brian and I would continue to grow in relationship—in Denver—and I would continue to practice being present and honest every day.

Then a friend named Mia drove with me to visit another friend, Andrea, in Kansas City over the Labor Day weekend. I was supposed to start my period that weekend, but when I was slowly awakening from a nap with Mia's four-year-old daughter, Emma, the thought that I was pregnant flitted through my mind. Mia had already guessed that I might be pregnant as we were beginning our trip, and though I was sure I wasn't, I had bought a pregnancy test to appease her. I decided to put an end to the silly thought that I might be pregnant, grabbed the test, and headed to the bathroom while Emma continued to sleep.

I knew the process, and I knew what the results meant. One line meant you were not pregnant, two that you were. I followed the procedure and looked down at the stick. There were two lines. I couldn't breathe. Was it really possible? Could I really be pregnant?

I read it again. There were two solid pink lines. I was pregnant!

I looked up and mouthed, "Thank you." My heart had opened, and a soul had chosen me her mother. I knew that Brian would not be expecting this, and I wondered how I was going to tell him. But I didn't care. I was delighted. I was pregnant, and something within me felt that I would give birth to a girl.

Both of my girlfriends were out shopping. I paced the house, growing more and more excited by the moment. I wanted to call Brian, but I knew I needed to tell him in person, so I continued to pace until I saw their car pull up. I threw the front door open and ran down the front steps while they were both still in the car with the engine running. Jumping up and down on the lawn, I held the stick with both hands above my head. Andrea looked at Mia, confused. Mia took another look at me and screamed, "She's pregnant!"

Tears began to stream down my face. My deepest desire had come true. My heart was open and alive, along with a second heart located deep in my uterus.

My life had become magical as I learned to live in the present moment, embrace my whole self—the good and the bad—and shift my thinking from the world being against me to the universe having everything that I needed. There was a life living in me.

I felt the weightlessness I had always dreamed of achieving when I was a little girl trying to fly. That feeling of flying included being light as a feather so mere air could easily lift me into the beautiful, big universe. At the same time, there was the sense of being wholly supported by the air—something unseen and, therefore, mysterious.

I had learned to fly. The life I had dreamed of when I was a little girl with a mind full of imagination and dreams was real. My gut had known to turn down that job because I was already pregnant. And I had finally learned to listen to my gut!

CHAPTER 29

A Difficult Delivery

The universe has its own way of doing things.

PREGNANCY WAS NOT ALL THAT IT WAS CRACKED UP TO BE. Since college, when I first knew I wanted to be pregnant someday, I had pictured having a perfect round tummy and being the envy of everyone around me. But that was not my actual experience. Instead, I gained fifty-five pounds and had heartburn, backache, and pre-term contractions starting at twenty-six weeks. Pregnancy was nothing like what I had imagined.

Brian adored my growing belly. His eyes sparkled as the little life inside me became strong enough to touch his hand with her powerful little kick. It was beautiful to watch his excitement win over his traditional views and logical argument that he was too old to be having a child with a thirty-six-year-old woman who was not his wife. And his Catholic upbringing definitely did not align with our current situation. But his ability to acknowledge the reality of the situation was refreshingly mature. He treasured what served him and easily released what didn't. This was notable because the pregnancy was not part of the plan we had discussed. It had rattled him for a bit, but he also confessed that in Mass he had asked God to miraculously make me pregnant.

His prayer was completely and unreservedly selfless and altruistic. Brian was already a dad with a daughter in college. But he loved me and wanted to give me the world, and it was no secret that my heart hungered to be a mother. Logic and reason kept him from talking with me about it directly. The church provided the mystical venue for his soul to talk with God.

I was convinced that the birth of our daughter would be easy and natural, even though the pregnancy was proving to be very uncomfortable. Brian and I had attended an eight-week class on natural childbirth during which we learned all the risks of the conventional drugs used in childbirth, including epidurals and Pitocin. I felt educated and mentally prepared to have a natural childbirth free of drugs or medical intervention. I was confident our daughter would come out when she was ready, and if I resisted the temptation to induce labor with drugs, labor would be easy, quick, and natural.

Unfortunately, my due date came and went—along with the next day and many days after that. My only solace was that in France, a woman's first pregnancy is considered full-term at forty-one weeks instead of forty weeks, as it is in the US. The discomfort of being kicked by a full-term baby coupled with an extra fifty-five pounds on my petite frame was nothing short of misery for both me and Brian. When I finally awoke with piercing labor pains at 2:00 a.m. nine days after my due date, I was ecstatic. It was Sunday, May 15, and I was confident I would be holding a baby girl by noon.

That was not to be. I labored at home for hours without drugs but with a doula, a professional we hired to help me deliver naturally. Finally, around 6:00 p.m., our doula decided that it was time to head to the hospital because my contractions were three minutes apart and the baby was coming.

Natural childbirth education taught expectant mothers to make a birth plan, which was a statement of what you did and did not want. I did not want to receive an epidural or any drugs, and after my baby was born, I wanted to have her put directly on my chest with the umbilical cord attached until the cord stopped pulsating. Then Brian would cut the cord. When I arrived at the hospital, I promptly handed multiple copies of my birth plan to the nurse and even brought tape to post a laminated copy on the outside of my hospital door, ensuring that everyone who entered was fully informed of my wishes. Instead of the healthy exercise of setting intentions, I had used my birth plan as a rigid definition for all involved in my delivery to follow.

I just forgot about handing my black-and-white script to the universe—not that it would have mattered. I had forgotten the classic spiritual caution that if you want to make God laugh, just tell him (or her) your plans. The universe has its own way of doing things.

My contractions were strong and consistently three minutes apart, but I was only one centimeter dilated. Even my doula was confused. She had watched me labor all day with consistent contractions. The hospital agreed to admit me only because I was over a week past my due date.

Once checked in to my labor and delivery room, I labored another two hours in the bathtub, which was provided for those desiring a natural childbirth. I breathed through the painful contractions that were now coming less than two minutes apart. When the nurse was sure that I must be close to fully dilated, I was taken out of the tub and put in the bed to measure my cervix. I was no more than one and a half centimeters dilated. I had been in active labor for twenty-four hours and was less than two centimeters dilated!

The nurse announced that it was time to take Pitocin, a drug used to strengthen labor contractions. The thought frightened me. Pitocin had side effects I didn't want, and my contractions were sure to become significantly more painful. I also didn't want an epidural. Women had delivered babies for millions of years without either Pitocin or an epidural, and I planned to deliver my baby naturally.

My mom had delivered both my sister and me naturally. My sister had delivered both my niece and nephew naturally. I *had* to deliver my baby naturally. I resolutely told the nurse that I didn't want any drugs. I wanted to keep laboring naturally.

Hours passed, Brian paced the room, and my contractions continued to come one on top of the other. Brian wanted to support my desires and wishes, and I could see that support in his eyes, but I could also see pain in them. He hated seeing me in agony, and he feared for my life. We had been to natural childbirth classes and had heard about the risks of drugs during labor and delivery, but what we hadn't researched was information about women who died in childbirth.

By 7:00 a.m. the next day, Monday, I was finally at four centimeters, but it was taking about five hours for me to dilate one centimeter. I had six centimeters to go, which meant another thirty hours at my pace. At noon, the doctor convinced me to get an epidural to see if that would help me relax and dilate. I was exhausted and knew I needed to sleep.

The epidural was heavenly. Within minutes, the pain was gone and I drifted off into blissful sleep. But abruptly and unexpectedly, terrorizing pain swept over me when my epidural catheter moved, which immediately impacted the flow of anesthesia. Going into labor at a slow, steady pace with the contractions getting harder and harder was one thing. Going from no pain to full labor with contractions one minute apart was pure torture.

The forty-five minutes I waited for the anesthesiologist to come felt like years. But when she finally arrived, I was quickly pain free again. The problem was that I was on my third bag of Pitocin. I was not dilating at a normal or acceptable rate. Once in a while, our little girl's heart rate would drop and alarms would go off, but each time, when they moved me around, her heart rate would return to its strong beat, and we would return to the hours of slow dilation.

At about 4:00 a.m. on Tuesday morning, my epidural catheter changed position again, and I was writhing in pain. My perfect labor was not going as planned! I didn't understand. Why wasn't my cervix dilating? Why wasn't I holding my little girl after a natural delivery? This was not the plan!

I wasn't going to have a C-section. I could handle this. I was a triathlete. I comprehended what it felt like to be miles from the end and energetically feel my body warning me that it was nearing deprivation. But I had mastered the art of using my brain to override my body. In short, I was skilled in successfully ignoring my body's rhythm and voice to achieve a goal. After a triathlon, I would do everything I could to help my body recover. I would also do that once I'd given birth, but right then, my body needed to be ignored and my will and determination needed to govern.

I was strong. I was Karmen! I could do this! And so I continued laboring without an epidural because administering a third epidural was off the table, and my only choice was to either labor naturally or have a C-section. After hours of heroic effort, the doctor came and checked on my progress. I was still only at eight centimeters and hours from the finish line.

With tears of disappointment and disillusionment, I looked at Brian. "I'm sorry. I can't do it. I want a C-section." I felt disgraced.

His eyes lit up. I had given up! I was finally asking for help! His lungs filled with air. He was able to breathe again. For over forty-eight hours, he had watched me go from a beaming pregnant woman to wounded, limping, weak human, trying for some unstated reason to achieve her documented-in-black-ink-on-white-paper birth plan. Brian had been patient. He instinctively knew that once my mind was set, I wasn't easily persuaded. But when I finally yielded and waved the white flag, his excitement permeated the entire room. He was halfway out the door and ready to wave down the doctor to get us into the operating room when our doula lunged onto my bed.

We hired the doula to help me maintain my goal of a natural childbirth. That was her paid purpose in being with us for over two days. Staying passionately focused on the job we hired her to do, she positioned herself right in my face. "You are not giving up! Do you want your baby cut out of you?" Without losing eye contact or changing her tone, she added, "Breathe. Relax. See your cervix dilating. Focus on what you want. Focus on giving your child the experience of the birth canal. Don't rob her of that because you're tired."

And with that, I was back. The coach had given me a swift kick in the butt, pointed to the finish line, and told me to get up and start running again. Brian was back on the couch, my doula was in my face, and I was focused and committed to a natural childbirth.

7:00 a.m. brought the shift change of both nurses and doctors. Kaiser Permanente believed in changing the staff every twelve hours, which meant that more than one doctor could be involved in the delivery of a baby. There was logic in the philosophy. Unfortunately, at each shift change, the doctor coming on saw me as a persistent mother desiring a natural childbirth. And the baby's vitals looked good. Because of that, I had been allowed to continue labor for fifty-three hours. The new doctor looked at my chart with shock, did an examination of my cervix, and proclaimed that I was at ten centimeters.

I was euphoric! I could push and get this baby out of me! It was going to be over. "Get the bar!" I nearly screamed to the nurse as I pointed to the metal bar that attaches to the end of the hospital bed. The bar was a delivery tool to hang on to so you could squat and push your baby out. Leaving my body for a moment, I witnessed a crazed wild woman, scampering to climb up on the bar,

screaming orders at everyone. If the physical surround-
ings had been a mental institution instead of a labor and
delivery room, I would have probably been sedated.

The nurses responded and started coaching me on
when to push. But once again, headstrong, stubborn, and
obstinate, I ignored my nurse's direction to rest after three
pushes and took a deep breath and bore down with everything I had. The nurse informed the doctor that the
baby's head could not been seen. At least an hour of
pushing would be required. The doctor left the room. I
didn't have an hour left in me, and dismissing a C-section
for the very last time, I pushed without stopping: big
breath, push, big breath, push. Seven minutes later, the
nurse announced that she had the head. The doctor was
called, and the finish line was within sight.

But when she entered the world, my beautiful baby
girl was blue. No cry, no movement. She was placed on
the tiny examination table, and within seconds, more doctors were summoned. After only a few more seconds, the
pediatricians announced to Brian and me that they had
to get her to the neonatal intensive care unit. Thanks to
medical intervention, she was breathing, but she was not
stable. Brian and I had discussed what he should do if
there was a problem with the baby. He would go with her
instead of staying with me. Panic and fright pooled in our
eyes as we connected momentarily before he ran after our
baby, who was being whisked away down the hall.

Meanwhile, my doctor had not moved his attention
from me and the massive amounts of blood leaving my
body. "You are not okay," he said with his eyes locked on
mine.

"I know," I replied. Even though my head had been turned and my eyes had not left the doctors working on my newborn daughter, from the instant she came out, I instinctively knew that my determination and resolution to push relentlessly had caused something very problematic inside my body.

"We need to get you into the operating room for an emergency hysterectomy or you are not going to make it," the doctor said matter-of-factly as the nurses started unhooking and unlocking the bed in preparation for getting me to the operating room.

The illusion of control had fully evaporated. My daughter and I were simultaneously fighting for our lives.

Somewhere in my pregnancy, I had reverted back to the old Karmen who fiercely demanded that she could control everything. Within my womb, my baby had been safe and warm, rocking back and forth in amniotic fluid, with all of her needs met effortlessly, free of wounds or pain. I had decided that I could keep her safe and continue this perfect life, even after she left the safety of my womb. Of course, I never consciously processed this. If I had, I would have quickly realized the foolishness of it.

With my pregnancy, I had somehow lost the habit of surfing life. I was no longer letting go and riding the waves. I had forgotten to just be curious and explore the energy around me. All the lessons of soul-body connection, faith in God, ease, and surrender had vaporized. They seemed millions of miles away—until I was again out of my body, seeing myself being rolled down a hospital corridor to an operating room where doctors would hopefully stop the bleeding and save me. I prayed that in the NICU, other physicians would keep my baby girl breathing.

Reese had been stabilized in the NICU. Reese. It was the name that jumped out after months of considering baby names. Brian had formed a habit of jotting down names while at work, and each night, he handed me one 3x3 yellow sticky note containing three to eight names that popped into his head that day. Reese was the name that stuck. After Reese was peacefully sleeping in a warm, safe incubator with IV fluids, Brian returned to our labor and delivery-recovery room with the good news that she was okay.

Instead of finding me resting and quietly recovering, he was met by a janitor mopping up pools of blood who seemed annoyed to have his cleaning disturbed. After a quick check of the room number outside in the hallway, Brian rushed to the nurses' station to ask where I had been taken. With dozens of nurses and patients on the floor, it was several minutes before he learned that I was in emergency surgery. Our perfect birth plan was a world away, and he returned to the NICU to sit beside his baby and pray for her mother.

Thankfully, before long, I was being wheeled into the NICU straight from surgery to finally hold my baby. My absolute resolve to march without hesitation to the beat of *my* plan had resulted in over a hundred internal stiches and close to a hundred external stiches. I had literally torn myself in two. I had shredded my cervix from a ball into tattered pieces and ripped my body open from front to back in my excessive, extreme, and unnecessary force—all because of an idealistic dream and the need to be superwoman.

My baby girl was finally in my arms and seemingly unbothered by the cords hooked up to her little body. She was content as she nursed. Reese was recovering quickly. I had not eaten for the two days that I was in labor. That and the trauma of labor had proven too much for her to handle on her own, but with the blessed medical intervention, she was quickly gaining color and life.

The trauma was enough to get my attention. I nodded in submission to simply *being* with my baby girl, completely surrendered to her fate and whatever our life together would be. I was ready to embrace the wonder and curiosity of the adventure called motherhood that lay before me.

CHAPTER 30

Motherhood and Fatherlessness

My sixth sense had blossomed as I faced and healed
my fundamental issues. Before that, I was like a bird trying to
take flight with fifty pounds of weight taped to its back.

"LOOK, MAMA! I'M SURFING!"

Her little body stood proud and glorious on top of the
long board—not in the water, but on dry land. She was
pretending to surf, just as I had pretended to fly as a little
girl. Reese was no longer a tiny newborn but a brilliant
and brave four-year-old little girl learning to surf. The last
four years seemed to have gone by as fast as a piece of ice
melts in the hot summer sun.

During the past four years, I had taken weekends to
write, continued to meet with my editor, and honestly focused on learning the craft of writing. I never questioned
whether my book would get finished, but it felt good to
simply let it grow organically. The need to command and
control was kept at bay by daily grounding activities such
as yoga, meditation, prayer, and breathing.

After Reese's birth, I had been prescribed four weeks
of strict bedrest. It was a gift that allowed me to start practicing the fine art of wonder. It also gave me the time to
get to know the little soul named Reese who was rich in

personality, disposition, and makeup. I felt no need to mold her. She was a fully formed individual who I had the pleasure of meeting and getting to know. That I could not walk, exercise, or be busy for those four weeks was a present from the divine. The myth that I would be the perfect mother with the perfect baby had evaporated along with any striving. I was fully engulfed in the magic of motherhood.

Four years later, she was a little girl playing in the water at the beginning of a summer vacation, and I had returned to the North Shore with her to work on my book. Only a month earlier, I had been lying in *savasana* (corpse pose) after yoga and my clear, empty, pure mind was flooded with the feeling of being tossed by the waves. It was clearly Hawaiian energy that was warming my body, but logic raced in behind with the argument and loudly reminded me that I had just returned from Paris, a reward trip for my employees. I couldn't run off to Hawaii to work on my book. Yet I had an itch to write that had been growing stronger. So I invited the waves back into my soul and asked if I was supposed to return to Hawaii to work on—and maybe finish—my book. The answer was clear, and it all came together beautifully and magically, as if by divine intervention.

Returning to the North Shore was delicious and en-chanting because the abandonment of my armor had begun in Hawaii, seven years earlier. It was there that I had welcomed awareness into my life. It was there that I had finally been brave enough—or exhausted from avoid-ing myself enough—to stop and sit in my grief, anger, em-barrassment, and regret. I had chosen to stay with the uncomfortable. I had chosen to let the shadows I had been running from for years encompass me.

My healing had begun in Hawaii, but it continued each time I chose to stay with the uncomfortable long enough to have insight about what was beneath it. I had reclaimed my soul by healing myself and inviting all of my parts—including everything I had rejected and suppressed for so many years—to take up conscious residence in me. I was more human, and therefore more authentic, than I had ever been. The need for personas and perfection had disappeared as naturally as clouds dissipating after a summer shower. What replaced them was a real woman with weaknesses as well as strengths and backsliding as well as forward movement. I had moments of arrogance and ego as well as moments of humility and genuineness. I was brilliant at some things and refreshingly inexpert at other things. And everything pleased and amused me. Being real has its advantages.

Being a mother had given me little choice but to be real, and I had brought everything I'd learned about myself to it. Reese had been an easy baby and an easy toddler. She was aware, inquisitive, and careful. The first time she shut a drawer on her fingers, she figured out that she should not repeat that move and understood how to avoid it. If she dropped something on the floor, all I had to do was ask her to retrieve it and she would comply.

All of that changed on her third birthday—literally. The morning of her third birthday, Reese dropped her fork as we were having breakfast at the kitchen table. As usual, I asked her to please pick it up, but instead of sliding off the stool and bending down to pick it up, her big blue eyes locked onto mine, she moved toward my face, and she screamed, "Noooooo!" Her body was shaking from head to toe. She was not just serious about it, she was adamant in the most dramatic way possible.

As I stared at her in disbelief, my first thought was that my little angel had just been possessed by a mean, scary, vicious spirit. I physically drew back in horror. My horror quickly morphed into anger. I refused to raise a brat who defied me. I needed to remind her of our roles as mother and child.

"Pick it up . . . *now!*" I commanded, loudly. Since I had never had to raise my voice to her before, I was sure that my tone, coupled with my towering authority, would whip her into submission and obedience straightaway. It did not.

Reese seemed to grow taller before my eyes as she straightened up and locked herself in position. "No. . . o . . . o . . . o!" she screamed for a good three seconds.

I was unnerved for a moment. Her behavior was completely unacceptable, but I was not sure what to do about it. Should I give her a time out? Spank her? Take away a toy? I was at a loss when it came to the appropriate punishment, but I was certain that some form of punishment was needed. I settled on a time out. It was her birthday, after all.

That incident was only the first in an ongoing battle of wills between my daughter and me. Over the next three weeks, the shouting matches, anger, and punishments seemed to subsume all of my time. Overnight, my daughter had transformed from a sweet, compliant angel into a wild-child demon. I tried every form of correction and every psychological strategy I could think of—within reason. Spanking had always seemed a bad idea to me, but I even resorted to spanking. I was exhausted. She had more stamina for the battle than me, but she seemed a bit spent too.

Just when I had resigned myself to the belief that the terrible twos were actually the terrible threes, my sister gave me a copy of the book *Positive Discipline* by Jane Nelson. My mouth dropped open as I began to read it. It described what had happened at my house on the morning of Reese's third birthday using words like *demon possessed* and *angel child changing overnight*. The book explained how, starting as early as three or as old as five, children realize that they do not have to do what you say. They begin to exert a bit of independence. This is a natural part of the development process.

As I read, I quickly made my own connection to how I reacted to someone in authority with a power trip when they confronted me. My entire body stiffened, just as Reese's did, and I wanted to disobey them just because I could . . . just as Reese did. Hmm. This author seemed to be on to something.

I read on. The book gave a method for dealing with the kind of defiance I was seeing in Reese. The method had nothing to do with telling the child to do anything, except when safety was involved, and the author was clear that it was to be used only until the child no longer felt the need to prove to the parent that she was, in fact, her own being, separate unto herself.

I devoured the book and decided to start applying the method, which involved an approach that was respectful, promoted connection, provided long-term benefits, and taught important life skills. A few days after I finished the book, Reese and I boarded a plane. With pure luck, we had the entire row of three seats. Shortly after takeoff, Reese used the middle and window seats to lie down. Her head was on my lap and her feet fell against the window. When she began playfully kicking the window, I employed the new approach instead of resorting to yelling, physically restraining her, or some other method that would have resulted in a tantrum.

"Do you think you could break the window?" I asked innocently and with curiosity.

She made a funny face and giggled at me. "No, Mama."

"What do you think would happen if you *could* break the window?" I asked.

I could see by the look on her face that her innate curiosity had taken over and she was now engaged. She thought for a few moments and then admitted that she didn't know.

I made a sucking sound. "All the pressure in the plane would be sucked out and we would be sucked out the window." To illustrate, I made a funny, smashed face.

Her little eyes widened, not with fear, but with wonder. I could see her putting it all together. She had been on flights before and had been through the safety instructions. She had also felt the pressure in her ears on many flights. "Mama . . . I should not kick this window," she proclaimed with assurance.

It was as if I had been through a month of bad weather that had begun with a tornado and had continued with hail, flooding, high winds, and continuously threatening skies. And now the clouds had parted, the wind and rain had stopped, and the sun was peeking through. No real damage had been done by the tornado. We were going to be okay.

The method continued to work if I treated her as a human being deserving of respect who desired to be seen as an equal and who saw herself as an individual, as opposed to treating her as just a child who was expected to obey my commands to eat, dress, and pick things up. If I stopped myself and gave her the space to be curious and play out what would happen in a scenario, we had no power struggles and no yelling matches. I knew I looked a little silly at times when I was in Target or at the grocery store, playing out the ramifications and crazy possibilities of what could happen if she stood in the cart instead of sitting in it. I was fine with that. It was working. Peace had resumed. My angel-turned-demon child had returned to angel form.

A year later, we were in Hawaii having a great time with one another. I continued to use the philosophy and techniques I learned from Jane Nelson, and I continued to learn, both as a mother and as a human being. I was continuing to discover and step into my full self.

And I needed my full self to be a good mother. Like any mother, I knew I would do anything to keep my daughter safe, but I also knew that I could not control my daughter's journey through life. Her soul had picked Brian and me as parents at a particular time during a particular century, in a particular part of the world. There was meaning and purpose to it. But her soul's purpose was unfolding as she unfolded in human form. I could protect her, guide her, and love her. But her journey was her own, and I could not chart its path any more than I could have charted the trajectory of the twists and turns my own life had taken.

Every day, I approached Reese with curiosity and respect for the underlying wisdom within her that nudged her forward much like the life force energy in a plant nudges it from seed to sprout. I got to be her witness to that growth. I got to be her partner in exploring life. And I got to mimic the sun, at least a little, in offering the warmth and light needed for her to thrive.

Reese woke up each day ready to play. Play was her laboratory for discovering who she was that day and what life was all about. Her curiosity was endless, and it reignited my own curiosity. Her life was an ongoing expression of what in Zen Buddhism they call beginner's mind. She was open and curious with no preconceived opinions about things. She engaged with life and allowed life to engage with her. Because she could not rely on her intellect yet, my daughter relied on her feelings and on her innate ability to read the energy of things and people.

I wanted to emulate my daughter, and on a good day, I did. Yes, I was her teacher where moving along the path from dependent child to independent adult was concerned. But in so many ways, she was my teacher too.

I was learning to put my business life in perspective. I had no choice. I was a mother now. My daughter was reminding me what it was like to play in an unselfconscious way, just as I had done when I had learned to surf in Hawaii, and this vacation was not just about turning my attention to my writing, it was about cutting loose and playing with my daughter. Reese and I were staying at a rental house on the North Shore of Oahu. We had spent days surfing, swimming, and otherwise playing, and I had meditated in a small garden just above the shoreline. I was happy, and it was not because I had a perfect child, partner, or life. I did not. I was happy because I saw the inherent perfection in every day, whether it was ordinary, troublesome, or unusually delightful. I was happy because I could sit quietly and hear the voice of the divine within me. I was happy because I was getting better at following the counsel of that internal voice. I had learned to fly.

"Look, Mama, I'm flying." The words flew out of her mouth. My little girl had no idea I was writing a book titled *Learning to Fly*. Yet she was giggling and expressing delight with flying in the form of pretend surfing. She was free, uninhibited, feeling the rush of the water, riding the adventure of life. I knew that the challenges of motherhood would change as Reese grew. But I was committed to helping her learn to fly, and I knew that in doing that, I was right beside her, learning to fly as a mother.

Feeling and intuition had become as natural to me as they were to my four-year-old daughter. She was free to feel, and so was I. In finding my way back to my soul, I had recovered the highly developed sense of intuition that all kids possess before they are socialized and life inflicts its wounds on them.

My sixth sense had blossomed as I faced and healed my fundamental issues. Before that, I was like a bird trying to take flight with fifty pounds of weight tied to its back. It was grueling and wheel-spinning instead of easy and natural.

The month after our trip to Hawaii, I got out of the shower one morning feeling overwhelmed by pure sadness. On almost any morning, I was positive and excited to start my day by the time I stepped out of the shower. This was so uncharacteristic of me that it was startling. At my core, I wanted to crawl back into bed and sob. There was nothing happening in my life to explain the depth of sadness washing over me, so I simply acknowledged it and got on with my day.

Peppa Pig was blaring from the television in the bedroom where Reese was enjoying her morning smoothie and favorite show. I got myself and Reese together and dropped her off at camp. Alone in the car, the surge of sadness returned. Ten years earlier, I would have rolled my eyes and chalked it up to fluctuating hormones, but I had learned to honor the wisdom of my gut feelings. The current gut feeling was pushing me toward tears. I welcomed them, along with the underlying sadness, knowing that some reason for both would eventually be revealed. After a few minutes of hearty crying, I collected myself and went to work.

Later, returning to work following meetings, I was surprised to find Brian there. My first thought was that he was in the area because he had clients nearby, and I was happy he had stopped by. But my enthusiastic hello was met with solemnity and even sadness. In fact, my energy and pleasure in seeing him only seemed to make him all the sadder, and his eyes began to tear up. With his eyes locked on mine, he began to move toward me with out-stretched arms.

Reese was not at any old camp, she was at tumbling camp. I panicked as my mind slammed my heart with the thought that something had happened to Reese. But before the thought could even crystalize, Brian spoke.

"Your dad died this morning."

Relief flooded me, followed quickly by confusion. It took a moment for it all to register. My dad had died, and Brian's tears were the result of his love for me and his concern for my heart and for the sorrow he expected me to feel.

I thought that I should react in accordance with his genuine concern for me. I should express grief. I should cry. But in truth, my dad's death changed nothing. He had left when I was four years old. The deep loss had happened then. He left again and again after that, often coming into my life and going out of it again without warning or explanation. For most of my life, I had felt rejected by him because I was not good enough, not perfect. His death had changed nothing in my life. Reese had never met her grandfather. In fact, she thought him already dead. I allowed her to think that because I could not tell a small child that her grandfather was alive but had no desire to meet her, let alone get to know her.

I did mourn for his wife, Betsy. I knew that she had loved him, and he had loved her.

But even though feelings of grief did not rise up within me upon hearing that he had died, the egoless part of me—my soul, my higher self, or whatever else I might call it—had risen up in grief before the human part of me knew. The sadness I had felt that morning had a name: death. When I began to realize that my intuition had informed me of his death or impending death before Brian spoke the words, I was stunned.

Then sadness washed over me again, but this time, it was for my fatherless life and the death of any hope that being fatherless could ever change.

A Line Boutique

*I wanted to create a safe place where stylists had the skill for
and love of making a woman glow through
the transformative power of clothes.*

IN LEARNING TO TRUST MY GUT, I had taken an enormous
leap a couple of years earlier by acquiring A Line Boutique.
A Line was one of the few specialty stores in the Denver
area that I enjoyed shopping at. The owner was your quin-
tessential boutique owner: a woman who had impeccable
style and an amazing eye for fashion and trends. She had
spared no expense and built out a stunning shop. The brick
archway and exposed ductwork were industrial chic. The
clothing racks had already caught my eye. In fact, that was
what first brought me into A Line. An artist who combined
steel and wood had crafted custom racks, shelves, and tables
for the store.

Initially, I walked into A Line to inquire about the
store designer—not shop—because every detail, from the
wallpaper to the lighting was astonishing and remarkable.
The collection of clothing designers and pieces was
equally well curated, and I began shopping at A Line.
Years later, when I went in one day, I learned that the
owner's husband had been transferred overseas. They had

thought it would be short-term, but two years later, they were still overseas and their lease was expiring. They decided to liquidate the inventory and close the doors.

As I stood in the boutique, hearing that this was about to happen, my gut stirred with excitement. Having learned to stay with the discomfort of my undigested feelings and unhealed wounds had also taught me to stay with the uncomfortable crazy thoughts we often call dreams and hopes. It wasn't my brain or logic talking. There was a swirling feeling in my gut. My head quickly began articulating all the reasons that buying a retail store was ridiculous: The margins were awful. I had no experience in retail. They were going out of business for a reason!

But quieting my head had become natural, and my gut had proven trustworthy. Ironically, it had become logical to trust my gut because when I did, things went well. So instead of giving in to the arguments swirling in my head and walking out of the store, I stopped and slowly looked around the boutique. The space was stunning.

I already had a vision of what a women's boutique should be, and it could not have been farther from the typical boutique. The goal of most traditional high-end retail stores was to have an exclusive brand list and fill the store with products that could not be found anywhere else in the city. That wasn't what my vision was about.

My love of fashion had never been attached to a label. And now that I was comfortable in my own skin and lived with a level of self-worth that had been hard won, I had no need to borrow social status by wearing or carrying an expensive designer piece. My attraction to designer pieces came from the simple fact that they were wearable art that left me feeling beautiful, seen, unique, and confident.

I had initially experienced the transformative power of clothes when building my first company in my late twenties and making presentations to multimillion-dollar Fortune 500 companies. I had purchased an Armani suit that cost enough to take my breath away. In no way did I think I could afford that suit at the time. But I bought it because of how I *felt* wearing something that fit perfectly, hung wonderfully, and was designed and constructed with such impeccability that I felt like the best version of myself when I wore it. I embodied power in that suit, but my power didn't come from the label sewn into it. The label was at best a promise, an assurance, a guarantee of quality and superior fashion. The power came from its capacity to make me feel so completely and unconsciously myself that I could easily stay focused on the business at hand instead of being distracted about how I was coming across.

I came to understand that the difference between a department store brand suit and a designer suit was all in fit and fabrication. Both garments represented what was trending and both could catch your eye hanging on a rack. But they were worlds apart—absolutely not contained in the same universe. At best, the department store garment covered the body and was flashy enough to get some attention. But the designer garment disappeared as I, the woman wearing it, appeared. The garment wasn't wearing me; I was wearing the garment! I was the focus. It was about me.

I also understood the difference a good stylist could make. With the help of a stylist, I was able to show up with confidence at any event: backyard BBQ; cocktail party; getaway weekend; important business function; dinner party at a friend's house. I would not feel over-dressed or underdressed, too preppy or too granola, too edgy or too conservative. There would be no chance of embarrassing myself—at least where my attire was con-cerned. Instead, I could interact with others and relate unselfconsciously because I would be stylish, beautifully put together, and appropriate for the occasion.

I knew that a stylist could break down why a style worked or didn't work for my body. I loved listening to their well-articulated, intelligent explanation of why a skirt that hit right at the center of my knee versus one inch below my knee resulted in my legs appearing twice as long and leaving me feeling gorgeous instead of short and stumpy. When a stylist first referred to a side tuck, I had no idea what it was, but I saw the difference it made on my body: A blouse transformed from looking merely cute on me to looking chic and cool because of a little tuck to the side. Instead of swallowing me up, it perfectly framed my waist.

Before discovering what a good stylist could do for me, I had often hated shopping. It meant going through racks and picking up three different sizes in each style I liked because I had no idea how that designer's clothes would look on me or what size I would be in that style or brand. I hated putting on a shirt I thought was cute and finding that I felt fat, frumpy, short, or wide-chested in it.

But at Dior in Paris, a stylist who had seen me select an item to try on did not ask if she could put it in a fitting room for me, she asked what I liked about that shirt. I replied that I liked the pattern because it was bright and fun. I was delighted when she grabbed several other styles for me to try on that might accomplish my goal of wearing something eye-catching and playful. And in fact, the items she selected not only did that, they also fit well and made my body look good—which made *me* feel good.

When I shopped on my own, I might fill up my dressing room with things to try on and find that one item in ten was, at best, okay. But when a professional stylist in a designer boutique pulled clothes for me to try on, eight out of the ten items were not just okay, they were sensational. I didn't confine myself to standing in front of the fitting room mirror. I strutted my stuff around the dressing room and through the store, checking myself out. I felt beautiful. I was instantly five pounds lighter and five years younger. Or when I wanted to look seasoned, I was five years older and the embodiment of understated sophistication and polish.

I already knew the transformative power of clothes, and I wanted to give other women the opportunity to experience how well-constructed and well-styled clothing could help them live their lives feeling confident, unique, seen, and beautiful. That was a powerful motivation for buying A Line Boutique. But I also wanted to meet other women in Denver who already enjoyed the power of self-expression through clothing. The tech company I owned was global, so I was not as connected to Denver as I would have been if it had been a small, local company. I was often envious of local restaurant owners because they were able to share their passion and their art with the Denver community. I wanted that.

I wanted a physical location where women could come and play dress up. I wanted to create a safe place where women were not sold as much as the stylist could get them to buy but where stylists had the skill for and love of making a woman glow through the transformation that the right clothes for her could provide.

If I ever wanted to combine my business skills and love of fashion, now was the time. The owner would get cents on the dollar for the fixtures, and the installed materials like brick would be worthless. My head told me that buying the store was illogical. I had a one-year-old child and a significant other. And a couple of years earlier, I had started another training company. I didn't have time for a retail store. But deep within my soul, I knew that buying the store was the right thing to do. I thought about the kind of smile that radiates across a face when a person thinks about something sweet. That was exactly what my gut was doing. I went home to talk to Brian about buying a boutique.

When Brian came home that night, I greeted him with, "Hi, honey. Can I get you a glass of wine?" I knew that walking into A Line Boutique before they publicly announced their closing was more than coincidence. But dancing with my soul's plan and convincing my partner that it was a good idea were very different things. Talking about it required a logical argument, which I didn't have. And the scary thing about disclosing a business idea that comes from deep within you instead of from dispassionate mental analysis is that sharing it not only makes *it* vulnerable to being squashed, it makes *you* vulnerable to *feeling* squashed. I didn't need help killing it. It was hard enough for *me* to avoid rolling my eyes at the idea. I was sure Brian was going to roll his eyes.

But I had become used to trusting my gut and being brave enough to follow its lead. So I got Brian that glass of wine and told him what I was thinking. Brian quickly saw that I wasn't looking for his experienced professional mind to analyze the business opportunity. With the apprehension and wide-eyed wonder of a child, I shared the idea of buying A Line Boutique. No hard exterior or commanding presence accosted him. The female standing before him was curious. It was as if I were reading to him from a new book that neither of us had read before, one that was full of adventure and hope. We could not know how it was going to end until we got there, but when the book is good, you keep questioning with interest, you keep exploring and discovering.

The next step on the pathway had lit up, and my intuition was telling me to explore it. The old Karmen would have figured it all out and then announced with fierceness and decisiveness that I was buying a boutique. But that commanding and controlling woman was long gone. In her place stood a vulnerable, open woman who had an idea and needed to explore it with her partner.

Of course, before any transaction occurred, financials would have to be analyzed. The savvy businesswoman had not disappeared. A Line needed business acumen, hard work, effort, and grit if it was going to work. It also needed the counsel of industry consultants if it were going to grow strategically. But before all of that, a swirling, dancing gut had to be listened to. And what it had said was being bravely shared with her family.

And Brian agreed that my gut needed to be listened to.

Sure enough, it made sense to the original owner to sell the store to me versus liquidate. Within ten days, we signed the deal, and I signed a new five-year lease!

CHAPTER 32

Flying in Business

*As the owner of A Line, I wanted stylists who had worked
through their ego impediments enough to be more interested in
the customer than they were in being interesting as stylists.*

IN ACQUIRING A LINE BOUTIQUE, I got the fixtures, the
name, the customer list, and the current stock of inventory.
But once the previous owners had decided to close the
store, all orders for future deliveries had been cancelled.
Thankfully, the lead sales person and stylist stayed with the
change of ownership. She was the stylist who had made
shopping easy for me by putting together dressing rooms
that flattered my body and met my lifestyle. She had confidence about taking on a greater role, and she was excited
about professionally growing and immediately assuming
the role of buyer.

The morning after the deal was done, we jumped on a
plane headed to New York City for "market," the quarterly
opportunity to meet with designers, see their collections,
and buy—right along with the buyers from other retail
stores. I wasn't a buying expert, and I had no ego about
turning that responsibility over to another team member,
but my experience with fashion and my eye for it made me
the perfect consultant in making buying decisions. I was

like a one-person fashion focus group. My expertise as a visionary and business orchestrator was something in which I *did* have confidence.

Being a boutique owner in the fashion industry was a world apart from being a consumer of fashion, but I was a quick study and my right-hand person was a great teacher. We were the perfect team. She brought the eye, styling skill, and knowledge of the industry. I brought the vision of an effortless shopping experience and years of savvy in assessing whether a piece of clothing or accessory was worth more than the price tag listed.

Once again, I was the student, learning a whole new language and a whole new science—the science of retail. Not only was I clueless about the meaning of terms like *market*, *line sheet*, *ATS*, and *open to buy plan*, I did not know what and how *categories* played into a buying strategy. Fortunately, I loved not being the smartest person in the room. I quickly invested in those with industry experience. We not only made good buys on that first buying trip, but both of us got up to speed quickly on how to analyze the performance of our buys and make adjustments as needed.

The most exciting part, though, was simply witnessing the reaction women were having to the A Line experience. These were women who didn't know how to pronounce designer names, didn't know what good fit was, and mostly hated shopping. They were emerging from fitting rooms transformed, looking beautiful and confident.

Mary Brown was a perfect testimony to all that I longed to do with the store. Mary came into A Line Boutique for a charity event. I loved supporting women and the causes they were involved in by giving a percentage of sales that evening to the charity close to their heart. Mary had never been in the store before and was looking lost when I approached her and asked if anyone had begun styling her yet. She shuddered as if the very idea of being styled was horrifying and shook her head. "Oh, I'm just here to support the cause and my friend. I'll buy something like this candle, or maybe I'll get a scarf."

As Mary talked, I observed her. I saw a woman who was beautiful but who looked as if she dressed to fade into the background. She was nondescript. Beneath the jeans, slip-on shoes, and plaid shirt, I saw potential. I guessed her to be in her mid-forties. Her skin was radiant and her hair was simple. I was pretty sure there was more to Mary than she was projecting.

I explained that at A Line, we had a team of professional stylists who were all on salary and actually tried on the inventory themselves so they would understand how they fit, if the style was running big or small, and how it looked on—as opposed to how they looked on the hanger. In short, they had already done the hard part. Combined with asking the customer a few questions about their lifestyle and personal style, that expertise with the inventory allowed them to quickly pull pieces that would look great on the customer. I encouraged her to let us put together a few things she might like in a room for her, and if she decided to try them on, we could have a little fun. Of course, she could just get a little something for her friend to support a good charity, but why not take advantage of the chance to be styled while she was at the store?

She meekly agreed, and Emily, a seasoned stylist on the team, went to work. Within minutes, Emily had assessed

Mary's style, determined her size, and grabbed some things for her to try: jeans, tops, a dress, and the perfect shoe. Emily walked Mary into the dressing room and began describing why she had pulled what she did and how Mary could wear the items. Emily showed her how the items could be mixed and matched and how they could be dressed up or down.

Despite her reluctance, I could tell that Mary was curious. I asked if she just wanted to try one outfit. "I guess," she replied. "I'm here. What's the harm."

The curtain was pulled shut and when it opened again, the meek woman who only moments earlier was trying to fade into the background had emerged with a new gait, confidently walking out of the room and heading toward the full-length mirror. "This is so me!" she blurted out. "It's just version 2.0 of me!"

Mary was radiating poise and confidence. She couldn't stop talking about how she felt transformed and yet the same person. Emily had not made her into something she was not. She wasn't fussy or fancy. She was still comfortable and casual, but as she exclaimed, "I'm styled and put together!"

Woman after woman emerged from the dressing room appearing to have come back to life after entering the dressing room looking depressed, beaten down, and suffering from a negative body image. They strutted their stuff, moving as if on the catwalk. One of my all-time favorite comments came from a woman who walked into the store after work announcing that she only had a few minutes before meeting a friend at the restaurant next door. She needed something for that weekend but was sure we didn't carry her size because she was a size 10–12.

I was committed to A Line Boutique not being a skinny girl store that only carried sizes 0–4. I knew from my own experience what usually happened to a woman with a career that included a lot of travel or who was otherwise so busy that she ate out most of the time and had little or no time to work out. She might be a 0-4, but as likely as not, her hectic life would take its toll on her dress size. So we carried larger sizes for styles that worked on larger frames.

A stylist immediately grabbed a turquoise-blue pencil skirt and a black-and-white V-neck striped top, and when the woman came out of the dressing room, she said, "Honey, I look small and I am *not* a small woman." Once again, the power of well-styled clothes had instantly made this hardworking travel warrior feel beautiful, feminine . . . and small.

It wasn't just the customers who experienced the ease of being styled at A Line. In many ways, I remained the client who enjoyed professional stylists crafting looks that evoked the image and style I wanted to elicit. I struggled with the fact that my personal style morphed from conservative, to polished, to edgy and fun during my constant movement between my company in the tech industry and my company in the fashion industry. The stylists helped me exhibit different aspects of myself in different arenas and environments. I loved being able to be the client who didn't have all the answers.

It took vulnerability and self-awareness to be able to articulate my desire to move from playful and edgy to more polished and sophisticated without being boring. Just as my daughter moved from baby to big girl, I wanted to evolve into the next version of myself. What bubbled out of my soul was a pronouncement: I *am* forty-five, but don't write me off. I'm not done. I wanted to be seen and visible.

The manifesto I wrote for A Line and loved seeing on the wall was not just a statement about how we viewed our customers and how we wanted them to feel. I saw it as my intention for how I wanted to feel and the power I wanted women everywhere to be able to access through fashion.

A Line Boutique Manifesto

You are beautiful. You are unique, and we're your biggest fan. Here, you are at home, in the comfort of good friends. Explore the world and imagine. Experience serious style with laid-back love. Try on the new you. Coax out the shy one. Give her confidence, head-to-toe. Move from invisible to invincible.

A Line Boutique was designed to be a playground for women, a place where they could try on a new version of themselves knowing they had the safety net of a team who loved and protected them from appearing silly or inappropriate.

The annual revenue of A Line was around $300,000 when I bought it, and the first year I owned it, it increased to $700,000. The following year ended with $1.4 million in revenue. It turned out that I wasn't the only "normie" (normal woman, as I liked to call myself, versus fashionista) who hated shopping but still wanted to feel beautiful, feminine, powerful, sexy, and age appropriate.

My vision for A Line Boutique was to help women step into their power more fully using the confidence boosting, transformative, powerful ability of clothing to breathe life into them. And I knew I needed a team of strong stylists to execute that vision. I never knew it would be so hard to find the talent that had the styling skills *and* was self-confident enough to avoid making it about them and their ego. I wanted stylists who kept their focus on what the woman they were styling wanted and brought their talent to give them the best version of that possible. I wanted a team who would laser-focus on the women, not themselves, and pierce the customer's deepest desires of the heart, extracting that emotion and expressing it through fashion that would make their heart sing and give them the power to step onto the stage of life.

The work Emily did with Mary Brown epitomized that. Mary wasn't transformed into a fashionista who would be stopped on the street and drilled about what designer she was wearing. Mary would not have wanted that. Instead, Emily honored her desire to be comfortable and not fussy, but she elevated that look with clothes that had great fit and fabrication.

I knew something about letting your ego get in the way. I had done that myself, needing to show off and prove my worth to the world through my grades, accomplishments, money, and power. I had worked through that and had learned how to fly without the encumbrance of an over-stuffed ego in my personal life. Now, as the owner of A Line, I wanted stylists who had worked through their ego impediments enough to be more interested in the customer than they were in being interesting as stylists. They needed to have an eye, and they needed to have good experience, but it was critical for them to be comfortable enough in their own skin to help the customer be comfortable in hers in clothing that helped her step into *her* own power.

Interestingly enough, I learned that being brilliant at styling was actually less important than being able to put the client first. Eighty percent of my clients were normies, and my stylists needed to be able to anticipate their styling needs and be their "easy button." Our customers had calendars with social and business events. They had lifestyles that required them to go from the conference room to their child's kindergarten talent show and from making dinner for the family to a charity event. The stylists had to care more about the women they were styling than the brands or products with which they were styling them. Finding stylists like that was not easy.

I had another challenge. I had a team working for me that was selling products that they personally could not afford on their current salaries. I discovered that at least some of them were reluctant to pull together everything that would serve the customer because they were adding up the cost in their head—and the cost was nothing that would fit in their own budget. I had to do a little one-on-one development training to help them see past their own wallets and be able to keep their attention on what their client wanted and could afford.

I was attracting millennials onto my team and knew that many business people complained that they were not loyal, did not know how to do grunt work, did not want to pay their dues, and expected constant praise and recognition. But what I saw in them was their deep desire to be a part of something bigger than them. And that was perfect for me and my mission, not just my company. I needed a team who wanted to have an important impact on women, who wanted to help them transform themselves into the next great version of themselves—one with more confidence, power, and prowess. Millennials who needed to be part of a cause and a mission were perfect for me and A Line.

What I was finally learning was that learning to fly in business included becoming aware of and respecting that a company is a living thing, an organism. It is not just an amalgamation of ideas, vision, buildings, merchandise, employees, vendors, and customers. It is, itself, a living thing. Somehow, the origin of the word *corporation* had escaped me. Its root was the Latin word *corpus*, meaning "body." A corporation, or a business in any form, was a collection of beings forming one body. Each being within the corpus that was the business impacted every other being.

I had long understood that when it came to the people working within a business, there was a gestalt at work. The whole was definitely more than the sum of its parts. That was why I felt so strongly that business tactics needed to be discussed collaboratively, even if I had often clumsily lapsed into dictator mode once the path became clear to me. I knew at a gut level that the business was a living thing and that ignoring a part of it would be at the expense of the entirety. The organism could become sick or even die. I simply had not moved that understanding from my gut to my head. My purpose and vision for A Line had always been elevated and lofty. I wanted to create something beautiful, but in the early years of A Line, I did not treat my team in a beautiful way. I had not yet learned to lead with love instead of fear. I didn't even think that was possible in business.

Fortunately, I had some strengths. I was willing to look inside myself without making excuses, and I had learned to do that with compassion instead of self-criticism. I had also awakened and come to trust my innate intuition. Those tools, which I wielded to unearth what was true, fundamental, and sacred in me—my authentic self—were also tools I could use to acknowledge what some Native American groups called "the long body," that energetic quality in us that extends beyond us and is connected to all things.

I wanted to be a kind of spiritual woman warrior. I had been a woman warrior before, but not this kind of woman warrior. Instead of manipulation and control, struggle, and command, my tools were now insight and intuition. And my secret weapons were the energy that underlies all things and a fundamental attitude of love.

CHAPTER 33

Empowering Women

It struck me that I wasn't just a shop owner, I was a cause.

BEING A WOMAN WARRIOR OF THE SPIRITUAL VARIETY required me to acknowledge and change some ways of seeing myself in business that I had held for a long time. There was a point in my life when I would have never opened a boutique for women. I was going to prove myself in a man's world. And for a few years after acquiring A Line Boutique, I found myself secretly being professionally embarrassed that I owned a clothing store. It had initially felt girly and silly in the serious technology world that I had played in with Fortune 500 companies, but I had developed some serious business acumen and a track record in that world. So much of my identity and confidence was still tied to that, and owning a boutique felt like taking a step back.

When I was in the store with the team or with customers, I was happy and content. This was exactly where I wanted to be and what I wanted to be doing, but as soon as I left the company of the team or customers and was in a casual gathering at an event or friend's house, I felt small and insignificant owning a women's clothing store. I constantly caught myself talking about building and selling GBSynergy to establish that I was much more accomplished and successful than a woman who owned one little clothing store.

It took me a while, but when I finally caught myself being embarrassed, I realized that there was a connection between my self-worth and my business résumé. Something within me needed to keep proving that I was enough, irrespective of career, and I knew that I was mostly trying to prove it to myself. It was less effort to do an hour of fitness boot camp than restrain my lips from blurting out my prior business success in technology when I met new business-minded people.

I could have meditated on why it wasn't enough to be a shop owner. Instead, I started asking myself why I was so happy and content when I was with the women who shopped with us. I absolutely loved owning A Line Boutique. If I had such a need to be a serious business-woman, why was I so happy in my shop with my customers and my team?

The answer was easy. My mission had never been to merely sell pieces of clothing. It had been to help women feel confident, relevant, and beautiful. Fashion had always been my art, my creative expression, and my secret weapon. A well-tailored designer suit had given me confidence when I met with large corporations. An evening dress that draped my body, delicately showing my physique, produced the equivalent of fairy dust that made me float through a room with mystique and intrigue. When another woman radiated quiet confidence, I had often wondered what her secret was. My own secret was simple: It was being clothed in a perfectly crafted garment that was wearable art.

For years I had seen clothes as a tool, weapon, and shield. I had long since evolved past a company's marketing tactics being able to convince me that I was cool when I wore their label. The Guess label might have given me a tiny boost of confidence in seventh grade, but the real power wasn't in a label, it was in the fit, fabrication, and construction, along with how that piece combined with other items of clothing.

Many women did not tap in to the power of clothing because wielding the weapon of fashion took skill, knowledge, and experience. Fortunately, I had grown up watching my mother use clothes. My mother had been a fashion model before I was born, and as my mother, she modeled the conscious work of constructing a look that expressed her mood while also enriching her disposition. She never shamed me for working at putting together just the right look because she put herself together with care. She never said, "Just put anything on. It doesn't matter." Instead, she taught me through example that walking out of the house knowing you looked good was powerful. There was so much you couldn't control, but starting the day feeling beautiful, special, feminine, and expressive through fashion was a given at our house.

When I was small, most little girls had a treasure chest of dress-up clothes. Mine ranged from cowgirl outfits to princess gowns. I used the cloth and fabric to transport myself into the magical fantasy world. The truth was that as an adult, I was doing the exact same thing. I was using fabric to step into the day I wanted to unfold. I was consciously playing out my day and readying myself through my attire just as I did when I prepared the slides for a presentation or the ingredients for a meal. I was consciously and purposefully dressing myself to embody the emotion I wanted to feel and elicit in others.

Cowgirl and princess costumes are easy to pull off when you are five. But adult life had challenged me to define and put together a costume for the badass business woman I was at twenty-six, playing in a man's world, and the cool, relaxed woman in her thirties hosting a dinner party at her home with her husband. Now it was challenging me to come up with edgy looks as a fashion professional who ran a boutique but also ran errands and took her kid to casual birthday parties. Each day, each event, each month, and each year produced new situations, and it took work and skill to construct the look that allowed me to levitate above the challenges of the day.

Of course, a kick-butt outfit does not replace the knowledge needed to run a business or the emotional maturity to know when a friend needed a hug at the end of a hard day. But it did inject a surge of confidence, happiness, joy, and energy in me.

We were not just attracting the fashionistas of Denver at A Line. The population was simply not big enough to explain how we had grown the business by over five hundred percent in five years in a city no one in the industry thought of as fashion forward. We had done it by making everyday women feel relevant by applying exceptional skill and joyful effort to the work of styling them.

I loved hearing "This is the 2.0 version of me! I love it!" Watching a mom who had spent every minute of every day taking care of her kids, family, and household walk out of the dressing room beaming, glowing, and brilliantly radiating her personal power was just one of the perks of the best job in the world.

I personally knew what it was like to wonder if I still had it. I personally knew what it was like to consider laser peels to make me look five years younger and crazy diets to make me five pounds lighter. But I also knew something that many women didn't: A well-constructed outfit can make you look five years younger and five pounds lighter. And it can do it instantly, with no down time and no suffering.

Many women had not tapped in to the power of fashion because fashion is work, and it is only accomplished with knowledge, skill, and experience. Styling was no different than being a master sommelier or architect. It required the expert to continuously stay abreast of their field to stay at the top of their game. Not many retailers provided highly trained and serious stylists. And not many women could afford to pay an hourly wage for a stylist. But every woman who goes shopping for clothes is seeking an emotional goal, whether consciously or not. They might be feeling heavy and bloated, outdated and maternal, or unsexy and frumpy when what they want is to feel trim, stylish, sexy, and age-appropriate.

The stylists at A Line were being trained to ask customers what emotion they had come into the store for that day. If we handed them a clipboard with a list of emotions, what would they order up for the day? How did they want to feel when they left the store?

It struck me that I wasn't just a boutique owner, I was a cause. And it was such a cause for me that I opened three more locations. By the fall of 2019, I had four boutiques in the Denver metropolitan area. My book and my stores had spontaneously converged. I wasn't embarrassed because I was in the fashion world. In fact it was the right place for me to make a difference in the world. I had finally embraced the fact that A Line Boutique was a women's empowerment brand. I knew my book was about empowering women. I knew my book was literally my heart's cry to tell women that they were enough, that they were worthy, and that their uniqueness was needed in the world. And I had created a store, a team, and four physical locations that did exactly that through the power of fashion.

This commitment to empowerment was put to the test on a very personal basis for me and my team during the worldwide pandemic of 2020. The way we did business and the way we supported our customers had to change overnight when we were forced to close all four locations indefinitely. Could the boutiques survive under those conditions? Did my staff and I have the ability to innovate our way through the crisis? Did we have the internal resources—the personal power that comes through empowerment—to respond quickly and elegantly? A part of our mission was to help women move from invisible to invincible, but could we find that place within ourselves and collectively—the combined energy that *was* A Line Boutique—to be truly invincible?

Fortunately, A Line had never been solely focused on the presentation of cool inventory at hip stores in the most fashionable parts of town. I had great stores in great locations. And I had great inventory and a great staff. But what made A Line unique was that my staff and I embraced being professional stylists . . . with inventory. With the most dedicated team a woman could have and working fifteen-hour days, we launched an online store within seventy-two hours of our brick-and-mortar closure and began serving our customers through virtual styling.

The power of teamwork when this committed group of people on a mission applied themselves to a crisis was a testament to the magic of empowerment. We were a living force to be reckoned with as we demonstrated that A Line Boutique really fit my favorite description of it: *A Hospitality Company with Inventory*.

CHAPTER 34

Taking Flight

Imagine the ambassadors of peace we can be for those who are frantic when we are in the process of healing our wounds, developing knowledge of our worthiness down to the cellular level, and moving through our days without needing to search, prove, or defend anything.

BOOKS OF FICTION CAN WRAP UP WITH NICE CLOSURE and fairy tale endings that include the words *happily ever after.* But real life is an ongoing adventure and challenge.

I haven't become a new and improved version of myself. Far from it. Instead, I have returned to the confident, trusting soul I had been as a little girl who tenaciously practiced flying every day and tap danced confidently for her grandma. The need to control everything and everyone is no longer essential for my sanity. My ego isn't calling the shots—at least not 24/7—nor does it need to be constantly fed.

Months after my father's death, I was snowshoeing alone near Breckenridge, Colorado. There is a quality of silence possible in Colorado when you are up in the mountains and at a place where there is a deep base of snow. The crunch of snow under my snowshoes and the gentle pulse of my breathing were the only audible sounds. The peace within and without, coupled with the raw beauty of the landscape, opened both my outer and inner senses. I felt light and soulful.

With the awareness of my own soul, I also became aware of my father's soul. His body had died, but his soul felt very close.

I did not grow up talking to dead people. I grew up praying to Jesus and welcoming the Holy Spirit into my soul. As my personal spirituality developed, I abandoned the more constrictive teachings of that church and came to a more inclusive sense of the numinous. But it took meeting spiritual medium and author Rebecca Rosen to free me from the leftover discomfort with the spirit world.

Interestingly, it was Brian, one of the most literal, practical people I know, who made the first experience with Rebecca possible. He bought me a ticket to see her at a large-venue event. A beautiful, down-to-earth woman, Rebecca took us through a meditation inviting in only the spirits with a loving purpose. She surrounded herself with a circle of light and love and taught us how to do that too. Then she spoke to nearly fifty departed souls who were connected with some of the people in the room—brothers, lovers, children. I left the event enlightened, excited, and encouraged.

No one connected to me came through at that event, but I still left feeling the love and healing in the room as so many people heard from loved ones. Beautiful messages of hope, healing, and beauty had been offered and received. I decided to book a small group session with

Rebecca, one in which only five other people would be present. I realized that my dad might come through, though I doubted it. He had abandoned me in life, and I doubted he would behave any differently in death. I was not interested in hearing from him, but I hoped that my mom would have a message for me.

It was my dad who came through, and what he had to impart was exactly what I needed to hear. Rebecca reported that she saw him with his hands on my shoulders. She said that he was proud of me and sorry he had been such a bad communicator when he was living. He was apologizing, but while I seemed to be receiving what Rebecca was saying in a neutral way, I was not very receptive.

My mother came through briefly. She wanted me to know that she had forgiven my dad long ago. She also wanted me to know that she had sent me Reese to heal me. My dog Bagley, who had taught me unconditional love, also came through. He reported that he was with Reese all the time in something like a guardian angel role.

I left feeling grateful for the messages from Bagley and my mother but skeptical about my father's message. Rather than reject his message altogether, I just sat with it for a while, and as I did, the message sank in and softened me. He could no longer hurt me, and I no longer needed to defend myself. I could let down my boundaries. If the message he had sent through Rebecca Rosen was true, it was good to hear.

After my experiences with Rebecca, I felt more comfortable with the idea of talking to the dead, something I had never been comfortable with before. So while I was in that open, receptive, loving state while snowshoeing, I welcomed my father's presence. I asked him why he had not wanted to spend time with me when he was alive in his earthly body. Why had he chosen the pursuit of money and prestige over me? It might not have really been an either-or choice, but it had long felt that way to me. I was alone, so I asked aloud, "Dad, why didn't you choose me?" as I visualized him.

I did not see a burning bush, but I did see my father's face in my mind, complete with all the creases, wrinkles, and details. And I received a reply.

"I thought I was going to make us money and then have all the time in the world with you and Kyla. But one week turned into a month, which turned into a year, which turned into a decade."

I immediately understood. The weeks, months, and years had created a fissure between us, one that became wider and deeper with every misunderstanding, mistake, and slight. Alone in the deep silence around me, I was shocked with the simple realization that my dad had not set out to miss my childhood, nor had he wanted to miss the rest of my life. He had just felt he needed to prove his worth by making a lot of money. And the more he wasn't there for me, the more he felt he needed to prove himself. That led to him being even more absent, widening the chasm between us even further. It was a vicious cycle. He had no awareness of or even the faintest idea that his pursuit of money to prove himself would cost him his family. I knew that ego and pride had been involved, but I had never put the pieces together.

I thought about all of the parents in the world who justify not being there for their kids because they are trying to make a better life for them through long hours of work and equally long absences from their family. The thought was painful to me because I understood, at a soul level, how misguided it is. Every parent wants a good life for their children, but there is a point of diminishing returns when it comes to time spent away from family making money. If the family is safe, fed, has a roof over their head, and has a reasonable level of comfort, the pursuit of money over time spent with family becomes not just counterproductive, but damaging. I knew that from my own experience.

I asked a few more questions, more of myself than him. If he had made enough money to make him feel worthy when I was ten or even fifteen, would I have held a grudge against him for the time he had spent apart from my sister and me? The answer was no. What if he had not managed to become as successful as he wanted but saw the error in his absence and had come to my sister and me asking to be forgiven for not being around? Would I have forgiven him? The answer was yes. Success and money were important to him when I was growing up, but they were of no importance to me. I just wanted my dad.

When my dad behaved as if I needed to be perfect to be good enough to receive his love, it was coming from his own deep wounding. He felt that he would not be good enough if he was not perfect. He never felt perfect, and it was painful to him. He did not want me to experience that pain, so he pushed me toward perfection. It was convoluted, but it made sense in a twisted kind of way. And none of it mattered now. I could let it all go and forgive him. In fact, I could let it all go with the realization that at the soul level, there was nothing to forgive.

His behavior after my mom's death now made sense to me. My mother had been bigger than life. My dad had never felt as capable, confident, or good as her. He never felt needed by us because she was there. Once he was the only surviving parent, he felt needed. He wanted me to skip a semester of school and come live with him to prove that he had not completely demolished his relationship with me. He wanted me to show my love for him and prove that I would not reject him by choosing him over college. I had no idea how needy he was. I was trying to prove that I needed no one, and he was trying to get some demonstration from me that I needed him. It was as tragic as a Shakespearian drama.

That semester off was not enough proof for him. He wanted me to take the next semester off too, and when I chose to return to school instead of doing that, he perceived it as rejection. It was all so pointless and all such a waste.

But as I continued snowshoeing in the deep silence of a wilderness that seemed to be on the liminal edge between this world and the otherworldly realms, I felt at peace with my dad, at least in that moment. I knew that I might have periodic bouts of angst over what was lost, but I also knew that he and I had healed a fundamental rent between us. He was now flying on the other side; I was still learning to fly on this side.

✎✎✎

Growing up is an ongoing adventure. I love raising and enjoying a little girl who is figuring out the world, learning

about possibilities and consequences, and treating everything as a grand experiment. I grew up feeling that I had
to prove my worth, just as my father had felt he had to
prove his worth. His parents before him probably felt that
they had to prove their worth too, and theirs before them.
But it stops with me. I am trying to model confidence,
self-worth, innate beauty, and authenticity for my daughter. I love that she does not have to prove herself, her
power, or her growing individuation to me.

Among the other detritus, my father's push to make
me prove myself led to a mind-set of ongoing competi-
tiveness in me. As I have learned to fly, I have stepped into
the power of cooperation over competition, and it is an
honor and privilege to teach Reese that she can challenge
herself and, conjointly, celebrate her friends' successes instead of competing with them.

I was reminded of this at a dude ranch in Colorado.
I was with a group of mothers and kids, all of us on
horseback. Some of Reese's newfound friends decided
to barrel race instead of ride with their parents that day.
Before I rode away from Reese, I repeated a bit of coaching she has received from me many times before. "Don't
forget to celebrate your friends' wins today. You know
how good it feels when people celebrate you and don't
compete with you."

I was so focused on Reese and what I was telling her
that I was oblivious to the other mothers . . . until my
coaching was met with a way-to-go-mama cheer from the
other mothers.

That kind of coaching flows naturally from me when
I am operating out of a sense of my own worthiness, when

I am not fighting to prove my worthiness or gain some sort of purchase in a steep climb up a hill of personal and business success. I was not striving to be the best rider at that dude ranch, let alone the prettiest, wittiest, or smartest cowgirl. I was just being, and I was just having a good time with my daughter, Reese. And because I was not expending effort or narcissistically focusing on myself, I could encourage my daughter to have the same sense of self-worth, which then allowed her to celebrate her friends and not compete against them.

ᗡᐤᗡ

It could be argued that I am still a fledgling at learning to fly in relationships. In truth, I was not capable of deep intimacy before I unpacked some of my baggage and dealt with it. Brian gave me the best gift of my life when he gave me Reese. The gift of motherhood is the richest role I have ever been given by the universe. Brian also was instrumental in A Line's growth and success. His support of me in building the company will always remain an unmeasurable contribution. While we never had a wedding ceremony and we haven't chosen to grow old together, we are both grateful for the time we had together. I'm a single mother these days, and while it isn't always easy, I cherish every bit of it.

It took me many years to love myself enough to be comfortable flying solo. I now see my own strength, embrace my femininity, and have trust in myself. I let down my guard and fully opened my heart to love when Reese was born, and because of that, I'm now ready to open myself to the possibility of relationship with someone who is ready for big love and soul connection. When I was able to heal some fundamental wounds within me and stepped into fuller authenticity, sex moved from being an act of power to being the spiritual connection it was always meant to be. Along with that, I've come to appreciate romance and delayed gratification. Relationship has far more dimensions for me than it once had, and I would love my daughter to have the gift of seeing me with another in the beautiful dance that is relationship between two people who love one another. My life has shown me that many good things are possible, so I hold the image of that kind of relationship in my heart.

I am also still learning to fly in business. I used to think my role was to muster the troops, command them into high performance, and maintain strict control. Now I see my role as more like that of an orchestra conductor. My woodwind, brass, percussion, and string sections are all in place, and the musicians are good at their instruments. As a conductor, I am not the first violinist. A conductor is not the best musician, even though they may play more than one instrument. And they may not even be a composer, even though they know how to read music. Their job is to put it all together. They can hear and see potential, and they know how to bring out the best the orchestra has in it, benefiting both the audience and the musicians.

I am not the designer, the buyer, or the stylist. I have some skills at those things, but I do not claim any of those roles, and I am not the best at any of them. My role is to have vision and orchestrate something beautiful.

I now realize that this is what I did best when I owned software training companies. I saw a need and I saw a solution. I had the lofty goal of creating self-sufficient, confident software users instead of just creating accurate and thorough documentation. At A Line Boutique, I saw the need for women to feel confident, edgy, cool, and hip at any age, and I saw the solution through well-fabricated clothing and great styling.

I always heard the music, and I always seemed to know what combination of skills, behaviors, energies, talents, and hearts were needed to make that music beautiful. What has changed is that I am a better conductor than I have ever been, and in my not-trying-too-hard way, I plan to keep improving at it.

Not long ago, I was sitting in meditation during a brief retreat at a spiritual center. I was with other meditators in a large tent when a bird flew in, hit one of the tent's plastic windows, was stunned for a bit, and flew around, finally landing on a woman's shoulder. There were meditation cushions without occupants, but the bird chose the woman's shoulder over one of those cushions.

I watched the bird as it settled in. It had been a bit frantic, but on that woman's shoulder, it slowly regained its composure. Its head stopped darting, its desperate, fearful movement ceased, and it settled into what looked to me like a peaceful state.

I saw the bird's activity as a beautiful message about how we all behave when we are in the presence of peace and love. The bird was drawn to that woman because it sensed her energy, sensed the tranquility and harmony she was emanating. It stayed on her shoulder for much longer than I would have anticipated, and when it finally lifted up, it took off effortlessly and flew out the tent opening. It had reoriented itself, differentiated sunlight through a plastic window from sunlight streaming in through an opening, and chose the right route—the one toward light, wind, life, and movement.

Isn't that like us? We all recalibrate and center in the presence of someone who is centered and oozing love, joy, and peace. We can all feel the energy of those around us, even if we are unaware of it. Imagine the ambassadors of peace we can be for those who are frantic when we are in the process of healing our wounds, developing knowledge of our worthiness down to the cellular level, and moving through our days without needing to search, prove, or defend anything.

That is real flying. I'm still learning. I'll always be learning. But there are moments of feeling a current of air under my wings, effortlessly lifting me higher, when I stay in a state of beginner's mind, always learning to fly, never hallucinating that I have become an ace pilot. In those moments, I realize that the intended outcome of being in human form is the process itself. So I take joy in learning to fly.

And I wish that for you too.

Acknowledgments

WHAT SEEMS LIKE MANY YEARS AGO NOW, I felt inspired to write my story and read, over and over, "Just start writing." So I did. In fact, I became engrossed with the writing, and for months, I poured out my soul onto the page. When I finally finished it, I sent it off to an editor a colleague had referred me to. In my naïveté, I thought she would work on it for a month or so, and then I would publish my memoir.

I was shocked when I met with the editor and heard the words, "You definitely have something worth saying, but this manuscript is not ready to be edited. The story is compelling and needs to be told, but right now it reads as a self-indulgent, superficial, and somewhat narcissistic story that only your enemies and a few friends will actually be willing to read. The woman standing before me has way more depth than the woman portrayed in that manuscript. The book needs work to represent you and what you have to say to the world."

My response was simple. "Great. Ghostwrite it for me."

Her small under-five-feet-tall frame remained stock still until she shook her head and said, "I might be able to do that, but it wouldn't serve you because you want to learn to write."

Melanie Mulhall was absolutely correct. I wanted to learn the craft of writing. She and I had no idea that it would take me over ten years to learn the craft and grow myself enough to feel complete in the telling of the tale. We had no idea how much collaboration and heart-based effort would be spent together conspiring to craft something real and true, teasing out what different parts of my story were really about, working to find just the right word or feel for a paragraph or chapter, knowing, intuitively, when more needed to be lived before the memoir that wanted to be written was done, and knowing, also intuitively, when there was wholeness to it and it was time to birth it. Thank you, Melanie, for taking this journey with me.

I am crazy excited to share this beautiful story with the world.

The rest of the people to thank are contained in the story. I have come to believe that all of us comprise a beautiful web of symbiotic growth. We couldn't be farther from alone or isolated. I am thankful for *everyone* who has been a part of my journey—both the beautiful and ugly parts of it—because I am the woman I am today thanks to everyone I have encountered on that journey, whether it was just as the passing of pilgrims on the way, as comrades traveling together for a time, as adversaries sparring and moving on, or as true companions trekking the path with no foreseeable end. Many of the names have been changed out of respect.

I am overwhelmed by all the Earth angels who exist in my life, including my team and my brilliant assistant

Brandon who deserves a world-class juggling award. I seriously couldn't have built another company, written a book, opened four stores, and remained remotely sane without Brandon at my right side.

My daughter Reese has healed my heart, taught me to love fiercely, and shown me how to fall courageously. Reese, contained in these pages are all my best lessons and my deepest wisdom. I pray that you will never need them. My hope is that you will never attach your worth to accomplishments or achievements. Your heart is big. I am doing my absolute best to protect it. One day, when you read the entire book, you will understand why, every night, I rub your back and whisper in your ear, "You are perfect. You are whole. You are worthy of love just as you are." Thank you for teaching my heart to love again, un-restrained. I love you, baby girl!

I have the deepest appreciation and gratitude for Brian, who gave me the best gift in the world. Thank you.

Lastly, to the leaders of the spectacular movement of vulnerability who helped put words and intelligence to my journey—including Brené Brown, Reese Witherspoon with Hello Sunshine, Gwyneth Paltrow with Goop, Elizabeth Gilbert, and Oprah Winfrey—thank you! My soul's purpose is to breathe life into women, help them heal the ugliness that spurts from wounds, paint the beauty of worthiness, and inspire them to fly! And then, just as I have healed and grown enough to be able to fly in my personal life and in business, I send love for their flights, with the vision that to-gether, we can help nudge the world in the direction of joy and love.

About the Author

AFTER CUTTING HER TEETH in the technology industry, where she founded and sold companies, Karmen Berentsen combined her business expertise with her lifelong love of fashion to become the CEO of A Line Boutique. She has put Denver on the fashion map with her four A Line Boutique stores. Karmen sees her business and personal successes as having flowed from the hard work of learning to fly as a person and living that wisdom in all aspects of her life. She and her daughter Reese live in Denver, Colorado.